Please renew/return this item by the last date shown.

So that your telephone call is charged at local rate, please call the numbers as set out below:

	From Area codes 01923 or 0208:	From the rest of Herts:
Renewals:	01923 471373	01438 737373
Enquiries:	01923 471333	01438 737333
Minicom:	01923 471599	01438 737599

L32b

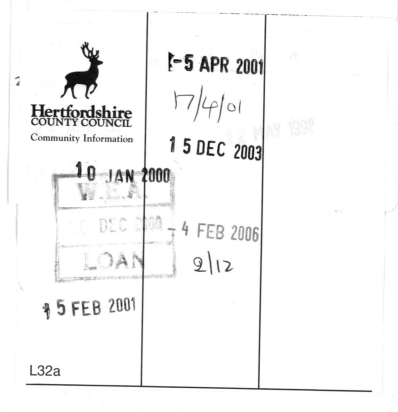

Hertfordshire
COUNTY COUNCIL
Community Information

L32a

The Prehistoric Settlement
of Britain

Archaeology of Britain

Edited by

Barry Cunliffe

*Professor of European Archaeology in
the University of Oxford*

The Prehistoric Settlement of Britain

Richard Bradley

Department of Archaeology
Reading University

Routledge & Kegan Paul
London, Henley and Boston

First published in 1978
by Routledge & Kegan Paul Ltd
39 Store Street,
London WC1E 7DD,
Broadway House,
Newtown Road,
Henley-on-Thames,
Oxon RG9 1EN and
9 Park Street,
Boston, Mass. 02108, USA
Set in Baskerville
and printed in Great Britain by
Lowe & Brydone Printers Limited
Thetford, Norfolk
© Richard Bradley, 1978

British Library Cataloguing in Publication Data

Bradley, Richard, b.1946
    The prehistoric settlement of Britain.
    – (Archaeology of Britain).
    1. Man, Prehistoric – Great Britain
    I. Title   II. Series
    936.1'01   GN805   78–40619

ISBN 0 7100 8993 7

For Bari Hooper and Collin Bowen

Men are made of what is made,
The meat, the drink, the life, the corn,
Laid up by them, in them reborn.
And self-begotten cycles close
About our way; indigenous art
And simple spells make unafraid
The haunted labyrinths of the heart.

Edwin Muir, *The Island*

Contents

Figures

Tables

Preface

This book has happened over a long period and many debts have accrued in its composition. The most obvious are for the use of published and unpublished material and these are acknowledged at appropriate points in the text. But beyond these are other debts which no such acknowledgment can pay. I owe more to my teachers and colleagues than they might care to agree. Two of them, Barry Cunliffe and Michael Fulford, have read and commented on the manuscript. I have also discussed much of this material with John Barrett and Brendan O'Connor. None of them, I suspect, has coaxed me from the errors of my ways. Alan Dingle also read the text and is responsible for the English translation. Verna Care and Julian Richards kindly drafted some of the original drawings and Sonia Burgess produced a clean typescript from an almost unreadable palimpsest. Bill and Judi Startin put me up when I began work on the book and Katherine has put up with me as I brought it to a protracted conclusion. It is dedicated to two friends: Bari Hooper, for reminding me, more than anyone else, how intellectual curiosity is a source of enjoyment; and Collin Bowen, who has shared his ideas so liberally that any merits of this book are not the author's alone.

Chapter 1

Introduction
Still Life of Sherds

*A word about this Royal Myles na gCopa-
leen Institute of Archaeology. . . . It would
be rash to suppose that the Institute was
just a gatherum of clay-minded prodnoses.
Each branch of research has a sub-institute
of its own. . . . Within the Royal Institute
you have, for instance, the Institute of
Comparative Bronzes. This body is concerned only with time-bronze progressions.*
Flann O'Brien, from
The Best of Myles *(1968)*

This book was planned as synthesis and has
emerged as speculation. In between came a
phase of Binfordian fellow-travelling. Why this
uncertainty of aim? Why so many changes of
plan?

Complete synthesis is always impossible since
it presupposes finite data and the exhaustion of
all approaches. But it is particularly difficult
when so little of this basic data has been properly
collected or recorded. Add to that the frustration
that little carefully collected material is ever
accessible. Few excavations reach the printer;
academic distinction is apparently measured by
the number of projects abandoned. But to turn
entirely to theory would be dull for both author
and reader, and to discuss methodology without
appropriate data is as likely to win converts
as a party political broadcast. For these reasons
alone, what has emerged is a trial piece, from
which outlines can be copied or erased. It is a
personal interpretation of biased and elusive
evidence.

The title is of course caricature. It is borrowed
from a painting by Klee, who, on this occasion,
was innocent of satire. Flann O'Brien was not.
But, like all creatures, it seizes on real features
of its subject. The framework of prehistoric
studies is based upon both of these sources. The
bronzes provide a chronological scheme which
unites local sequences over much of Europe and
eventually relates them to a historical chronology.
The ceramics can locate more restricted phenomena. The problem is when these objects lose
all connection with the men who made them
and are studied as an end in themselves, a hermetic
exercise in self-validating skill. About the time
that O'Brien was writing, the American archaeologist, Walter Taylor, was lambasting the same
evasion:

Fellow students . . . have accused the
archaeologist of tatting endless taxonomic
rosettes out of the same old ball of 'material
culture' and maintained that his findings are
next to useless for the purposes of history and
culture study. It seems that archaeologists
are becoming, as Tolstoy once said of modern
historians, like deaf men answering questions
which no one has asked them (1948).

The 'time-bronze progressions' were inevitable.
Without this framework there would have been
no time-scale, and its long time-scale is the one
contribution that prehistory can offer to other
disciplines. The study of pottery could have served
a similar end, but here chronology and explanation have become so tangled together that
discussion often ends in deadlock. To show chronological relationships, cultural relations are
inferred. These have then taken over, at times

leaving a dubious historical narrative in support of a circular argument. The Childean 'culture' is not a testable hypothesis, but it is sometimes an *idée fixe*. When Childe's scheme fails to offer the acceptable solution, the questions are changed to accommodate the answers:

> Judged by these [Childe's] standards, the early La Tène invasions from the Marne have been found defective by several authorities. . . . If . . . we are obliged to apply less rigorous criteria, then . . . the Marnian invasion . . . stands upon firmer ground (Harding, D., 1974, p. 230).

The result has been a cultural framework which owes something to changes in metalworking and not a little to a suspect ethnology.

Now it seems that the main areas of study, at least by those in the field, are to be settlements and even whole landscapes. There is nothing new to economic prehistory. Grahame Clark produced his great classic in 1952 and his achievement has not been matched since. It is not particularly constructive to trace the development of this climate of opinion. There is a temptation to disciplinary autobiography that reveals the frustrated historian, and on this occasion it is better resisted. Settlement archaeology is certainly popular, but in Britain it seems to rest on a compromise. It is *de rigueur* to study 'settlements in Belgic Britain' (Rodwell, 1976) or 'the Food Vessel economy' (Herity and Eogan, 1976). But is this any help? It must be asked whether landscape history can really be studied using an intellectual structure formed almost entirely around artefacts.

Two developments may provide a release. The development of radiocarbon dating at last holds out some prospect of building sequences independent of diagnostic artefacts, and indeed of putting traditional chronologies to the test. Despite the statistical uncertainty attached to every date, an intelligent application of this technique should eventually provide both an absolute time-scale and a measure of rates of change. At present controversy over the tree ring calibration of radiocarbon rules out any dogmatic conclusion. But again there is a danger of abuse:

'Radiocarbon dates for Midsummer Hill Camp have now indicated that the La Tène invasions were as early as perhaps *c.* 390 b.c. (420 ± 185 b.c.)' (Stanford, 1972, p. 308).

The second area of development has been in the environmental sciences, and in particular in pollen analysis. This is no longer just a technique of compiling botanical and climatic sequences, but has proved itself a discriminating judge of human activity. Much can now be learnt of early land use, and studies of the dissemination of pollen may eventually reveal the size and location of the occupied areas. The analysis of closely spaced samples has shed surprising light on early agriculture, particularly when all the pollen grains have been counted. Three-dimensional pollen analysis, the study of separate cores over a limited area, can also help to localise prehistoric activity. Since peat can be carbon-dated, many periods of land use can be tied directly to an absolute chronology. Previously palaeobotanists had shown undue deference to the archaeologist's assumptions: 'The Late Bronze Age communities in this area are regarded as having been nomadic with a predominantly pastoral economy and are thus equated with episode C 3' (Birks, 1965).

Given these opportunities, it seems worthwhile to explore the evidence for prehistoric settlement. A number of basic economic practices are discussed in the next four chapters. The final chapter, which is much the longest, is an attempt to draw this evidence together and to suggest how it might eventually form its own framework for the study of settlement patterns. This is perhaps a worthwhile ambition, but the reader must be warned that it is still very much an ideal. This book asks more questions than it can answer and avoids more problems than it solves. But the attempt is still worth making, provided it is understood that this is a study of the information that is already accessible. The emphasis repeatedly falls on its potential, rather than its present shortcomings.

There are four areas which drastically need to be explored before all the propositions in this book can be put to the test. Until then a few gnomic assertions can be useful in setting exams.

The most important of these problems is the selective destruction of evidence. Christopher Taylor has argued that the prehistoric landscape can be divided into a 'zone of survival' and a 'zone of destruction' (1972). He considers that this division cuts across the settlement pattern so completely that it can no longer be understood. This depressing conclusion is nearly justified. But it is still possible to locate some sites in the zone of destruction, although it is unlikely that a large sample can now be achieved. It is also true that the quality of the evidence will vary radically between these zones. Certain areas, for instance the Wessex downland or Dartmoor, dominate the archaeological literature for reasons which are themselves part of landscape history. The continuous pressure placed on the best resources means that the quality of the remaining material can be in inverse proportion to its original significance. The way forward is perhaps to consider each area in relation to its potential for field survey and to weight all distributions accordingly.

But fieldwork needs to be planned on a more rigorous basis. Since it is unlikely that the whole of the British Isles will ever be examined, all surveys will be a form of sampling. It would be sensible to make proper use of the techniques which have already been devised for obtaining a representative pattern. These have been widely discussed in America (e.g. Mueller, 1975), but their potential has been almost ignored in this country, with the result that financial resources are still dissipated in hunting for biased information.

It is because so little information has been collected on an appropriate basis that hypotheses are so hard to test. There are very few reliable figures for the movement of settlement between different soils, or for changes in the number of sites from one period to another, even though such processes are widely claimed in the literature. Only a few case-studies can be used, without any real way of knowing whether they reflect a general trend. Few of the ideas in this book can be tested for statistical significance, since the sample which has been used is an accident of academic history.

The main reason for this situation has been a pragmatic avoidance of formal analysis. There is a general terror of theory. Some reviewers obviously think that New Mexico is the seat of the Spanish Inquisition. Methodology is widely portrayed as a tiresome retreat from the data. But the evidence never speaks for itself, and without questions there *are* no answers. Controversy of a sort can be felt, but reappraisal soon turns into reminiscence. Objectives are rarely discussed. The critics have not been wonderfully constructive. They are content to parse the polemic and to criticise its sentence structure. Repunctuated, reworded, the charges are exactly the same: 'Archaeology [here British archaeology] is undisciplined . . . an intuitive skill . . . a manipulative dexterity learned by rote' (Clarke, D.L., 1968, xiii). Without better collection of the basic materials, this is not likely to change.

Lastly, the bias towards economic evidence also means a bias towards a functionalist interpretation. The poor recovery of economic data weakens these explanations still more. Archaeology and anthropology in Britain have quite different emphases, although one cannot help noticing that kinship models can look like bronze typologies. By avoiding the social meaning of his material, the archaeologist is choosing a rather narrow personal mythology. Leach's recent strictures were rude but not quite unfair (1976). This book is another exploration of economic evidence, since this is almost all that has been recorded. Because of this self-denial it is not a complete interpretation.

These gaps may seem fatal. But to bewail the limits of inference is finally an unproductive exercise. It has led too many prehistorians into the pessimism of Samuel Beckett: 'I have nothing to say, but I can only say to what extent I have nothing to say.' Alternatively one can be more foolhardy. To quote Walter Taylor again: 'Why should every archaeological hypothesis have to stand and be correct for all time? . . . Why should archaeology assume the pretentious burden of infallibility?'

This book contrives its own obsolescence.

A Pure Soil
Clearance and Colonisation

I like a plantation in a pure soil – that is, where people are not displanted to the end to plant others. . . . Planting of countries is like planting of woods, for you must take account to lease almost twenty years' profit and expect your recompense in the end. . . . In a country of plantation first look about what kind of victual the country yields of itself to hand, as chestnuts, walnuts, pine-apples, olives, dates, plums, cherries, wild honey and the like, and make use of them. Then consider what victual or esculent things there are which grow speedily and within the year, as parsnips, carrots, turnips, onions, rádish, artichokes of Jerusalem, maize, and the like. For wheat, barley and oats, they ask too much labour. . . . For beasts and birds take chiefly such as are least subject to diseases and multiply fastest, swine, goats, cocks, hens, turkeys, geese, house doves and the like. The victual in plantations ought to be expended almost as in a besieged town, that is, with certain allowance.

Francis Bacon, 'Of Plantations' from
Essays, or Counsels Civil
and Moral, *1625*

Said Ysbaddaden Chief Giant. . . . 'When I have myself gotten that which I shall name to thee, then thou shalt get my daughter. . . . Dost see the great thicket yonder? . . . I must have it uprooted out of the earth and burnt on the face of the ground so that the cinders and ashes thereof be its manure; and that it be ploughed and sown so that it be ripe in the morning against the drying of the dew, *in order that it may be made into meat and drink for the wedding guests and my daughter's. And all this I must have done in one day.'*
'It is easy for me to get that, though thou think it is not easy.'

'Culhwch and Olwen',
The Mabinogion,
trans. G. and T. Jones, 1949

INTRODUCTION

When John Aubrey was writing his *Natural History of Wiltshire* in the second half of the seventeenth century, his views of early agriculture were not surprisingly coloured by what he knew of America. As so often, his speculations have proved remarkably acute.

> In Jamaica, and in other parts of America, e.g. in Virginia, the natives did burne down great woods, to cultivate the soil with maiz and potato-roots, which plaines were there made to sowe corne. They doe call these plains Savannas. Who knows but Salisbury plaines, etc. might be made long time ago, and for the same reason?

This suggestion, which would have seemed so peculiar when it was finally published in 1847, would hardly have surprised the anonymous author(s) of 'Culhwch and Olwen'. But, by the nineteenth century, little or nothing remained of the native forest, and these apparently simple processes of clearance had long since given way to more complicated patterns of management (Rackham, 1976). Even within the prehistoric period, the evidence for land clearance is remarkably complex. It is the purpose of this chapter to consider some of the ways in which the natural landscape was prepared.

The opening part of this chapter deals with actual methods of clearance, although some attention will be paid to chronology, and to those modifications of the forest which fall short of complete removal. Otherwise, clearance will be taken as a deliberate preparation for farming. This definition confines the discussion to the Neolithic and later periods, and the relevance of changes in the course of Mesolithic hunting will be considered separately. Even with this limitation, much of the evidence is controversial and almost all of it uneven. There are few archaeological sites showing environmental evidence and even fewer palaeoecological studies which allow a clear correlation with these. The ecologist's long-standing interest in forest history has also meant that much of the evidence emphasises Neolithic practice at the expense of later developments.

The second part of this chapter will be concerned with the transfer of settlements into the newly cleared areas.

THE BEGINNING OF AGRICULTURAL CLEARANCE

The actual onset of Neolithic clearance is not easy to recognise. There is still no real agreement on the nature of the Elm Decline, which marks the division between zones VIIa and b in the botanical literature and between the Mesolithic and the Neolithic in archaeology. Its clearest characteristic is its virtual synchroneity across the British Isles (Smith, A. G. and Pilcher, 1973). There is difficulty in choosing a single explanation, especially since the Elm Decline is such a complex phenomenon. Iversen interpreted the initial fall in elm pollen as a purely climatic effect and only saw its later curtailment as a 'landnam' or land-clearance phase (1941). More recently there has been a tendency to extend the cultural interpretation to the earlier episode, and it has now been partly explained by the selective gathering of leaf fodder (Troels Smith, 1960). Proponents of

this view draw analogies with contemporary practice in northern Europe and with undoubted evidence for leaf collection in the Swiss Neolithic.

There are difficulties in the uncritical extension of these views. Groenman-van-Waateringe has argued that similar phenomena can be created naturally (1968), and Pennington, in particular, has shown how the Elm Decline actually occurred in a period of increased rainfall (1975). This had the effect of changing the composition of lake sediments and of increasing the rate at which pollen grains were deposited. There are, of course, ambiguities in this evidence, since increased rainfall and humanly generated erosion can both have played a part. Other authorities see a fall in temperature and a deterioration of soils within this crucial phase (Frenzel, 1966; Pennington, 1975).

It is essential to separate the different strands in the argument. Some of the difficulties may now have been partly offset by work in north-west Scotland (Pennington *et al.*, 1972). Here the situation is simplified in two very important ways: the areas chosen for study showed no archaeological evidence for clearance at this early date; and in any case they seem to have supported too low a proportion of elm in the natural forest for any economy *based* on its exploitation to have been worthwhile. In fact, elm was only really common in parts of Ireland, south-west Wales and Cornwall (Birks, Deacon and Peglar, 1975). Despite these qualifications, there was still evidence for an elm decline in this area, an observation which makes it difficult to accept a purely anthropogenic origin. This agrees with another observation, one which has always created difficulties: although the representation of elm pollen seems to have dropped abruptly close to 3000 b.c., the detailed variations in other species at this time are not particularly consistent and, taken on their own, would not always be enough to suggest human activity. To some extent the presentation of pollen diagrams by percentage rather than by absolute frequency may be to blame for this confusion; it can even produce quite spurious episodes which are a product of the method itself (cf. Pennington, 1973, p. 96).

A more rewarding approach may be the one adopted by Sims at Hockham Mere, where a complex Elm Decline was revealed by absolute pollen analysis and certainly included cereals and other indicants of human activity (1973, Table 1). Sims himself views the Elm Decline as a result of man's interference, but also accepts that there is evidence for climatic deterioration in this period. He has suggested that a result of this change in climate and of soil deterioration might have been to force the population to 'change from a nomadic existence to one where a stable community was built up', in effect a change from 'incipient agriculture' to the more intensive system in evidence on this site.

The archaeological implications of this suggestion are interesting, whether or not Sims's detailed arguments are accepted. They suggest that the Elm Decline does not mark the beginning of Neolithic clearance but may correspond more closely with a period of intensified activity. If so, it becomes less of an *archaeological* problem, and the pioneering phases of clearance must be sought at an earlier date.

There are three reasons for accepting this revision. The most serious objection to connecting the first period of clearance to the Elm Decline is its very synchroneity. This poses two problems which this model could not contain. It runs counter to the distributional evidence for a slow expansion of settlement from lighter, well-drained soils into less favourable areas; and, on a larger scale, it also contradicts the notion that farming was gradually introduced across Europe from south-east to north-west. In the second case, Ammerman and Cavalli-Sforza have tried to show that the earliest radiocarbon dates for Neolithic activity in different regions support the spread of agriculture from its traditional areas of origin at an approximately constant rate (1971). Although their detailed selection of radiocarbon dates has met with criticism (Evett, 1973), the general trend which they expose still seems to be correct. It conflicts absolutely with the synchroneity of the Elm Decline.

A second difficulty arises if an attempt is made to set the Mesolithic/Neolithic transition as late as the Elm Decline. The greatest problem with the late Mesolithic is simply its failure to meet up with the succeeding period. The majority of radiocarbon dates still seem to lie in the fifth millennium b.c., with only a small number in the earlier fourth millennium. This applies particularly in southern England, where Mesolithic and Neolithic distributions overlap, but not, for instance, in western Scotland, where Clyde Cairns and Obanian shell middens show an almost complementary distribution. In Ireland the degree of overlap is controversial (Woodman, 1974b). What apparently happens in most parts of Britain is that the frequency of dated sites declines, following a classic S-shaped

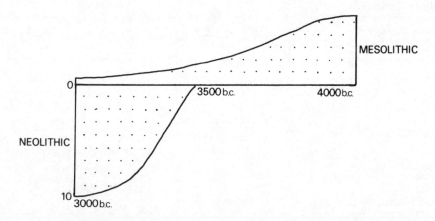

2:1   Chronological distribution of late Mesolithic and early Neolithic radiocarbon dates from southern England, plotted at two standard deviations.

curve, before any Neolithic activity replaces them (fig. 2:1). This suggests three alternative solutions: to invoke an independent demise of Mesolithic activity, for which there is no other evidence; 'to assume that this is a fortuitous product of archaeological sampling; or to postulate that the pioneering stage of the Neolithic began in the earlier fourth millennium b.c. and led to progressive acculturation.

There are good reasons for accepting this last alternative. The dates at present available for extended clearings are very much the same as those for large Neolithic monuments. Case has argued cogently that the difficulties of pioneer agriculture, particularly after settlement by sea, would not allow such undertakings until the population had achieved a 'stable adjustment' to its new surroundings, perhaps at a time when hunting was already less viable (1969, cf. Sims, 1973, p. 234). If this were so, Sims's suggestion might be partly correct, and a climatic fluctuation, mirrored to some extent in the Elm Decline, would also correspond with the first period of extended farming. This could account

for the presence of open grassland on the chalk at this time, and Limbrey now considers this to be related, not to an initial large-scale clearance, but to a developed stage of settlement after earlier activity had depleted the soil, with the loss of part of its molluscan fauna (1975, p. 185).

The extent to which the public monuments may relate to this level of organisation can be demonstrated by a simple example. The clearing at Hockham Mere seems to have lasted about 230 radiocarbon years, with an initial date of 3036 ± 115 b.c. (Q– 1048). Following the work of Tauber, Sims has attempted to relate the position of his sampling site to the pollen catchment which it represents (1973, p. 233). His smallest estimate is an area of 36 sq. km. Assuming that this overall episode (or episodes) lasted roughly 250 *calendar* years, it is possible to estimate the minimum effort involved in stripping this area of trees, assuming that no part was cleared more than once. This calculation makes use of the felling rate for stone axes provided by Iversen. This suggests that the smallest work-effort required for clearance would

TABLE 1: *The Neolithic clearance at Hockham Mere*

Effects on forest	Agricultural indicators	Interpretation
Temporary local reduction		Pioneer settlement and woodland grazing
Second temporary reduction		As above
Clearance of major trees	**ELM DECLINE**	Young trees felled; older trees ringed
Some colonisation and scrub		Drying of timber
Clearance of scrub		Burning of dried wood
		Shifting agriculture with woodland grazing. Reduction of nutrients
	Appearance of grassland	leading to greater grazing.
Start of regeneration	Cereals and grassland	Mixed farming. Two phases, the second on a greater scale
Regeneration of elm and ash		Depletion of soil nutrients
		Abandonment
Full secondary forest		

Minimum pollen catchment *c.* 36 sq. km.
Elm Decline to fall of herb pollen *c.* 236 radiocarbon years.
Based on data from Sims 1973.

have been about 4,000 man-hours per annum. This corresponds quite closely with estimates of the work requirement for building an earthen long barrow (Renfrew, 1973a, p. 547). But it must be added that Sims himself admits that his calculations are tentative – and this applies even more to the present scheme.

These arguments imply clearance before the Elm Decline, but none of them *prove* it. However, there is pollen evidence which is quite consistent with this outline. Six sites in Cumbria have demonstrated clearance before the Elm Decline, and work in Ireland and elsewhere is giving similar results. Most botanists have so far treated these episodes as a Mesolithic phenomenon, not because of their particular character, but because of the demands of the prevailing Neolithic chronology. A. G. Smith, however, has cast doubts on this procedure, pointing out how the date of the first clearance at Ballyscullion corresponds very closely with those from the Neolithic settlement at Ballynagilly (1975). Woodman has also argued that hunting, with or without burning, was not important in the Irish Mesolithic (1976). Pennington, working in Cumbria, has preferred a Mesolithic context for similar episodes, although she specifically noted that the early clearance at Blea Tarn was not very different from a later episode on the same site: 'the Neolithic effect on the primary vegetation was, though more intense, *similar in kind to one of Mesolithic date for which no material evidence in artefacts remains*' (1975) (my italics). Elsewhere in the Lake District there are perhaps five other sites demonstrating clearance before the Elm Decline. At Storrs Moss, where worked timber was recovered in excavation, there were two such episodes, the later possibly associated with arable farming (Oldfield in Powell *et al.*, 1971). At Williamson's Moss there is greater ambiguity, since both Mesolithic and Neolithic artefacts are known near the sampling site. At Williamson's Moss and again at Barfield Tarn, these minor episodes were followed by clearance for cultivation at the Elm Decline (Pennington, 1975, p. 84). Another precocious clearing was at Ehenside Tarn (Walker, 1966); it was a radiocarbon date for the Neolithic settle-

ment here which was partly responsible for the extension of this period back from the later third millennium b.c. It now appears that even this date may belong to a developed phase. In no case is the Cumbrian evidence decisive, but it is perhaps significant that five of the six sites with possible pioneer clearings are situated near the coast (fig. 2:2).

Evidence is not confined to Cumbria and Northern Ireland, although these are the areas where pollen analysts have been most active. In East Anglia, Dimbleby and Evans concluded that the first forest clearance at Broome Heath took place about 3500 b.c. (in Wainwright, 1972, pp. 86 ff.), and recently published work on the North Yorkshire Moors raises similar issues (Spratt and Simmons, 1976):

> A feature of the period around the *Ulmus* decline is the conglomeration of small forest recessions just prior to that event, so that the decline of *Ulmus* itself . . . appears as the culmination of a series of clearances rather than suddenly. Such interference phases might represent the end of Mesolithic occupation or might equally be due to initial Neolithic incursions.

Once again the nature of these early episodes is not apparent, and the authors suggest that they might show some opening of the upland forest for hunting. They note that the specifically Neolithic clearings on the moors 'were more pronounced than those of Mesolithic times, *but not different in kind*' (my italics).

As this last quotation makes clear, it is not easy to characterise these early clearings. Not all were of short duration, and the first episode at Ballyscullion may have covered a century. There is little evidence for the use of fire, except at Storrs Moss, where arable farming is also a possibility. None of these clearings seems to have included cereals but these are in evidence from the Elm Decline onwards. John Coles has argued, on the basis of more recent pioneer agriculture, that the earliest interference with the forest would have left little or no pollen evidence (1976). If this is true, it may be more rewarding to isolate the archaeological traces of this early phase. ApSimon has already suggested an 'Earliest Neolithic' period ending about 3500 b.c. There need not be any conflict between this suggestion and the pollen record (1976). As A. G. Smith has remarked, 'It may be that the decline in elm is overemphasised both in the pollen diagrams and in the literature' (1970, p. 91).

THE CLEARANCE OF WOODLAND

Evidence from analogy

The location of clearings In all pioneering agriculture the choice of clearance site is especially crucial, the more so since the farmer may have no experience of the area to guide him. How-

ever, there is widespread traditional evidence that the ecological preferences of particular trees and plants are normally well understood. John Coles has recently considered the archaeological implications of pioneer agriculture in Canada and Russia (1976). Here tree types were certainly employed as a guide to local fertility and windfalls were also used as a means of examining the subsoil. Another clue to soil conditions was the ease of splitting these windfalls. Because of the time required to prepare the ground for agriculture areas with natural plant foods were also favoured, a procedure which was recommended by Lord Bacon.

There have been suggestions that early Neolithic farmers specifically sought out areas where

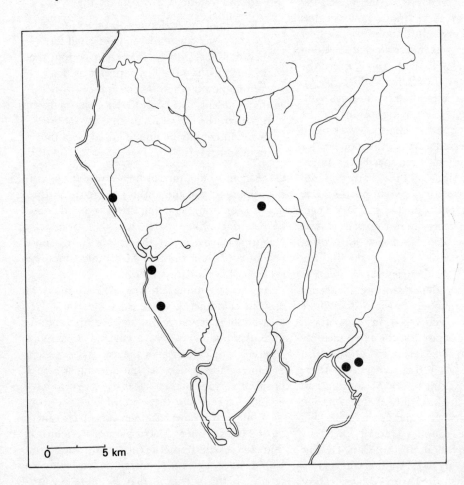

2:2   The location of pre-Elm Decline clearings in Cumbria.

particular trees were growing. This is one explanation of the events in those parts of Ireland where elm was the commonest tree. Mitchell (1956) has suggested that the pioneer settlers in such areas selected relatively pure stands of elm, partly as a source of leaf fodder, but principally as a clue to local fertility. The one difficulty with this argument is that elm is notoriously difficult to work. Very much the same approach may apply to the later fall of lime pollen (Turner, J., 1962). This was at one time seen as another climatically induced phenomenon, but now it appears to result from human interference. Lime may have been selected as another source of fodder, or indeed of bast, but again its chief importance may have been as a guide to better quality soils. There is the further complication that both elm and lime are slow to recover from interference and do not release pollen again for several years.

Selective clearance One extension of this principle is through forest management, the careful manipulation of woodland areas to fulfil specific timber requirements. It is difficult to use pollen analysis to investigate selective interference of this kind, mainly because the intervals between regrowth and pollination vary from one species to another. The regular culling of one particular tree can lead to its virtual exclusion from the pollen record and the over-representation of others of far less economic importance (cf. Rackham, 1976, p. 82). Even so, the high proportion of hazel pollen in the Somerset Levels does suggest Neolithic and Bronze Age coppicing, and preserved wood showing appropriate growth patterns has now been excavated (Coles, J. and Orme, 1976; cf. Turner, J., 1965, p. 351). Pollarding would also have been employed in later prehistory to supply the many oak timbers used in defensive and domestic architecture.

Other forms of selective interference are equally hard to confirm on the basis of physical evidence. One alternative to the total stripping of tree cover is the deliberate removal of the upper canopy, retaining only the trunks. The cut material can then be spread on the ground

and burnt, leaving the forest floor open to light-loving plants. A further alternative was suggested in Walker's study of Neolithic activity in Cumbria (1966), that trees might merely have been ring-barked and the intervening spaces used until these had died. This might be five to fifteen years after the bark was removed. There is some evidence for this type of procedure from the Swiss site of Niederwil. This was a settlement providing remarkable evidence of waterlogged timber buildings. One curious feature of the site was that the sequence of houses established in excavation did not correspond to the sequence of felling established by dendrochronology. The excavator, Waterbolk, argues that some of the trees were not actually felled, but were ring-barked, and then left standing until the timber was needed (1972). A variant of this arrangement is to attack the smaller trees initially and to fell the larger ones a year or so later.

In each case, once the initial opening had allowed light-loving plants to flourish, the effects of grazing animals would assume increasing importance. Cattle, and particularly pigs, have a most destructive effect on woodland, not only by suppressing secondary growth, but also by attacking the trees themselves. A. G. Smith has observed that in winter cattle can even strip elm bark (1975, p. 65). It is possible that by carefully controlled grazing at the right intensity forest clearings could be maintained and even extended. Conversely, cattle will not attack the young shoots of hazel and this may be one reason why it increases its holding in secondary forest. Groenman-van-Waateringe has recently argued that controlled grazing of this kind can also lead to the creation of hedges (1972). She points out that a number of characteristic hedge plants are already recorded as pollen or charcoal in British Neolithic contexts. On a rather similar principle, Pollard has used the species composition of some modern hedges to suggest their origins in medieval woodland (1973).

Complete clearance Full clearance proceeds in two ways: by felling or by fire setting. The actual choice of method will probably be governed by both the size and the hardness of the timber.

There is now a valuable body of experimental work on the problems of felling and from this it would appear that stone axes can be almost as efficient as metal tools. The best-known experiment (Iversen, 1956) suggested that one archaeologist could clear about a hectare of forest in five weeks. In eighteenth-century Canada the felling rate using a steel axe was roughly double this figure, but in modern Brazil clearance with metal tools is at a rate of about one hectare a month (Coles, J., 1973, pp. 20 ff.). There are many imponderables, such as the precise way in which different tools were used, and the time needed to fell trees of different sizes. Startin (1976) gives estimates which range from 7 minutes for felling a tree 15 cm across to 90 minutes for one 60 cm across. Evidence from preserved timbers shows very clearly that felling normally depended not on brute force but on splintering off chips around the trunk to create a 'sharpened pencil' outline. Tool marks on felled timbers found in the Somerset Levels suggest the use of an axe rather than chisels and wedges, although wooden wedges were almost certainly used in cleaving planks (Coles, J., Hibbert and Orme, 1973). Fire setting would normally be reserved for the larger or more resistant trees. Startin suggests that those of more than 60 cm diameter would only be cut down to supply building material (1976, p. 11). This is consistent with the practice in Somerset, where the larger trees were used. Carefully managed, fire setting need not be labour-intensive and Shaw has described an instance in West Africa where a tree 44 m high was despatched in six hours (1969). Burnt tree stumps are on record from Storrs Moss in the Neolithic and Thorne Waste in the Late Bronze Age (Powell *et al.*, 1971; Buckland, 1976).

In either case a large amount of debris would then need to be burnt, not only to clear the ground but also to eradicate weeds. And for clearance to be fully effective it might be necessary to remove the boles of dead trees, although these would eventually rot in the ground. Burning would need to be thorough, and carefully controlled. Conklin's observations show that it could be undertaken in several stages until the ground was fully prepared (1957). Felling might have taken place in early summer, when the sap was no longer rising and when there was time for the wood to dry. In Russia bark was stripped from felled trees to hasten this process (Coles, J., 1976). Slow fires were essential and needed careful management. One technique was the rolling of logs. Not all timber was equally productive, alder, for example, providing more ash than other trees (Coles, J., 1976). In some cases felled timber was actually imported to be burnt, and Estyn Evans has pointed out how up to 4 hectares of woodland could be burnt to nourish the soil in a tenth of this area (1975, p. 3). In any cycle of shifting exploitation firebreaks might also be needed to protect the secondary cover in adjoining plots (cf. Conklin, 1957). There would also be a need for fencing. The eventual clearance of the secondary forest, though rather easier, would have followed similar lines.

Artefact evidence

The archaeological evidence is limited but certainly conforms to this scheme. There is above all a large corpus of artefacts, conventionally associated with clearance, and spanning a period of perhaps 2,000 years. For all its abundance, this material is little understood. The chronology of flint and stone axes is only documented in part; their overall distribution has never been compiled; and there are even difficulties in understanding their use. There can be little doubt that many of the tools normally described as axes had very varied functions, despite an evident similarity of form. Some of these 'axes' are far too small to have been used directly in forestry and may have served as chisels or leatherworking tools. Others again are too large to have been used at all. In some cases their very quality gives them away; the jade axes imported into Britain in the Neolithic are one example (Campbell Smith, 1963), the chalk 'axes' from Woodhenge another (Cunnington, 1929, p. 113). The symbolic aspects of the larger items have been considered by Sherratt (1976) and Tyler has shown that the weights of flint axes can fall into three distinct groups (1976).

There are probably four functions to be distinguished: axes *stricto sensu*, adzes, stone wedges, and hoes or mattocks for use in cultivation. Although some progress can be made in separating the first two on morphological grounds, the others are better distinguished by analysis of edge-wear patterns. Sonnenfeld (1963) has done experimental work on hoes, but this approach has yet to be extended to British material. Startin has shown evidence that stone wedges might well have been perforated towards the butt. A comparatively slight shaft could then have been used to hold the wedge in place from a position of safety (1976, p. 9). This interpretation could well be applied to European shoe-last adzes and to some of the British axe hammers, both of which have been claimed, amongst other things, as agricultural tools (cf. Fowler, 1971; Bradley, 1972). One site where this could apply is Barmston in Yorkshire, where Varley found a quantity of felled and apparently shaped timber associated with three of these tools (1968). Apart from edge-wear analysis, work is in progress on the extant remains of felled timbers, and the evidence from Somerset certainly shows the use of axes, adzes and wooden wedges early in the Neolithic (Coles, J., Hibbert and Orme, 1973). The few British 'axeheads' with hafts have now been reviewed by Savory, but only in terms of panoramic cultural diffusion (1971).

The chronology of stone axes is still uncertain, and there is conflict between the evidence from the production sites and the few discoveries of these tools in Bronze Age contexts. Indeed, on Middle Bronze Age sites they have been dismissed as rubbish survivals (e.g. Stone, 1941, p. 136). In fact, there are dates as late as the fourteenth century b.c. for antler picks from flint mines and the twelfth century b.c. for the production of other axes. It was only in the Late Bronze Age that a full range of woodworking tools was developed, and it is doubtful whether bronze implements played much part in primary clearance (but see Godwin and Clifford, 1938, p. 394, for waterlogged oak and pine trees felled

with Late Bronze Age axes). It was not until the Iron Age that a suitable replacement for the heavy stone tool was found. In this period also the modern type of saw was developed. Iron hoes were another innovation at that time (cf. Manning, 1970).

It is only in the Neolithic that these items show really clear spatial patterns. Whatever the precise functions of 'axes' as a class, some relationship with clearance and cultivation is inescapable. But there is a problem, in that their numbers on the ground cannot be treated as any index of the intensity of clearance. In Cumbria, where the chronology of Langdale axes offers some control, there is an inverse relationship between the intensity of activity, as measured by pollen analysis, and the distribution of Neolithic axes in the field (Bradley, 1972). These are most frequent in the areas with less durable or extensive clearance. In Wessex and the Cotswolds, the same relationship exists between the areas with public monuments, which may have been constructed in grassland, and the main distribution of axe finds (cf. Tyler, 1976). In each case this distribution is a measure of repeated but limited onslaughts on forest or cultivated land, and fewer finds are made where the ground remained open for longer. Similarly, in the early Bronze Age axe hammers are absent in those parts of Cumbria with pollen evidence for grassland (Bradley, 1972).

Chronological trends

There are some chronological trends within this evidence. These relate to the location of clearings, the techniques of felling and the economic possibilities of pioneer agriculture.

One way of viewing the gradual retreat of the forest is to compare the ratios of arboreal and non-arboreal pollen between a series of sites, but the use of this method for dating does of course presuppose a fairly simple and uniform process of clearance. One area where it has been employed with some success is the New Forest, where Dimbleby has suggested the relative sequence of a number of barrows and other earthworks (1954). It is possible to make a different use of this same principle. Figure 2:3 summarises this ratio for all the reliably dated clearance phases in England, Scotland and Wales. The basic sample is that used by Godwin (1975), with some subsequent additions. Only clearings with radiocarbon dates or direct archaeological associations have been used. To ensure comparability soil-pollen analyses are not included. This ratio is plotted on a 400-year moving average, omitting the later Neolithic where too little data is available for calculations of this kind. The resulting diagram merely summarises the local environment of these particular clearance horizons. For this reason it may be regarded as some reflection of the processes described above.

Setting aside the later Neolithic where there is not enough evidence, there seem to be two general cycles towards open country, one beginning in the earlier Neolithic and *possibly* gaining momentum only by the second millennium b.c.; and a second, more rapid cycle, beginning with the first millennium. There are two ways of viewing this pattern: either as a prolonged cycle of clearance, regeneration and renewed clearance, or as a series of successive onslaughts on the landscape of different areas. The second interpretation seems more appropriate, and on this basis the higher ratios of arboreal pollen might denote those phases in which clearance was directed into more wooded areas, including primary forest. Conversely, lower ratios might represent activity in those zones which had already been strongly affected. What this diagram implies is that the cycle of forest clearance discussed so far is one which was not specific to a single period or to a single economic regime. Much of the discussion of Neolithic pioneer agriculture might apply to the Late Bronze Age too.

It is possible that other changes in the nature of forest clearance can be recognised from more conventional sources. One such change may in fact span the conventional Neolithic/Bronze Age division. It is perhaps first seen in the massive timber constructions of the southern English henges, which necessitated the shaping of oak uprights up to a metre in diameter. Those at Durrington Walls were almost certainly brought

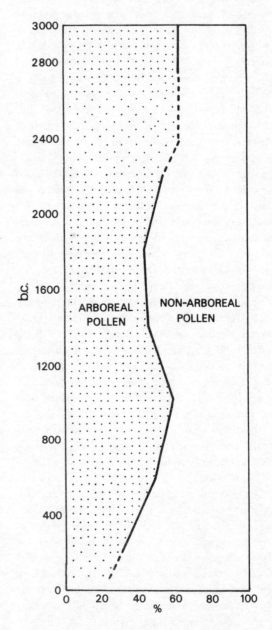

2:3   The percentages of arboreal and non-arboreal pollen in dated clearance horizons, plotted on a 400-year moving average. Dates were originally plotted at two standard deviations.

to the site from alluvial or Greensand deposits some distance away, and yet the artefacts from the excavation included only seven possible woodworking tools (Wainwright and Longworth, 1971, p. 222). This is in complete contrast with the number of antler picks abandoned after digging the ditch. The implication must be that much of the preliminary shaping work was carried out at the felling site, a reasonable enough procedure considering the weight of wood to be moved. But this does not explain the rarity of smaller tools at the site itself, and it is possible that the detailed carpentry was carried out with metal implements, reworked when they were blunted or broken. This problem becomes acute with Musson's reconstruction of the circles as roofed buildings (in Wainwright and Longworth, 1971, pp. 363 ff.). A bronze axe has in fact been found in an equivalent context at the Mount Pleasant henge (Wainwright, 1970). This difficulty may be solved by Burgess's chronology for the period (1976a).

The major transition may be a little later, and should perhaps appear with the adoption of axe hammers early in the second millennium b.c. If any of these were used in felling there could have been a gradual change from Neolithic techniques of clearance to the use of the beetle and wedge. It is quite possible that in the second millennium b.c. clearance may have been directed towards soils which could support more substantial trees and, if so, the assembling of timber for the great henge monuments might be only the start of a process. In the earlier Bronze Age tree trunks over a metre in diameter were adapted as coffins (Ashbee, 1960, p. 86), and recent radiocarbon dates also reveal that a number of dugout canoes are of the same period, some of them made from trunks up to 1·6 m in diameter and 15 m in length (McGrail and Switsur, 1975). Other hollowed tree trunks may have been used as cooking troughs (Sayce, 1945). In the Late Bronze Age there is a similar relationship between the second cycle of forest clearance and the building of hill forts.

In each of the major onslaughts on the forest, the range of economic options will have been limited and for this reason changes in the extent of clearance may have permitted corresponding changes in the economy.

Burning is not just a means of clearing away debris. In an equilibrium ecosystem there is a limit of about 10 per cent to the energy which can be passed to the consumer, while the remaining 90 per cent has to be recycled through the litter food chain. In a wooded environment much of the biomass is concentrated above the ground in trunks, branches and foliage, with a finite humus component in the subsoil. Burning can release these mineral nutrients, but they are dispersed once a few crops have been taken (cf. Welinder, 1975, pp. 28 ff.). If the burning is too rapid, or if dense surface cover generates too much heat, these advantages are put at risk, and iron-rich soils can be harmed. Although the advantages of burning are relatively short-lived and crop yields soon start to fall, this can be partly due to competition from weeds. As the nutrients acquired by burning are gradually lost, a lengthy period of fallowing becomes necessary, but if burning is resumed at the scrub stage this will be less productive and the soil itself may need more attention. As Boserup has pointed out, a shortening of the fallow period can mean an increase in individual work effort (1965). To some extent this may be mirrored by the use of more elaborate agricultural tools, but Coles has observed that the plough can only be used in forest agriculture after the tree stumps have rotted (1976). Because pioneer clearings are often short-lived, this restriction would mean that the plough might only be used on soils which had already proved themselves more than usually resilient. It may have been the conscious application of manure to *these* areas which did most to sustain the extensive clearings known in several regions of Neolithic Britain.

There are also limitations on stock raising in a forested environment. In an interesting study of this problem, Andrew Fleming argues that there was little scope for the emergence of pastoralism until a grassland landscape had developed (1972a). He distinguishes between the evidence from small clearings and that from the larger open areas. In the smaller forest clearings it *would* be possible to obtain enough leaf fodder to support a herd of animals, but this would be a considerable burden. 'If 20 or 30 . . . cattle required a square kilometre of forest browsing during the summer, and the best part of another for their winter keep, domestic animals at this stage could never have been more than a supplementary source of food.' In the case of the larger open areas, he offers a series of alternative estimates, drawn from ethnographic evidence, for the relationship between population and the total extent of clearance. His figures show that if half the land were in fact used for cattle – and this would be essential if the soil were to remain productive – no one would be able to keep more than about five animals. Once again a pastoral economy is seen to be rather improbable until woodland had given way to grassland.

THE CLEARANCE OF GRASSLAND

There seem to be two possible routes to the creation of open grassland. The first is evident from some of the earlier examples. In these cases grassland came into being less because it was specifically required than as a consequence of mounting pressure on woodland. Once the primary cover had been disturbed, the pioneer farmers initiated a cycle of diminishing returns, in which land that ought to have reverted to forest was cleared at decreasing intervals as crop yields fell. Ultimately, all that might have been needed was the regular burning of scrub. This procedure could be consistent with population pressure, and each reduction of the fallow period would involve an increase in work effort which was not completely offset by an increase in production. To this extent the creation of open grassland might be fortuitous, even unwelcome.

The second approach was perhaps more carefully calculated. Here John Evans has suggested that the ard might have been used to break up the surface in order to create pasture. This is an interesting reversal of Boserup's argument, that the plough can be adopted as the one means of continuing cultivation under grassland fallow. It is a view that Dr Evans first put forward to

account for the ard marks beneath South Street long barrow (1972, p. 364), but it might also explain the equally short-lived cultivation which preceded the building of Wayland's Smithy. In the Late Bronze Age, the presence of woodland snails in the lynchets at Rams Hill invites a similar conclusion, and here again it was shown that cultivation was succeeded by grassland (Evans in Bradley and Ellison, 1975, p. 143). Once established, these conditions lasted a millennium.

There is a considerable difference between woodland and grassland conditions. Grassland has more humus per unit area than woodland, and for this reason properly maintained grassland has a greater potential under cultivation. Welinder has suggested that land used for growing crops may feed ten times as many people as it would when used as pasture (1975). There seems little doubt that alternate husbandry, the alternation of cropping and grazing, is usually more productive than the maintenance of permanent pasture. The difficulty is in clearing areas of grassland once they had become established.

Grass roots are resistant to ordinary burning, and therefore Boserup argues that a plough would be needed to clear grassland fallow (1965). This may be appropriate to modern conditions but, as Estyn Evans points out, there are grazed swards in Ireland which even today are too tough for the plough (1975). This is a serious objection, since practical experiment has shown that an ard would not be equal to the task of clearance, particularly if it lacked an iron tip. Therefore, two alternative courses of action might be open: to retain the grassland as pasture without attempting cultivation; or to break it by hand preparatory to a fresh phase of ploughing. This runs counter to Estyn Evans's own view that in the Neolithic the ard might have been used to break the soil before hand-ridging.

There is some evidence for the treatment of grassland before iron was available for ards and mattocks. Spade irons are a Roman innovation (Manning, 1970). Two Neolithic sites are instructive. At Windmill Hill it appears that the turf had been stripped from the site before the enclosure bank was built, an illogical procedure unless it was intended to release the subsoil for tillage. This layer showed signs of possible disturbance (Dimbleby in I. F. Smith, 1965, pp. 34 ff.). Later work on the associated snails supports these observations, and Dimbleby has suggested that this was an early instance of paring and burning (cf. Dimbleby and Evans, 1974). This consists of stripping off the sods, allowing them to dry and then burning them to nourish the soil (cf. Gailey and Fenton, 1970). There may also be some analogy with Dalladies, where 0·75 hectares of turf were cut for use in the long barrow (Piggott, S. 1972a). The total effort required for this operation was estimated to be 5,750 man-hours, the equivalent on other sites of digging a quarry ditch. The excavator commented that this was an extremely wasteful procedure, since the whole of this area had been 'rendered useless for plough or pasture'. Some of this material certainly incorporated oak charcoal, but Piggott's reference to layers of 'burnt turf' calls to mind Dimbleby's earlier suggestion, although it may be that the sods were stripped to such a depth that too little soil was left. There may be some analogy with Crawford's description of traditional turf walls: 'These were once common in the . . . south of England where they were erected round intakes

from the waste, the turf being pared off the surface as a necessary prelude to cultivation' (1936). A rather similar method was adopted in Dutch 'Celtic fields' (Brongers, 1976, pp. 60 ff.).

Further evidence comes from Bronze Age sites. A number of barrows, some in marginal areas, were originally built over furrows, possibly a result of stripping off the surface in this way. These barrows include Latch Farm in Hampshire, Simondston Cairn in South Wales and Wind Hill in Lancashire (Piggott, C., 1938, fig. 2; Fox, C., 1959, fig. 50b; Tyson, 1972; see fig. 2:4). On these sites the furrows appear in the drawn sections but were not identified in excavation. At Ascot in Berkshire the furrows under a bell barrow were associated with scattered charcoal and a peak of cereal pollen (Bradley and Keith-Lucas, 1975). There was some similarity between the size of turves used in this barrow and the width of the excavated furrows.

The tool used in turf stripping may not always have been the same. In some cases a stone or bronze axe, mounted as a mattock, might have been sufficient, and there is certainly evidence that both were used in digging chalk in this period. Anthony Harding has now suggested that some bronze 'axes' were agricultural tools (1976).

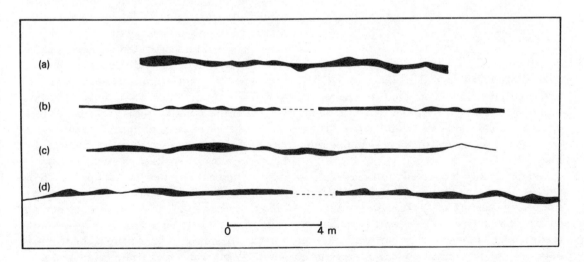

2:4   Profiles of buried soils showing possible furrows: (a) Ascot (Bradley and Keith-Lucas, 1975); (b) Latch Farm (Piggott, C., 1938); (c) Wind Hill (Tyson, 1972); (d) Simondston Cairn (Fox, C., 1959).

Otherwise, a wooden spade would have been perfectly adequate and there is evidence for these in the Bronze Age at Gwithian and Skaill and in the Iron Age at Danebury and Rudh' an Dunain (Thomas, C., 1970; Shepherd, 1976; B. Cunliffe, pers. com.; Scott, L., 1934, p. 221). Other tools traditionally used in paring and burning include flaying spades, foot ploughs and breast ploughs, and the irregularity of the Ascot furrows could imply that a different implement was used there.

If the changes in woodland clearance during the Early Bronze Age mark one transition, this onslaught upon open grassland must mark an equally significant threshold. The two changes may be related to one another and it is possible that as the land cleared rather earlier was invaded by grassland, fresh areas of forest may have been brought into use. Fleming has in fact suggested that mobile pastoralists could have driven farmers off the best land. And just as renewed forest clearance provided a valuable source of raw material, the second millennium b.c. also sees greater use of turf. This remained the case until the adoption of more durable agricultural implements in the later Bronze Age. By this time too there is evidence for fresh inroads into the primary forest.

STONE CLEARANCE

So far, the evidence has mostly applied to lowland areas of Britain and to those with light, fertile soils. For this reason, the major emphasis has been placed on Neolithic activity. Stone clearance usually became a problem with the expansion of settlement from its Neolithic outlines.

Stone clearance has already attracted an extensive, if inconclusive, literature, most of which concerns the nature of cairns. For this reason, only a short review of the principal points is needed. One comment must be made at the outset. Normally, stone clearance is not a feature of the first man-made landscape and may not be associated with preparation for crops. A normal requirement is for the natural forest soil to be

eroded or deeply disturbed before quantities of boulders are released (Fleming, 1971a). This applies as much to erosion through over-grazing as it does to cereal agriculture, and field clearance today is as characteristic of pasture as it is of arable land. There are frequent references to charcoal layers underneath upland cairns, whether the function of these individual monuments is understood or not. In these cases, it is noticeable that hazel is almost always present and is often the only species identified. Hazel will resist clearance by fire and normally regenerates rapidly. It is shunned by grazing cattle and a number of writers have noticed how it can increase its density in secondary forest (Smith, A. G., 1970). The burnt layers under these cairns may possibly show that forest after modification.

The main evidence for stone clearance comes from cairnfields, and is rather ambiguous since so many of these sites were used for burial. For the Neolithic period, Atkinson has commented on field clearance as one mechanism by which materials for stone monuments were accumulated (1965, p. 127), and there seems no reason why the processes of land clearance and burial should have been any more exclusive in the Bronze Age. It is a moot point whether burials were attracted into an area where cairns already existed, or whether the adoption of one particular place as a cemetery offered a means of disposing of field stones; but in the Early Bronze Age there is sometimes evidence for the placing of funerary monuments in situations where any other use was impossible. For example, Graham has noted the siting of cairns on bosses of rock that could not be farmed (1956). On other sites large natural rocks, which were perhaps too heavy to move, were incorporated into stone-built monuments. Among the examples given by Lynch are a number of ring cairns (1975a), whilst there is also a widespread tendency for stone heaps to develop around one or more earthfast boulders. In later periods the relationship between cemeteries and clearance plots is equally problematic, and Jobey has commented on the association of cairnfields with hill forts in northern England (1965, p. 54).

There is some evidence for the way in which these cairns were accumulated. In a pioneering study of Scottish cairnfields, Graham commented on the changing density of surface boulders and suggested that clearance proceeded outwards from a central point (1956). This is consistent with Feachem's view that small cairns often lie in rough alignments, or along slight banks which could mark the edges of plots (1973). This does not apply on every site, however, and cairns could always develop inside fields, provided cultivation was carried out by hand. The clearance of plots towards their edges resembles the accumulation of field walls. Some insight into this process is given by a settlement at Blissmoor in Devon where the clearance of one enclosure was never completed (Fox, A., 1954, fig. 3).

The intensity of activity can be quite impressive. In one study of cairnfields Scott-Elliott noted that clearance heaps were normally spaced at about 12 m intervals, although this could fall to as little as 6 m (1967). In part of Wales, Hemp also showed that the large burial cairns fell into distinct size groups (quoted in Bowen, E. and Gresham, 1967, p. 75). The larger systems have been described by Feachem and may cover more than 40 hectares (1973). One of the most extensive cairnfields was at Chatton Sandyford in Northumberland. Here Jobey observed plough marks against the edge of one cairn and a characteristic layer of charcoal on the surface beneath it (1968). He also noticed plough damage on stones protruding from a pit sealed by the monument. Interestingly, clearance cairns are still being built on agricultural land in this area.

There is little evidence of how large stones were cleared, where they could not be incorporated in cairns. There have been few claims for 'stone holes' in the literature, and it is not always clear how far surface rocks will bed themselves in the ground to a detectable extent. At Cerreg Samson, however, a large hole underneath a portal dolmen may have been made in removing the capstone from its original position (Lynch, 1975b). In some cases fire would be used to break up large surface stones. Sarsens certainly need this treatment, as Stukeley witnessed at Avebury in the eighteenth century (Smith, I. F., 1965, p. 180). This practice may explain a layer of burnt fragments in the Bronze Age ditch at Rams Hill (Bradley and Ellison, 1975, pp. 35 and 50), and also the use of burnt sarsens in field walls at Overton Down (Bowen, H. C. and Fowler, 1961, p. 105).

The evidence from walls and similar boundaries is less open to confusion, despite the wide range of possible techniques. The structure of such features can give clues to the progress of clearance. Crawford took the view that early walls would be based on a series of 'grounders', large rocks which would need moving before thorough clearance could proceed (1936). He argued that the superstructure of these walls would tend to use smaller boulders, and applied this argument himself in deducing the extent of early clearance in part of Cornwall. This general outline certainly has its attractions, but another sequence of events is equally likely, and neither must be given any overall application. In this second sequence, the structure of linear banks betrays the difficulties of maintaining cultivation as upland soils were progressively depleted. At Beaghmore in the Neolithic and at both Swine Sty and Achnacree Moss in the Bronze Age, the lower material of a boundary was composed of soil and small stones, and as erosion bared larger rocks these were incorporated in the upper layers (Pilcher, 1969; Machin, 1971; Barrett, Hill and Stevenson, 1976). At Achnacree Moss the boundary banks were associated with shallow ditches cut through the underlying podsol, and the excavators suggested that this was done to improve the local drainage and to bring degraded land back into use. Such an approach might have been combined with burning to control the quality of the browse. There may be some analogy between the basic structure of these boundaries and the sequence from turf to stone seen in so many round barrows.

One example may clarify this last point. In 1937 Sir Cyril Fox excavated two neighbouring round barrows in south Wales, Pond Cairn and Simondston Cairn (1959, pp. 78 ff. and 105 ff.). Both belonged to the Early Bronze Age and on pottery evidence Fox concluded that Simondston Cairn was probably the earlier. The stones in each cairn were taken from separate sources within a small area. There was varying evidence for cereal agriculture on the two sites. The earlier barrow overlay a series of furrows, probably produced with a spade. Although they were not recognised in excavation, they are clearly shown in the section drawing, and represent a very shallow treatment of the soil before the cairn was built. They did not affect the natural bedrock and some of the stones employed in this phase were definitely quarried. There was no physical evidence for cultivation under the later site and the main mound was of turf construction. A cairn ring was added to this core and the fact that it was built entirely of surface stones suggests that the surrounding area was now more intensively used. Cereals were recognised in a pit of this phase and it is tempting to suggest that the stones were collected in the fields.

Fairhurst and Taylor have argued that the changing intensity of agriculture may be reflected by different methods of stone clearance (1971). At Kilphedir they showed that the first Iron Age occupation had been associated with clearance cairns and probably with the use of hand tools like the spade and the hoe. After an interval, a second occupation followed, during which the most productive land was divided up by a series of linear banks, which they connect with the introduction of the plough to the site. Their physical layout certainly suggests a more orderly arrangement and perhaps a more intensive regime. There is possible evidence in support of this succession from the pollen analysis of nearby peat.

At first sight this sequence of agricultural techniques seems to resemble the increasingly exacting sequence of lowland areas, from forest clearance through to paring and burning. But there is an important difference: most of the environments in which stone clearance was necessary were already so precariously balanced that they held little prospect for prolonged or intensive agriculture. In this sense these highland clearances only achieved archaeological visibility in their terminal phases. If the pressures were

rather the same, the responses had to be different. In areas where stone clearance was important there is much to commend Feachem's generalisation that agriculture was significantly curtailed by environmental decline in the later Bronze Age (1973).

COLONISATION

These processes of clearance have shown two very clear tendencies. One is towards more demanding land use and may be a sign of population pressure; while the second is towards gradual environmental decline, which dislocates the settlement pattern. There is direct archaeological evidence for an increase in the area of the settled landscape, and for thresholds beyond which certain zones would fall from use or would only permit exploitation of a different kind. Despite this varied background, these changes could be accommodated in just two ways: by the expansion of existing settlements or by the creation of new ones.

These questions have been reviewed in a theoretical study by Hudson (1969). He suggests that the formation of a settlement pattern might go through three successive stages. The first would be the location of sites in more favourable environments but in a random distribution. These settlements then expanded outwards from the pioneer holdings, giving rise to a series of unevenly spaced clusters. Only later, when resources became the subject of competition, would sites space themselves into more regular patterns. This sequence was initially demonstrated for a series of documented settlements in North America, but the same model has been used in analysis of prehistoric settlements in Poland (Hodder and Orton, 1976, pp. 89 ff.).

There is now one study of the expansion of early settlements in two areas of southern England (Ellison and Harriss, 1972). It makes use of site catchment analysis to demonstrate that from at least the Middle Bronze Age onwards settlement sites were located so as to obtain a varied and increasingly productive range of soils. This seems consistent with demographic expansion, and the extension of settlement into areas of greater agricultural potential will have made more demands on manpower. A particularly arresting, if controversial, aspect of this study has been its application to the Saxon period, through the analysis of sequences of place names. The results of this territorial analysis seemed to suggest two main models for expansion from the primary areas: the development of new settlements in a virtual ring round a parent site and their simple replication at an approximately even spacing. These are basically equivalent to Hudson's two stages of expansion, and the same range of procedures is apparent in the Middle Ages (Chisholm, 1968, p. 127).

There are two aspects of the model to consider from the prehistoric information: the evidence for internal expansion and the evidence for thresholds beyond which the cleared areas could not support further growth. It might be at this second stage that the new settlements would form.

One initial problem is to distinguish settlement expansion from the process of settlement drift. The latter can be defined as the gradual linear or lateral movement of a settlement, and is comparable to the horizontal stratigraphy characteristic of cemeteries. It is a process best documented for Saxon and medieval villages (Beresford, M. and Hurst, 1971) and was usefully defined by D. L. Clarke in a discussion of Beaker settlements (1969, i, p. 57). It can arise from such basic factors as rotting house foundations, insanitary living floors, eroded arable plots and contaminated pits. It is known on extensive open sites like the Iron Age occupations at Twywell, Fengate or Puddlehill (Jackson, 1975; Pryor, 1974a; Mathews, 1976, pp. 44 ff.), but also extends to the location of individual features in enclosed compounds. This is possibly seen at Gussage All Saints, where the distribution of features in the first two phases is almost mutually exclusive (Wainwright and Switsur, 1976, fig. 3), and again at Burradon, where individual houses were replaced in the adjoining plots (Jobey, 1970, fig. 5). An intermediate case is at South Barrule, where the stone-built huts inside a hill fort formed clusters, in which the construction of new houses on the periphery blocked all access

to the earlier buildings. Interestingly enough, these later huts were also the largest (Gelling, 1963, fig. 1).

There is one important regional study of settlement growth, a paper by Jobey on the Roman stone-built settlements between the Forth and the Tyne (1974). He demonstrates, mainly from surface evidence, that many of these sites did in fact show expansion: in upland areas the proportion was about 31 per cent. Excavation inside these enclosures has shown quite clearly that the number of houses did increase, and on sites with limited space this tendency is confirmed by a fall in the size of the later buildings. This estimate compares with a figure of 30 per cent for those hill forts in southern Scotland which show field evidence for an increase in area (data from RCAM Scotland, 1956 and 1957 and RCAHM Scotland, 1967). It is interesting that in Jobey's study, which covers much of the same region, 19 per cent of the hill forts are overlain by Roman native settlements, but that these settlements include 50 per cent of the largest sites.

In other cases it is not possible to use the internal area as a basis for analysis; but here rather similar results can be achieved by considering the human effort invested in the basic enclosures. For instance, over 40 per cent of the palisaded enclosures known in northern Britain seem to have been replaced by earthworks, although not all of these should be classed as 'forts'; and over 20 per cent of these palisaded sites show evidence for at least one replacement of the basic stockade, whether or not an earthwork was constructed later (data from Ritchie, A., 1970). There is some tendency for greater development to take place on the double-palisaded sites, where the work effort would in any case be greater, but the size of the sample is unacceptably small (cf. Griffiths in Bradley and Ellison, 1975, p. 228).

There is also evidence for local thresholds to expansion within an occupied area. Stanford, for example, has shown that a number of hill forts in the Central Marches increased their area by different proportions, but that the final enclosures show an optimum size of about 8 hectares

(1972, p. 316). In a similar way, the earthwork-defended enclosures of Wales show distinctive regional size ranges. These have been discussed by Hogg, who has defined eleven different groups on this basis and has shown that there is very little overlap between them (1972). In each area it seems that these enclosures did not develop beyond a certain threshold. In another paper he also argued that there is a regular density of houses inside hill forts (1971). If this has a wide application, it might reveal another limit to expansion. It is certainly apparent that this density was greatest inside the smaller earthworks (Atkinson, 1972, p. 64). On the boulder clay of north-east England Jobey has observed a comparable pattern among the stone-built native farms (1974). Here there is certainly evidence for an increase in the number of houses on each site, but this increase was apparently curtailed at a lower limit than in upland areas nearby.

This last observation is especially important in view of the constant process of selection by which less successful settlements went out of use. This placed correspondingly greater pressures on those sites which were optimally located. Until this happened, it may have been rare for settlements to remain in being for long. But once this occurred settlement mobility became increasingly wasteful. At Chalton, for example, the later Bronze Age sites which fell out of use were replaced in the Roman period. In the Iron Age these had appeared as gaps in a quite regular pattern of settlements (Cunliffe, 1973).

RESOURCE CATCHMENTS

The relationship between resource catchments and settlements is much more complex. There is a practical limit to the number of people which an area of cleared land can support, just as there is an optimum size for this territory beyond which it would have been simpler to create a new settlement (cf. Chisholm, 1968). Unfortunately, there is no completely reliable method of estimating population or total territory from settlement area. Again, medieval experience can be helpful, since the full extent of

individual field systems can sometimes be recovered by fieldwork and checked against documentary evidence. After detailed fieldwork in Bedfordshire, David Hall has suggested that a fairly regular relationship existed in this area between the maximum size of villages and the extent of their arable land. On good soils the greatest size of the settlement is 7 per cent of the area of its arable land, but this would fall to just 2·6 per cent if the arable were entirely on the less productive clay (Hall, 1972). That the relationship is so regular is an argument for population pressure (fig. 2:5). It would be useful to establish a series of comparable parameters for prehistoric sites, but this is rarely possible.

As an alternative, the resource catchments of early settlements have been much studied. These have two possible implications for the spread of sites. In a study based partly upon modern peasant agriculture, Chisholm has suggested that restrictions of mobility may have limited the distance over which it was profitable to exploit land from a single centre (1968). In the Middle Ages the minimum distance between English villages was about 1·6 km and in most areas all the land was within 4 km. When agricultural land expanded beyond this limit, it might be more practical to create another settlement. Unfortunately, this principle is hard to recognise in operation. Where there *was* competition for space, equally placed settlements might be closer together, and in areas where there was still room for expansion there is no way of inferring the changing boundary. Analogy with Chisholm's work suggests that the 2-km-radius catchment area adopted by Ellison and Harriss would only be appropriate in this second situation. This radius works moderately well when the authors consider the parishes of the Saxon period, but the problem is that the villages were more extensive than most of their prehistoric counterparts. The range of areas is from 2 to 5 hectares (Rahtz, 1976). There are two ways of checking the usefulness of this hypothetical catchment area: by relating it to other estimates of the cleared area based on excavated data, or by measuring it against the actual spacing of prehistoric sites where proper field survey is available.

One site on which it is possible to check the Ellison and Harriss interpretation is Little Woodbury. Here Bersu used the assumed number of storage pits and granaries to calculate that 73 bushels of corn were probably being stored each year (1940, p. 64). This figure was based upon an unfortunate mathematical error and should be corrected to about 666 bushels (Bowen, H. C., 1969, p. 11). The same correction must be applied to Bersu's estimate of the arable area needed to produce this quantity of corn, increasing his figure of 20 acres to roughly 180 acres (79 hectares). In Ellison and Harriss's hypothetical area, based upon a 2-km radius about the site, the best potential arable covers no less than 700 hectares. Whatever allowance is made for fallowing, there is a great difference between these figures, and the second estimate seems much too large. If the estimates were reduced proportionately the catchment area would have a radius of 0·7 km. One way of tackling this problem could be the use of sherd scatters to discover the extent of manuring.

The same conclusion, that a 2-km-radius catchment is too large, may be drawn from published field survey. In at least six areas field survey seems to show a roughly regular pattern of settlement which lends itself to simple calculation, although the sample is too small for nearest neighbour analysis. In each case the quality of the original work does suggest that a representative pattern has been recovered. The smallest spacing of apparently contemporary sites is in the Iron Age at Chalton, and on Portsdown Hill, Hampshire, where sites are on average 0·8 km apart (Cunliffe, 1973; J. Johnston, pers. com.). On the boulder clay of north-east England Jobey noted that native settlements could occur roughly 1 km apart (1973, p. 48), while extensive fieldwork in Cornwall shows that the densest distribution of rounds is at intervals of 1·3 km (Thomas, C., 1966). This compares well with

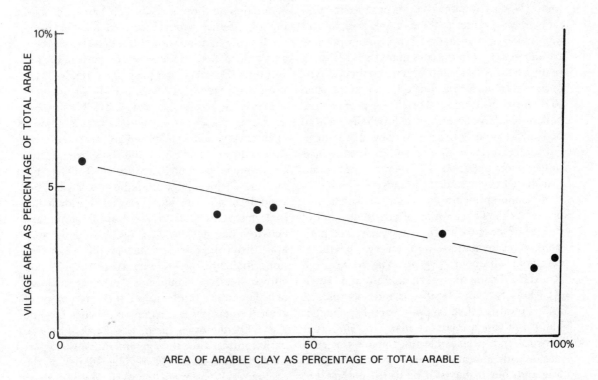

2:5 The size of medieval villages in Bedfordshire in relation to the extent of their arable land. Source: Hall, 1972.

the revised estimate for Little Woodbury. Similar work in Bedfordshire gives an average spacing for Iron Age sites of 1·5 km (Hall and Hutchings, 1972), a figure which also applies to settlements and 'forts' around the excavated site at Harehope in Peeblesshire (Feachem, 1960). The general agreement of these figures is quite striking. To place these estimates in perspective, a catchment area 1·6 km across would be the size of the average Irish townland (Buchanan, 1973). The fact that these sites are fairly evenly spaced would be explained in Hudson's model as the result of spatial competition. The degree of 'packing' may of course mean that these territories were about the minimum size that could sustain a settlement based on an Iron Age economy. Examination of another class of site tends to support this view.

One of the most distinctive of all field monuments is the broch. Fortunately, these sites are not easy to remove. Their distribution includes parts of the Scottish coastline bordered by many small islands. Although changes of shoreline present certain problems, these islands are particularly useful in that they set a maximum possible territorial extent to the sites upon them. If there really is a threshold below which a particular type of site could not be sustained, it may be possible to define it in this case. For all the peculiarities of their defensive architecture, brochs do seem to be suited to this approach, in view of the agricultural equipment found within them. It is immediately apparent that they are not found distributed evenly among islands of all sizes: is there a minimum size of island on which they occur? With the exception of one island and of several offshore rocks, chosen as defensive positions, a clear pattern does emerge, giving a threshold of about 3·75 sq. km (data from RCAHM Scotland, 1911a and b and 1928; RCAHM Scotland, 1946). Islands of this size and upwards often support brochs; smaller islands, of which there are many, do not. It is obviously not permissible to compare this conclusion with those arising from a study of southern England, but it may still be worth noting that this area is roughly equivalent to a territory extending from the broch in a 1-km radius, half

the figure adopted by Ellison and Harriss and a quarter of the figure suggested in Chisholm's study. This disparity might emphasise the importance of the sea as another resource.

So far, it appears that there is a body of evidence for the internal expansion of settlement and for local thresholds at which this growth was curtailed. There is also some evidence for the minimum area which could support a settlement at all. In each case this limit ought to be the point at which a new settlement was founded. The basic difference between the parent site and this newer settlement could be that while one gradually grew towards its limit, the other could be established in one operation, whatever its potential for subsequent expansion. If the parent site was in the same area, as Hudson's model might suggest, some problems of pioneer agriculture could be avoided.

Several writers have drawn a basic distinction between imposition and organic growth in the planning and operation of settlements. This distinction has been seen in their basic plan and in their internal layout. Little attention has been paid to the first question, although one study is available of Roman native settlements in part of Cumbria. Here Webster proposes a simple classification of settlement plans, mainly on the basis of previously published work (1971). He suggests a division between the enclosed sites and those open sites which had grown by accretion. He subdivides the enclosures into three groups, distinguishing those which are specifically defensible and those which show secondary expansion beyond the original nucleus. Webster considers that the construction of an enclosure is a unitary activity that sets his first two groups of sites apart from the others. One may have reservations about this point, since there is no reason why an open site should not have been enclosed at a later date, and indeed there is plenty of evidence that this was common practice in some areas. On the other hand, it is hard to deny a basic contrast with the agglomerative sites, particularly in view of the regular shapes of the enclosures. Webster goes on to suggest that these sites represent pioneering settlement and that the open sites show a more gradual expansion.

In this sense his enclosed and his aggregate settlements form two stages of the colonisation process, with the enclosed sites with external additions occupying a transitional place in this sequence. There is some pollen evidence in favour of this outline, and it appears that his aggregate sites were on raised ground, in open woodland or grassland, while the enclosures were mainly located in woodland. Webster himself suggests that the open sites were the later development, but it might be more logical to reverse this scheme. It should not be treated as an overall chronological sequence, and much depends on how the model accommodates settlements found by renewed fieldwork in this area (cf. Higham and Jones, 1975, p. 42).

An analogous distinction has been made by Graeme Guilbert in considering the internal plans of hillforts (1975). Following his discovery of regular zones of buildings inside Moel Y Gaer, he suggests that a distinction should be made between planned hillfort interiors and those which show organic growth, either overall or as a secondary development from a planned nucleus. He has drawn attention to the orderly rows of buildings of different types inside a variety of defended sites, including Crickley Hill, Croft Ambrey, Fridd Faldwyn and Danebury. In each case the internal plan makes it clear that the buildings conformed to a coherent design and were probably erected together. At Grimthorpe and Rams Hill they were possibly prefabricated from timbers which had been cut to length at the felling site. At Grimthorpe this also applied to the timbers used in the rampart (Bradley and Ellison, 1975, fig. 4:1). Such a pattern is

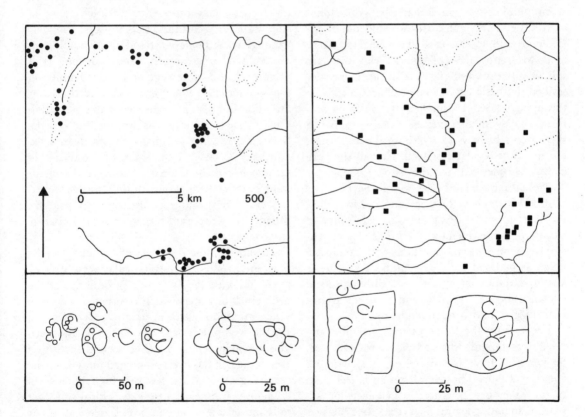

2:6   The distribution of Romano-British settlements in two areas of north-east England: (*left*) on the edge of the Cheviots; (*right*) on lower ground. Sketch plans of typical settlements below. From field surveys by George Jobey.

'imposed' on the site and contrasts with the usual palimpsest of overlapping buildings. Such a view was anticipated in 1924, when Reginald Smith claimed that rows of Iron Age pits at Wisley in Surrey showed 'the rudiments of town planning'.

So far, it has been possible to illustrate a number of the pressures and influences which determined the process of colonisation. Since so little adequate fieldwork is available, it is not possible to illustrate all of these from a single area, and discussion has for this reason been founded on scattered examples. This cannot be rectified entirely, but the major points in Hudson's theory *can* be illustrated from a single region. It is worth returning to Jobey's study of settlement growth between the Forth and the Tyne. Within this area he has drawn together a quantity of reliable fieldwork to provide basic material for analysis.

An initial distinction is made between stone-built settlements in the uplands and others on lower ground to the east. This second group tends to occupy areas of boulder clay that are still in intensive use (fig. 2:6). Clack has described the basic arrangement of settlements in the upland areas as 'smaller sites in twos and threes . . . with the average distance between these groups being 2–3 km' (1973). These clusters are not very regularly spaced. Not all sites are completely enclosed, and they show evidence for horizontal movement or expansion. Seventy per cent of the sites have between one and five huts; the average is five, but there is a wide range of variation. Some resemble Webster's class of enclosures with external additions and cannot be taken as planned settlement units. Too little is known of the basic environment, although local evidence for peat growth and stone clearance both suggest a fairly open landscape.

The sites on the lower ground are often defined by rectangular ditched enclosures. Of these, 86 per cent have five or fewer huts, with an average of four. The overall range is less than in the other group. There is evidence for expansion in both geographical zones, but this was on a smaller scale on the clay. The sites in the latter area were spaced at approximately 1-km intervals, although a few are found in pairs.

They resemble Webster's regularly planned enclosures. This environment may have been rather more wooded, but there is no evidence that it was settled later than the uplands.

This information may be summarised as follows:

1 Despite evidence for an overall expansion of settlement, this seems to be curtailed at a lower threshold in the clay than in upland areas.
2 This distinction may correspond very broadly with that between ditched enclosures and other sites.
3 It is also reflected in a contrast between the irregular spacing of upland sites and the more regular placing of those in the lowlands.
4 The spacing of the lowland sites is close to the minimum seen in earlier discussion.

It seems likely that the settlement pattern in these two zones represents different types of colonisation according to Hudson's model: 'contagious' settlement around initial holdings in the upland areas, where land was not at a premium; and more regularly spaced units on the boulder clay, where the land needed greater attention but also possessed a greater potential. Only in the latter area was there spatial competition, despite clear evidence for an overall expansion of settlements. Minor variations in settlement plan between these zones could mirror some of these distinctions. In this case, however, it seems likely that the different patterns are broadly contemporary responses to two separate environments.

To sum up: the first part of this chapter has been concerned with the physical process of clearance and with the economic possibilities of the different landscapes which resulted. Because so much attention has been paid to early farming, the main emphasis has been placed on the third and second millennia b.c. The second section of this discussion has been concerned more with the surviving settlements, few of which have been recognised from earlier periods. This means that only at a late stage in prehistory can their sequence and spacing be described.

But this is not just a consequence of poor survival. The apparent contrast conceals a single structure and for this reason the two halves of the account can be brought into relation. Instead of considering the different types of land clearance, it may be useful to look at the frequency with which these occurred. This has been attempted in figure 2:7, which represents the relative number of clearance episodes for which radiocarbon dates are available. Each date was initially plotted at two standard deviations. The time-scale is truncated at both ends. In the earlier Neolithic this has been done to leave out sites on which the Elm Decline presents problems of interpretation. In the Iron Age a false picture can be given, since the upper levels of many peat beds have been disturbed in later activity.

There is a broad correlation with the changing forms of clearance. The first phase of activity took place largely in woodland; these areas rarely remained open. The second peak of activity more frequently led to the appearance of grassland or heathland, and it was in this phase and later that stone clearance became a common phenomenon. The third and most sustained period of clearance began in the late second millennium b.c. and continued on an increasing scale through to the Iron Age and probably beyond. This corresponds to another cycle of activity in which areas of closed forest may again have been selected, as well as more open country. The implications are clear. Greater pressures were being placed on the landscape and more areas were apparently being used.

It was in this phase that the settlements themselves began to take a durable form. Because certain sites were occupied for a longer period, more of them can be recognised from earthworks and other features. Settlements were conceived on a more lasting basis and were sometimes associated with well-defined boundaries. The implications of these changes will be considered in the final chapter but it may be no accident that it was about this period of sustained colonisation that the settlement evidence should be so informative. There are the first signs that domestic sites were competing for resources and there are hints of an organised process of colonisation, both in the internal planning of some settlements and perhaps in their overall conception. There are indications of a steady expansion on some of the sites and perhaps of local limits to this growth. The second main cycle of clearance, then, shows the same processes at work as the newly created settlements themselves. If Hudson's model has the applications which have been suggested, by the Iron Age, if not earlier, parts of the landscape had been transformed and competition for its riches had begun.

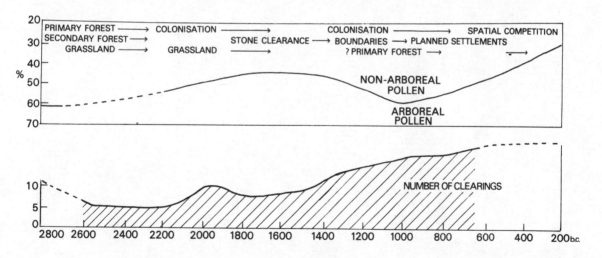

2:7   The relative frequency of dated clearance horizons compared with the percentage of tree pollen. Outline interpretation above. Dates were plotted at two standard deviations.

Tillage and Hard Labour
Arable and Pasture

Chapter 3

*In North Wiltshire, and like the vale of
Gloucestershire (a dirty clayey country)
the Indigenae, or Aborigines, spake drawl-
ing; they are phlegmatic, skins pale and
livid, slow and dull, heavy of spirit;
hereabout is but little tillage or hard
labour, they only milk the cows and make
cheese; they feed chiefly on milk meats,
which cools their brains too much, and
hurts their inventions. These circumstances
make them melancholy, contemplative and
malicious . . . and by the same reason
they are generally more apt to be fanatics:
their persons are generally plump and feggy:
gallipot eyes, and some black: but they
are generally handsome enough. It is a
woodsere country, abounding much with
sour and austere plants, as sorrel etc. which
makes their humours sour and fixes their
spirits. In Malmesbury Hundred etc. (ye
wet clayey parts) there have ever been
reputed witches.*

*On the downs, sc. the south part, where
'tis all upon tillage, and where the
shepherds labour hard, their flesh is hard,
their bodies strong: being weary after hard
labour, they have not the leisure to read
and contemplate of religion, but go to bed
to their rest, to rise betime the next
morning to their labour.*

John Aubrey, **Natural History
of Wiltshire** *(1656–91,
first published 1847)*

THE PROBLEM

If Aubrey's views on forest clearance have proved
especially perceptive, the quaint environmental
determinism of this second passage only prefigures

another aspect of archaeological thinking. Arable
and pastoral farming are usually two component
parts of a harmonious economic regime, but in
the literature they are often set in opposition.
Calvin Wells, for example, has tried to distinguish
between pastoralists and agriculturalists from
skeletal evidence alone (1974); and ever since
the cautious and rewarding work of Cyril Fox
archaeologists have tended to treat his division of
highland and lowland zones as an inflexible
economic frontier. Fox's own view was sensibly
limited: 'The surface conditions in a highland
area tend to limit arable farming and to encourage
pastoral farming, but the great contrasts in the
highland and lowland zones in Britain . . . render
the economic life of the two . . . unusually distinct' (1932, p. 53). None of his twenty-five
'propositions' equate this very general division
with that between two exclusive economies. And
yet by 1958 Stuart Piggott was arguing that

> the type of Iron Age economy associated with
> intensive corn growing . . . is in fact a
> specialised form of agriculture having a
> restricted distribution. . . . On the whole its
> north western boundary is the Jurassic Ridge.
> . . . There is evidence that an economy
> which was not specifically concerned with
> corn growing flourished beyond [this] line.
> It was based on pastoralism . . . with a
> probable element of limited nomadism.

This argument has been influential. Six years
after Piggott's initial statement Dr Isobel Smith
extended his ideas to the Neolithic period (in
Field, Mathews and Smith, 1964). Having
noticed that the distribution of Neolithic and

Beaker pits resembled that of Iron Age examples, she suggested that a similar economic distinction was observed in the earlier periods:

> Professor Piggott has shown that in the Early Iron Age the Jurassic Ridge forms the effective boundary to the north and west beyond which few pits are known. . . . He has inferred that 'in the south alone' corn was grown in substantial amounts. . . . It can also be inferred that the Neolithic and Beaker folk who inhabited the same region . . . had something to store which was not available to their counterparts elsewhere.

The argument was now less flexible.

In Piggott's paper the arable economy of lowland Britain was represented by six elements. For his Stanwick economy 'much of the inference must be based on negative, rather than positive, evidence'. Indeed, the direct field evidence amounted to one group of enclosures in southwest England, a restricted area of linear earthworks in Yorkshire and the possibly unique site of Stanwick itself. Smith's evidence for arable farming depended upon three positive elements and on analogy with the Iron Age arrangement. With so limited a basis for discussion, it is worth returning to Fox's original statement. How far do the natural constraints which he describes impose a division on land use today? Of particular relevance are the maps collected by Coppock (1964).

Fox placed his main emphasis on differences of rainfall. In general terms, heavy rainfall threatens the harvest and can encourage the development of acid grassland, whilst lower rainfall is more suitable for crops. The basic division now falls at about 90 cm per annum; a much higher precipitation favours grassland, and a lower favours cereals. It is surprising then that Fox's own map, which was based on figures for 1930, shows rainfall below this threshold over only a very limited area, running from south Yorkshire through most of East Anglia to the Thames Valley. This zone contains only 16 per cent of the Iron Age pits mapped by Piggott and just under half those considered by Smith. Such a discrepancy cannot be attributed entirely to climatic change. Further investigation reveals that the figures used by Fox were unrepresentative and the rainfall average for the years 1901–1930 shows more agreement with these distributions (Coppock, 1964, fig. 3). In general, rainfall increases from east to west, and some Neolithic sites in western Britain and Ireland are in areas well above the threshold figure. What is really important is not the absolute, but rather the *relative* intensity of rainfall and, adopting this wider framework, Fox's original argument would have to admit the feasibility of cereal farming along most of the coastal belt of eastern England and Scotland. There is increasing evidence for Neolithic cultivation of these areas.

Temperature is equally important. The growing season for cereals begins at about 42°F (6°C) and has been usefully mapped by Coppock (1964, fig. 8). His results emphasise the advantages for pioneer agriculture of those coastal areas with a long growing season. Towards northern Britain the length of this season decreases at a rate of about 10 days for every 80 m of altitude. The normal limit of cultivation is about 200 m, at which height the growing season is a month shorter than at sea level in the same region, but wheat can be grown to a height of 300 m and barley as high as 475 m. In these cases a southerly aspect is particularly important. High-altitude cereal growing in prehistory has been discussed by Fleming (1976) and by Kirk (1974). There is less risk from frost on the coast, but raised land is at some advantage in areas of thermal inversion. One restriction on cereal farming is topography, rather than absolute height; where an area shows abrupt changes of altitude, local variations in the growing season can give problems.

All these statements are based on modern experience, and for this reason they must be modified to take account of the very large areas where environmental change, frequently combined with human interference, has turned arable plots into moorland. The present distribution of moorland is not directly related to altitude, and the moorland edge is lowest to the north and west and highest in those areas where the uplands are most extensive. Cultivation is also infrequent in very dissected landscapes.

Modern cereal yields are highest in eastern England, which has the greatest proportion of cultivated land. To this extent the pit distributions are not unhelpful. It is in the east, where the largest holdings are found today, that major defended sites are elusive until the late Iron Age. The relatively low rainfall here can make the ground too dry for extensive grassland. Soils impose further restrictions. A choice has to be made between lighter soils, which warm quickly and are easy to work, and rather heavier soils, which need more labour. The latter involve a greater element of risk and may be worked for a shorter period, since poaching of clayey subsoils will limit the growing season. The lighter soils are more vulnerable to drought and are lower in plant nutrients. Particularly crucial here are the calcareous soils which feature so prominently in the literature. These could have been depleted after forest clearance and are sometimes rather thin.

Pastoral farming has been defined mainly in negative terms. This does not do justice to its inherent complexity. Here again, climate is important. Modern grazing land becomes more extensive from east to west, with the gradual increase in rainfall. Cattle favour a range of 90 to 120 cm per annum, each animal needing about 10 gallons of water a day. Modern cattle densities are highest in south-west and west Wales and in a belt running northwards from Dorset to Clwyd. They are also high in some coastal areas. The growing season for grass is longest in the south-west. Although this basic distinction certainly takes in areas with over 120 cm of rainfall a year, it still avoids the main upland areas. Temperature is a limiting factor in pastoral farming also. The optimum temperature for milk production is about 50°F (10°C) and this ensures that dairy production will usually avoid the higher ground. Today dairy farms tend to be distributed around the fringes of the uplands. Although southern and western England offer the best conditions for dairying, summer milk production is actually highest in Wales. There is also the crucial question of shelter for dairy stock, and winter cattle housing is most in evidence north of a line from central Wales to south Yorkshire, and least in evidence in Wessex and parts of the south Midlands (Grundy, 1970). In upland areas, and also in south and south-west Wales, cattle may need protection from high winds. Beef cattle are less vulnerable and normally adapt more easily. They can be grazed on poorer soils and are suited to rather higher ground, although this can lead to some competition with sheep.

Sheep are in fact more mobile and will dominate in upland areas like Exmoor, the Cheviots, central Wales and parts of the Pennines. Their recent distribution includes converted arable, and where they have replaced cattle on moorland they may have an adverse effect on the land – this is particularly true in the west Scottish Highlands. In general, seasonal changes of climate and environment have led to more winter culling of sheep in the west. Sheep are basically resilient, but do not like damp, lowlying land, where they may be prone to disease. In spite of their general tolerance, they are quite sensitive to temperature and, in more severe conditions at least, the young of the flock may be brought down to lowland areas. Sheep farming is normally very mobile and one Herdwick may graze 2 hectares of hill pasture a year.

Pigs, on the other hand, are relatively undemanding. They eat little grass and can normally be left to fend for themselves. They have a natural preference for woodland. Their main limiting factor is a sensitivity to cold and damp, and for this reason they dislike upland areas.

From this it would appear that the balance of cereal and stock farming can vary greatly from one area to another. It is equally apparent that changes of rainfall, wind, temperature and soils can all modify the internal balance of pastoral activity. These relationships are in fact so complex that, even in prehistory, the geographical divisions described earlier must be considered too simple. They also ignore the extensive evidence for the interdependence of arable and pastoral practice.

There are two aspects to this last question: the widespread ethnographic evidence for the relationship between farmers and herders, and the ecological evidence for the balance of the two types of land use. Sahlins has observed that in the ethnographic literature pastoralists and agriculturalists are normally interdependent (1968). Piggott acknowledges this in his original discussion and Fleming has enlarged on the same theme (1971b). Without doubt, dietary considerations play a major part in this relationship, and many pastoral communities today obtain part of their nourishment from cereal products. Similarly, there is an effective limit of about 70 per cent to the extent to which a normal diet can be based upon grain and its products (M. Bowden, pers. com.). Sahlins likened the relationship between pastoralist and arable farmer to a marriage in which 'the nomad can't stand the farmer but can't live without him' (1968, p. 35).

The ecological evidence is more direct (Gilchrist-Shirlaw, 1966, pp. 49 ff.; Welinder, 1975). The most important element in cereal farming is nitrogen, and it is the hardest to compensate for once the system is in decline. The addition of animal manure to the soil will much reduce this decline, even though the nitrogen content can only be completely restored by the addition of fertiliser. Nevertheless, the manuring of cultivated land will offset an otherwise inevitable fall in production. Because manuring compensates only partly for the loss of nitrogen, fallowing will be essential. Unused arable land can increase its nitrogen content by half in twenty-five years. Not all manure is equally effective and it seems that sheep are more useful than cattle in this respect. The fact that there is more humus in grassland than in woodland also makes it more suitable for conversion to arable, a change which can bring about a considerable increase in the food supply. In the light of arguments of this kind, arable and pastoral farming should not be set in opposition unless the archaeological evidence specifically demands it. It is the nature of such evidence which must now be considered.

Crops

The principal crops in British prehistory were varieties of wheat and barley. Other major plants seem to have been flax, rye, oats and beans. Before considering the archaeological record, it is worth describing the properties of the two main crops.

Wheat favours heavy to medium textured soils, especially stiff and well-drained clay loams, and it does not grow well on wet clay or loose sandy or peaty ground. Although it does best on land below 200 m, wheat can be ripened at 300 m. Its modern distribution is mainly eastern England, but also includes parts of Sussex, the Midlands and south-west Lancashire. It can exhaust the soil faster than other crops. It has been suggested that spelt, which is an Iron Age introduction, could have been winter sown (Appelbaum, 1954).

Barley is less ecologically specialised and prefers deep, fertile well-drained loams. It is the most tolerant cereal in saline or alkaline conditions and does well on calcareous soils. Barley is especially sensitive to acidity, which is the main cause of crop failure, and gives low yields on sand. It has a shorter growing season than wheat and its present distribution extends further into northern England. Barley can ripen at heights of as much as 475 m. Its modern distribution is mainly Wessex, east Yorkshire and East Anglia. The use of hulled barley from the later Bronze Age has been associated with winter sowing (Cunliffe, 1974, p. 167).

It is depressing to turn from current practice to the archaeological evidence for crops. Cereals are of necessity the fundamental evidence for arable practice and yet this whole topic has seen virtually no development for more than two decades. During this time improved recovery techniques have been developed and applied, but few results of substance are available at the time of writing.

The conventional outline is easy enough to describe but, for all its repetition in authoritative texts, it does require critical scrutiny (Helbaek, 1952; Jessen and Helbaek, 1944). A welcome start is a recent paper by Dennell (1976). In the orthodox scheme, a mixed economy featuring both wheats and barley has been considered characteristic of the Neolithic. In general the wheats predominated but lost some ground to barley in the second millennium b.c., just as they did in Europe. In the later Bronze Age there was some movement from naked to hulled barley, and by the end of this period wheats again assumed greater importance. Apart from one find from Hembury, it seems that spelt was a new introduction at this time. Other plants, including rye, oats and beans, made their main impact later in the Iron Age.

This rather neat scheme has always had the attraction of matching the conventional cultural framework. The increased representation of barley has been associated with Beaker immigrants, just as the appearance of spelt has been one argument for early Iron Age colonists. It has even been treated as a clue to their area of origin (Harding, D. W., 1974, p. 81). However, there are serious difficulties in elaborating this framework.

The most basic difficulty at the moment is an imbalance in the sources of evidence, which is really limited to chance impressions in pottery or to more occasional finds of carbonised grain. The latter were normally recognised only when they occurred in large deposits and may not be a representative portion of the full grain spectrum. Robin Dennell has pointed out how cereal samples will reveal different stages of crop processing (1972) and it is important to decide the place of the individual sample in this sequence. Most of these deposits are from pits and it has been suggested that this form of storage might be more suitable for wheat than for barley (Evans in Wainwright, 1968, p. 116). If the latter were kept above ground, it might be under-represented in excavation. The impressions in pottery present different problems, since they can only be compared with carbonised material on sites where pots were produced in the home. This is an assumption which it is no longer safe to make. At Belle Tout neutron activation analysis does suggest that vessels with grain imprints were made in the domestic area (J. Hawkes, pers. com.), but at Windmill Hill,

the main source of information on Neolithic crops, some of the pots showing similar evidence were actually imported from a distance. As Dennell has pointed out, these cannot give any information on Neolithic cultivation of the chalk and it now seems likely that different crops were favoured in areas with distinct ceramic workshops (1976). This is hardly surprising when the modern distributions of these crops are so different.

The transition from the Neolithic to the Bronze Age is equally complicated. Hubbard has observed that the decline in emmer wheat depends entirely on imprints in pottery which show an apparent increase in barley (1975). This raises the possibility that the pattern could result from different storage or processing methods. It is not known where Early Bronze Age pottery was made, although it must have been produced more widely than Dennell supposes, and finds of barley are not limited to the chalk. It is possible that this crop was used to feed animals and perhaps stored less carefully than wheat. Developments in the Iron Age give more scope for bias, since spelt requires heating before it is processed (Helbaek, 1952, p. 231; for another view see Robinson, M. and Hubbard, 1977). This will increase the chances of accidental burning. It is also possible that spelt and hulled barley could have been winter-sown and harvested before the crops sown in spring. This might lead to the use of different storage areas. More important, these cereals may have had a greater chance of inclusion in pottery, since this is normally made in summer and the whole process might well have been completed before the second harvest was taken. This does seem likely with the impressions in briquetage from salt production (Bradley, 1975a).

But even accepting the most general trends at face value, there are problems of explanation. *Pace* Hubbard (1976), it is not very likely that particular crops would be grown because of 'cultural tradition', unless there were some specific advantages in doing so. It is worth returning to the explanations offered for these apparent changes. The most frequent have had recourse to cultural and climatic determinism.

In the second view, the change from wheat to barley resulted from a dryer climate in the Early Bronze Age (Godwin, 1975, p. 407). The evidence for such a change has recently been considered by John Evans (1975, pp. 142 ff.), but remains very limited. On the same basis, the climatic deterioration of the first millennium b.c. has been linked with the practice of autumn sowing. In Appelbaum's words: 'The climatic deterioration of the Early Iron Age *(sic)* might be expected to have led to an increase of wheat on light lands since it is better adapted to cold and wet and later springs favour autumn rather than spring sowing on chalk soils' (1954, p. 104). One difficulty here is that autumn sowing is almost impossible to prove, however efficient it might appear under modern conditions. There may be some evidence for this practice from the arable weeds at the Ashville site in Abingdon (M. Parrington, pers. com.) and if this were a common practice it would certainly have extended the overall period in which sowing and harvesting were possible. Such an increase in productivity would necessarily mean an increase in work effort and for this reason population pressures might be as likely a cause (cf. Bradley, 1971). John Coles has also pointed out how in pioneer agriculture winter-sown crops competed more successfully with weeds than those which were sown in spring (1976). Hubbard has made the additional suggestion that the change to hulled barley could have a social dimension and might be connected with malting (1975).

In Helbaek's original study, he commented on the fact that barley was less ecologically specialised than wheat and would be more useful in settling 'new and inferior areas' (1952, p. 200). Barley can of course tolerate a saline environment and there is certainly evidence for a greater emphasis on coastal resources in the early second millennium b.c. But this does not explain the entire change suggested in the literature, although it could account for some of the evidence from northern Britain. Many of the new areas settled at this time are now acid heathland or moorland where barley would not do well. If it did accompany the clearance of these regions, cultivation would have been short-lived and

can hardly have withstood any changes in the soil. The major problem, however, is that barley is well adapted to the calcareous soils, which were already settled in the Neolithic. Although the apparent emphasis on wheat has been modified by Dennell's work, some contrast with the Bronze Age still remains. This being the case, why should any change have occurred?

It is already apparent that the distribution of Neolithic pits does not entirely correspond with the areas having the lowest rainfall. It may now be possible to explain this. Recent work over much of lowland England has shown that significant areas were originally covered by varieties of loess, some of which has been concealed under more general descriptions, such as 'loam', 'brickearth' or 'clay with flints'. It appears that substantial areas originally capping the chalk have been dispersed by erosion. The distribution of early Neolithic sites extends beyond the chalk, limestone and valley gravels to take in East Anglia, Kent and the south-west, all areas in which loess has recently been found (Perrin, Davies and Fysh, 1974). It seems possible that Neolithic settlers were attracted towards these environments, which had much in common with the areas favoured for early farming in Europe. If this were so, it seems likely that the loess covering the chalk was exhausted within the Neolithic, particularly if the main crop was wheat. Limbrey has already suggested soil loss in this area (1975, p. 185), and changes in the downland environment might have made the region more suitable for barley. There could be a similar situation in the Iron Age, where Godwin observed increased barley growing on areas of chalkland in which it had apparently been absent before (1975, p. 410).

Livestock

The principal stock animals in early Britain were cattle, sheep, goats, pigs and horses. Sheep and goats are not easy to distinguish by their bones and cannot be treated separately at the moment. The basic patterns of modern stock-raising have already been considered: few general trends have been perceived within the prehistoric data, although Clark did suggest that sheep became more common at the expense of cattle (1947a). There may have been rather more pigs about the end of the third millennium b.c. and it was perhaps at this time that the horse was introduced in Ireland (Wijngaarden-Bakker, 1974). Each of these suggestions will be considered later.

Despite a widespread reluctance to take any notice of bones, these remain the most informative evidence of pastoral activity. Few sites have been dug with any attempt to secure adequate samples, and for fewer still are there any figures for species composition, meat weight, age or sex. Little attention has been paid to the social, ritual or even purely physical factors which can impede understanding of this material, and the majority of the acceptable data relates to a limited period and a limited region. This account is perforce biased towards the later prehistory of southern England.

Two immediate problems stand between this evidence and the prehistoric economy. The first is the importance of ritual. An early suggestion of this kind was made by Mortimer, who observed that Iron Age burials in Yorkshire could be accompanied by complete goat skeletons but by only the long bones of pig (1911, p. 50). He considered this to indicate the use of pig as a meat animal and suggested that the goat was kept for its milk alone, its flesh being taboo. There seems no reason to insist on this specific interpretation, but patterns of this type certainly recur (cf. Foster, 1977). A 'pig cult' has been suggested in the Neolithic of northern England, based upon repeated finds from long barrows (Piggott, S., 1954, p. 108), whilst in the chambered tombs of the period wild pig is more common than the domesticated variety (Murray, 1970, pp. 326–9). Animals might also be taken as totems and there is evidence that the horse was adopted by the Epidii of Kintyre (RCAHM, Scotland, 1971, vol. 1, p. 1).

The second difficulty concerns the assumption that the bones on any site will be a representative sample of the livestock actually raised there. In fact, it is perfectly possible that some animals were taken on the hoof for use or exchange elsewhere, and there is oblique evidence for a trade in salted carcasses from coastal areas (Bradley, 1975b). A useful project would be to compare the age structure of a series of contemporary fauna selected from neighbouring sites of different status. Thus at Hawk's Hill in the Iron Age the rarity of older cattle *could* suggest that they had been taken from the site, and the remarkable rarity of young at Croft Ambrey might imply that part of the livestock there was raised on neighbouring farms (Hastings, 1965, pp. 40–2; Stanford, 1974, pp. 215–22). If so, there could be an analogy with the range of excavated structures that could have stored other produce from these sites. Again there may be evidence that some young animals were eliminated in the course of transhumance away from the parent site. This will be discussed in the following chapter.

There is also evidence for the slaughter of livestock on certain sites and the introduction of joints of meat into others, although the problem always remains that different body parts may have been used or discarded separately. Differential preservation and scavenging also impose a bias (cf. Isaac, 1967). On at least three sites there have been claims that the remains show a bias towards the waste parts of the animals. These are a camp of the later Bronze Age at Mildenhall and two initial Iron Age enclosures at Portsdown and Harrow Hills (Kelley, T., 1967, pp. 53–5; Bradley, 1967, pp. 52–4; Holleyman, 1937, p. 250). At Harrow Hill the high number of ox skulls might alternatively be evidence of ritual, as indeed the place name suggests (Mawer and Stenton, 1929, p. 165). Evidence for the introduction of meat comes from other sites, where the edible parts of the body may be over-represented. This was most convincingly shown by Phillipson at Eldon's Seat (in Cunliffe and Phillipson, 1968, pp. 226–9). It also occurred at Rams Hill, the precise status of which is rather elusive (Bradley and Ellison, 1975, pp. 118–22). Kaimes Hill is another hilltop site showing this pattern (Simpson, 1969, pp. 26–8). The evidence from Nornour is more complex and only the cattle seem to have been brought in after butchery (Turk, 1967).

Each of the three main animals, cattle, sheep and pig, shows a variety of patterns which does a little to offset the minuteness of the available sample. Cattle bones may show two basic patterns. The first can be seen at Grimthorpe and Hawk's Hill (Stead, 1968, pp. 182–9; Hastings, 1965, pp. 40–2). At the latter site the majority of the bones were from animals under three years of age. The majority were possibly killed when they had completed the rapid growth to maturity, and before further fattening would make them less economic as a source of meat. At Hawk's Hill about 60 per cent were within this age range, whilst at Grimthorpe even more of the cattle were less than thirty months old. At New Grange in the Beaker period most of the animals were between two and three years old (Wijngaarden-Bakker, 1974). This should be contrasted with the hill fort at Croft Ambrey, where only 6 per cent of the cattle were under four years of age (Stanford, 1974, pp. 215–22), and again with the enclosure at Windmill Hill (Smith, I. F., 1965, pp. 141–5). At Ancaster more than 50 per cent of the cattle were over four years old (May, J., 1976, p. 137), and at Durrington Walls 75 per cent were fully mature (Wainwright and Longworth, 1971, pp. 338–50). In each of these cases it would have been uneconomic to keep these animals solely for meat, since the additional feed required would not have been covered by an increased yield. Cattle may have been kept for dairy products and the males, which included steers at Durrington Walls, might have been draught animals. On an Iron Age site at Abingdon the majority of cattle bones were from males and steers which may have been used in working the land (M. Parrington, pers. com.). This is a problem which could be considered in studies of bone pathology. At Rams Hill a compromise solution was adopted, by which most of the cattle were kept for dairy products but were eventually brought into the enclosure as butchered joints (Bradley and Ellison, 1975, pp. 118–22). It is possible that at Windmill Hill the cattle were collected from a wide surrounding area; this could perhaps account for the remarkably high proportion of dogs – 22 per cent –

in the causewayed enclosure, compared with 2 per cent in the earlier settlement (Smith, I. F., 1965, p. 143).

These two patterns emphasise the need for economic and social links between different pastoral regimes. The bones from Grimthorpe mostly postdate the use of the site's defences, as do those from Rams Hill. It is worth asking whether the specialised pattern at Croft Ambrey is any reflection of its local standing as a hill fort. Whitehouse and Whitehouse, who produced the faunal analysis, took a different view of the situation:

> The small number of immature animals suggests that meat was not over abundant: the inhabitants of Croft Ambrey were unable to indulge frequently in the luxury of young and tender meat. This is in contrast to the situation recorded elsewhere, especially in the lowland villages and farms such as Barley, Eldon's Seat and Hawk's Hill. It is probable that (this) . . . reflects . . . different population densities. The lowland sites contained small communities living in relative plenty, whereas the hill fort at Croft apparently housed a dense population of considerable size.

This has not been proved. Conversely Ewart and Ritchie claimed that the high proportion of young domesticates in the coastal caves of Fife was evidence that these animals were hunted (in Wace and Jehu, 1915, pp. 245–54). This contrasts strangely with the view that a high proportion of young game bones can show incipient domestication (cf. Collier and White, 1976).

Sheep offer an almost equally clearcut pattern, but few sites are available for study. In three cases the evidence emphasises the younger animals, although in the first year meat can be rather limited. At Grimthorpe 73 per cent of the sheep had been killed by the age of two; the figure at Eldon's Seat was 57 per cent (Stead, 1968, pp. 182–9; Cunliffe and Phillipson, 1968, pp. 226–9). In each case the evidence emphasised the second year of life. At Catcote, most animals were killed for meat after their first lambing (Hodgson, 1968, pp. 129–30). By contrast, the evidence from Hawk's Hill, and possibly from Rams Hill, suggests a more varied pattern, in which young animals were found with older sheep, but middle-aged individuals were rare (Hastings, 1965, pp. 40–2; Bradley and Ellison, 1975, pp. 118–22). Perhaps in each case a proportion were culled for meat whilst the rest were kept mainly for wool. This was the case at Ancaster (May, J., 1976, p. 137) and again, contrasts with Croft Ambrey, where only 2 per cent of the sheep were immature (Stanford, 1974, pp. 215–22). This suggests an emphasis on their wool. There are no comparable figures to hand, but a similar economy must have been practised at Glastonbury, where 92 per cent of the animals were sheep. The bone report is not very helpful but does not suggest an emphasis on the younger animals (Bulleid and Gray, 1917, pp. 648–72). The excavation also produced weaving equipment.

Pig presents a different problem. It does not offer many resources, and is mainly used for meat. It comes as a surprise therefore to find that the killing pattern is varied. At Durrington Walls 53 per cent of the pigs were juveniles, whilst only 21 per cent of those at Croft Ambrey were even immature, that is, less than three-and-a-half years old (Wainwright and Longworth, 1971, pp. 338–50; Stanford, 1974, pp. 215–22). At Grimthorpe 75 per cent of the pigs had been killed by thirty months (Stead, 1968, pp. 162–9). The best explanation is that pig was an occasional resource, used as a reserve against the failure of other staples. It is less nutritious than other animals, and pork is harder to keep. Pigs need very little management and can be fattened in an environment which has few other uses. They were quite common at Croft Ambrey, where not many animals were raised directly for food, and again at Hawk's Hill, where some of the lambs were too young to provide much meat. This suggests the use of pig as an undemanding supplement to the economy and surely explains its erratic representation on different sites. It may be especially common in the late Neolithic.

Published figures show that in lowland Britain pig can represent from $1\frac{1}{2}$ per cent to $33\frac{1}{2}$ per cent of the Iron Age fauna, in spite of Clark's proposition that it was progressively replaced by sheep (Clark, 1947a; Foster, 1977, p. 2). The actual ratio of sheep to pig at this time varies from 54:1 at Glastonbury to 0·9:1 at Croft Ambrey. Even excluding the rather special case of Glastonbury, the figure goes up to 11:1 in the Late Bronze Age occupation at Eldon's Seat. But Clark's original argument remains persuasive and pig would not have adapted well to an unsuitable environment. Medieval experience, however, suggests that its numbers might also be restricted if there were reserved areas of managed woodland. In the latter period this did more to account for the decline of pig than did the creation of grassland. In modern circumstances, on the other hand, pigs can be supported on the waste from dairy production.

Although the proportion of pig may not have fallen universally, the increase in the number of sheep does seem to be real. Cattle usually remained the dominant species, even before meat yields are considered. A valuable summary of the available bone reports was given by Hodgson in 1968 and when this paper appeared it still seemed that cattle were the commonest species on all pre-Roman sites but Glastonbury. Since then a number of Iron Age sites have revealed a preponderance of sheep and the true position is now harder to judge (cf. Foster, 1977, p. 2; cf. fig. 3:1). These new sites cover a wide area from the South Downs to the Western Isles. The two Bronze Age sites showing this new pattern are Tooth Cave, Gower, and Amberley Mount in Sussex (Ratcliffe-Densham, H. and M., 1966, p. 21; Harvey, Morgan and Webley, 1967, pp. 284–5). Examination of older reports, on the other hand, makes it clear that sheep were better represented in upland areas than the few exact figures can show. This matches an increased number of spindle whorls in the north (cf. Cunliffe, 1974, p. 199). Only in the upper Thames do any local contrasts appear and here it seems that the sites nearest the river favoured cattle, in contrast to those on the higher ground. The value of sheep manure should not be forgotten.

There remains the dog and the horse. The dog is practically ubiquitous from the Neolithic onwards and its importance to early communities is clear from the special circumstances under which it might be buried. There is no evidence for its restriction to sites with game bones and it is not possible to correlate it with the appearance of any one species. The horse raises other difficulties. It occurs frequently from the Neolithic or Beaker period onwards but the earliest horse trappings belong to the Late Bronze Age. It may be that it was originally a minor source of food but that from this date it was also used for riding. If so it could have facilitated large-scale mobile pastoralism, but this is impossible to prove. In the later Iron Age, however, certain regions do show concentrations of rich horse gear, and the additional evidence for wheeled vehicles suggests that mobile warriors and herders should be seriously envisaged. Ptolemy's Gabrantuici, a group who may be placed somewhere in Yorkshire, are literally 'horse-riding fighters' (Challis, 1975, i, p. 184). This in turn implies areas in which horses could be caught and broken, and specialised sites with a high proportion of horse bones may yet be found. The raising and breaking of ponies could be one activity associated with the later linear ditches of southern and north-eastern England.

DATED INNOVATIONS

Crops and animals have been discussed at some length, since these are on any reckoning the most direct evidence of economic practice. Unfortunately the information which they have to offer shows few clear chronological patterns. For this reason it is now necessary to turn to other forms of evidence which have a bearing on the development of agriculture. The objectives of this examination are deliberately limited. It is concerned simply with two questions: the actual relevance of each class of evidence and its broad chronological range. More general studies of prehistoric farming are already available and the one purpose of this discussion is to consider what chronological patterns such information can show. It must be clear from the outset that the whole body of this evidence is too limited for the formation of regional schemes and analysis

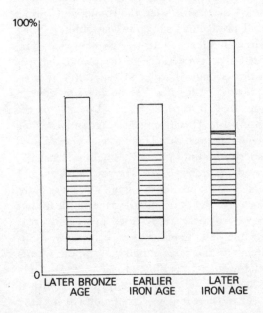

3:1   The percentage of sheep bones on later Bronze Age and Iron Age sites in England and Wales. The interquartile range is shaded. Data from Foster (1977) with additions.

must be conducted in very general terms. But pollen analysis provides some check on the usefulness of this approach and in the closing section of this chapter the two methods will be compared. In concentrating so closely on the sequence of innovations this discussion follows a recent study of Dutch prehistory (Brongers and Woltering, 1973).

Arable farming

Agricultural tools The physical evidence for cultivation shows an increasing elaboration and specialisation. The most basic implements are those for tillage.

Evidence for the use of the ard from the third millennium b.c. is now well known, and a valuable study of early ard marks has already been published (Fowler and Evans, 1967). Fragments of several ards have been preserved from Iron Age sites. It is necessary to add that the evidence for this form of cultivation extends over a wider area and a greater time range than at first seemed likely. There are ard marks on clayland sites in northern England starting in the earliest Iron Age (C. Burgess, pers. com.) and a number of examples have been preserved beneath Roman military installations (Breeze, 1975). There is similar evidence in the Northern and Western Isles from the Neolithic onwards (e.g. Lamb, 1974; Shepherd, 1976) and in the west of Ireland field systems, including plough marks of this date, are currently being examined (e.g. Caulfield, 1974). Ard cultivation is quite labour intensive and before it is adopted population may have reached a local level at which short fallow agriculture was practised. Stone shares were sometimes used before the introduction of iron (Fenton, 1963, pp. 265–9), but this was possibly unusual. There is no convincing evidence for a new type of plough before the Roman period.

Less demanding techniques were also available. These included the digging stick, the spade and the hoe. The evidence for digging sticks is naturally tenuous, but one has apparently been found with Late Bronze Age or Iron Age pottery at Garryeallabus, Islay (Newall, F., 1963). Other-

wise the best approach is through the weights which may have been added to these tools. The best candidates are usually described as hammers, net weights or maceheads, but in Cumbria, where detailed pollen evidence is available, their distribution corresponds to the areas with evidence of cereal farming (Bradley, 1972). Tools of this form are found throughout Britain and were probably most common at the end of the Neolithic.

The evidence for hoes is just as complex. These would have been especially important on steeper slopes where the ard could not be used. This evidence is both physical and botanical. The botanical evidence has been considered by A. S. Thomas, who has drawn attention to the occurrence of chalk heathland plants beyond the effective reach of the plough (1960). He sees this as an effect of hoeing and manuring and suggests that at Kingley Vale in Sussex one plot of this kind impinged on a barrow. It is also possible that some stone 'axes' were really hoes. Radley and Cooper suggested that fragments of these around a Neolithic site at Elton in Derbyshire had been broken in clearance and cultivation, and argued on the basis of carefully recorded flint scatters that these were found within an area manured from a domestic settlement (1968). And in Sussex Eliot Curwen published a series of 'axes' with a blunt polished end (1939). He felt that these were used in potting or leatherworking; but this interpretation supplies a third alternative. The Iron Age evidence is rather clearer, with the development of a distinctive iron hoe, but its full distribution is unknown (cf. Manning, 1970).

Spade agriculture poses different problems. Actual evidence of wooden spades has been found on at least three sites (p. 18). The use of an iron-tipped implement only dates from the Roman period. Spade furrows are probably more common than was once thought (p. 17) and are certainly distributed from Hampshire to Ireland and the Orkneys. Individual spade marks are known at Gwithian and Rosinish (Thomas, C., 1970; Shepherd, 1976), and complete Neolithic plots have been recorded in County Mayo (Caulfield, 1974). A similar claim for Late

Bronze Age plots at Albury, Surrey, has been withdrawn by the excavator (Harding, J., 1964). The evidence extends from the Neolithic to the Iron Age but does not imply any local sequence of techniques. The edges of the Middle Bronze Age ard plots at Gwithian had been dug with a spade, and an area originally of grassland may have been hoed before it was ploughed (Megaw, Thomas and Wailes, 1961). In Ireland Neolithic ard plots may have been prepared by hand digging (cf. p. 16).

The other agricultural tools are even less informative. Querns are virtually ubiquitous and the chronology of different types is increasingly uncertain. At Gussage All Saints there was unexpected evidence for rotary querns at an early stage of the Iron Age (Wainwright and Switsur, 1976, p. 36). Such a new chronology would agree well with other signs of intensified agriculture at this time. Nothing is known of the intensity of quern production in the Neolithic and Bronze Ages, but Iron Age querns are well known in Atlantic Scotland and Challis has pointed out that their distribution in northern England is inconsistent with the pastoral hypothesis outlined at the start of this chapter (1975, p. 158).

Sickles also pose problems. There is no proof that they were all used for cutting crops and Case has even inferred that their rarity in Neolithic contexts could indicate plucking of grain by hand (1976, p. 54). Alternatively, less distinctive types might also have been used. But it is not easy to recognise composite implements, and other flints conventionally classified as knives may have served the same function. Flanagan has suggested that this was the purpose of hollow scrapers in Ireland (Flanagan, 1962). Even the chronology of single-piece sickles remains uncertain. In the Netherlands they were in use up to the Iron Age (Brunsting, 1962; Groenman-van-Waateringe and van Regteren-Altena, 1961); in Britain the first metal sickles only appear in the Middle Bronze Age. Sir Cyril Fox used later literary evidence to suggest a possible use for sickles in ritual, an important point when so many have been found in rivers and hoards (1939). Sickles are especially frequent in Iron Age contexts and show a rather wider typological range, but scythes, which would often have been more efficient, were not available until the Roman period (McGregor, M. and Simpson, 1963). The distribution of these tools takes no account of Fox's zoning and shows a continuously enlarging field.

Field evidence   On the ground the evidence can be less difficult, although the mere appearance of enclosed fields or lynchets in no sense presupposes a single sequence of land use. It is important to remember that no field systems are likely to be visible in their original form. In areas of resistant stone the forest soil might be truncated before clearance would leave a visible trace and in some cases its poor quality could mean that land was abandoned before this ever occurred. For this reason the appearance of lynchets or field walls is not uniform throughout Britain. A near equivalent to the regular walled fields of the Irish Neolithic is only found in southern England in the Middle Bronze Age. Demographic and environmental strains may both play a part in this contrast.

The lynchets of southern England show a similar sequence. Lynchets are not created immediately cultivation begins and a basic requirement seems to be mismanagement on a large enough scale to precipitate soil creep. And for earthworks to form at all a regime of permanent boundaries is needed to trap the eroding material. Although individual lynchets are known under barrows of Early Bronze Age and even Neolithic date, the larger surviving systems probably begin towards the Middle Bronze Age (Fowler, 1971; Bowen, H. C., 1975). Two observations reinforce these arguments. By the first millennium b.c. extensive areas of fields were already being modified by the building of linear boundaries, some of which may run in a series of offsets respecting the individual headlands. But in some cases this distinctive pattern of offsets can be recognised where there is no evidence that lynchets had formed (cf. Bradley and Ellison, 1975, p. 185). This might be because these fields were of such recent creation that their boundaries had not been augmented by erosion. A possible corollary is the evidence for ploughwash or alluviation in valley bottoms. This can occur in areas without obvious fields, one instance of Late Bronze Age date being the valley of the Warwickshire Avon. Field boundaries may have changed too often for large earthworks to form, even though the ground was used thoroughly enough to lead to erosion. Ploughwash in chalkland areas will normally occur only when the soil structure breaks down. Most of these deposits belong to the first millennium b.c., although there are precocious cases at Brook in the Neolithic and at Pitstone Hill in the earlier Bronze Age (Kerney, Brown and Chandler, 1964; Evans, J. G. and Valentine, 1974). There is also evidence in the latter period for episodes of wind erosion, possibly of arable fields (Evans, J. G., 1975, p. 144). Given such information, it is feasible that the adoption of large field systems was an attempt to deal with land wastage, and that these accumulations of eroded soil are a measure of how far this failed.

On ploughed land a number of techniques were adopted to arrest this decline. The most basic was the use of manure. This is not easy to demonstrate from archaeological evidence and really requires the application of phosphate analysis. At Skaill manuring of an acid plough-soil is suggested by the incorporation of pieces of humus (Limbrey, 1975, pp. 331–2), but normally the only physical trace of manure deposits is a scatter of abraded refuse, presumably removed from the living area together with organic matter. At Elton in Derbyshire Radley and Cooper interpreted an extensive flint scatter as a Neolithic settlement with a manured area around it (1968); there is no doubt that these items are more durable than sherds in a cultivated soil. At Hurst Fen and at Belle Tout the distribution of pottery was more restricted than that of flints (Clark, 1960, p. 205; Bradley, 1970, p. 365) and, if the same principle applied, this might indicate an area of garden agriculture. At Belle Tout it is even possible that the excavated enclosure was only the 'infield' of a more extended unit. In two cases differences in the intensity of manuring can still be observed. At Gwithian the excavators noticed a different density of sherds and shells in the soil of two adjacent fields (Megaw, Thomas and Wailes, 1961), and in Dorset analysis has shown different phosphate levels on either side of an earthwork suggested as a farm boundary (H. C. Bowen, pers. com.).

This whole approach could be reversed, turning the focus on the settlement area. The excavators of Itford Hill noticed that only small parts of the pots used on the site actually remained to be found and suggested that the rest had been taken to the fields (Burstow and Holleyman, 1957, p. 199). The poor preservation of sherds dispersed in this way might mean that the stronger parts of the vessels would be over-represented. It is just as useful to consider which artefacts were left in the settled area. It is clear that the commonest finds from many Iron Age sites in Scotland are the larger stone tools, such as pounders or querns. This applies even in alkaline environments, where bones and pottery ought to survive, and it may well be that potential obstacles to cultivation were removed from the settlement debris before it was spread on the fields. Where smaller unused stones did reach these fields, they can be especially useful. Peter Drewett has produced valuable evidence for the manuring of fields on the downs from a Roman villa some distance away. His argument was based on the foreign stones incorporated in the ploughsoil (1970, p. 55).

The last example is perhaps the most satisfactory. Dimbleby and Evans have carried out both molluscan and pollen analyses on the Neolithic soil at South Street long barrow (1974). They concluded that the different preservation of snails and of pollen would mean that the latter could reflect only the latest period of land use. This argument seems to explain an apparent contradiction between molluscan evidence for open conditions and pollen evidence for bracken on the site. It was suggested that the bracken pollen perhaps originated in animal or human bedding added to the soil as fertiliser. Other comparable techniques are the addition of sea shells, shell sand or seaweed, but there is little direct evidence of these practices except at Gwithian (Megaw, Thomas and Wailes, 1961).

Marling, which was far more important, will be discussed on p. 44. But taking the evidence as a whole, there may be most *field* evidence for manuring from the later first millennium b.c.

'*Facilities*'   Cereal agriculture requires ancillary buildings and other facilities. Virtually all such evidence relates to the storage of grain.

The distribution of pits supposedly for storage underpins each of the hypotheses introduced at the beginning of this chapter. This distribution has now been given such wide implications that it is disturbing to find how little the basic question has been examined. The geographical limits to the distribution of pits have been treated as the limits of cereal growing and the rarity of pits from the later Neolithic to the Iron Age has become evidence for a general emphasis on livestock. The basis for these wider assertions is very tenuous indeed. There is experimental evidence that seed corn can be kept in pits of Iron Age type (Reynolds, 1974) but much less information on the smaller examples. Useful results might be achieved by pollen analysis (Robinson, M., and Hubbard, 1977). There have been discussions as to whether such storage is more appropriate to seed corn or corn for consumption (Bersu, 1940, pp. 60 ff; Collis, 1971a, p. 253), and indeed whether barley is not better kept above ground (Evans in Wainwright, 1968, p. 116). But in the Neolithic and Early Bronze Age hazelnuts are still the commonest remains in these pits. The increase in pit capacity in the Iron Age is just as contentious. It can be viewed either as one more sign of intensified arable farming, or as an attempt to hide the grain from raiders.

It will also be clear that the distribution of these pits is more narrowly confined than that of most other types of evidence. It is far more restricted than the distribution of fields and even of carbonised grain. Above all, it is inconsistent with the evidence of cereal pollen. Indeed, so many of these pits are on calcareous soils that there are few pollen analyses of any kind from the area in which they *are* found. It is also clear that Piggott's original distribution can be extended to the north and north-west,

although the relative density of sites will remain rather the same (Challis, 1975, p. 158). Two quite unrelated distributions could be informative here. Both are essentially comparable to the pattern provided by these pits.

The first is the distribution of Mesolithic pits, which, like the others, is virtually limited to southern and eastern England. The likely explanation is that most of these were winter shelters, although David Clarke did suggest that they were sometimes used to store nuts (1976a). It is not crucial to resolve this question: what is more important is that no one would suggest Mesolithic agriculture simply because this distribution is so like the later ones. The second distribution is of those shafts or wells which might give evidence of Celtic ritual (Ross, 1968). These are also clustered in Fox's lowland zone, so much so that Ross has suggested that they are a specifically 'Belgic' phenomenon. What seems as likely is that all three distributions are limited to soils suitable for digging pits.

The apparent decline in pit-digging from the later Neolithic has also been over-emphasised. The sample is far too small for any general statement, and other explanations are possible. Although it did seem likely that this decline might have been related to greater storage of barley above ground (Bradley, 1972), a closer examination of the form taken by the earliest pits suggests a quite different reason. The majority of such pits are circular or oval in plan and have a relatively shallow basin profile. In some cases they contain upright pots. Early Neolithic pottery includes an unusual range of large round-bottomed vessels, which are often recovered in considerable fragments. Some of these sherds would hardly have survived on the surface and it seems possible that some of the pits were specifically designed to hold containers. It is noticeable that large, flat-bottomed vessels became increasingly frequent as these pits fade from the record. This pattern is maintained into the later Bronze Age when other pits may have taken specially fired linings. If this is so, their overall frequency reveals changes in storage methods rather than in farming.

In the early Iron Age it would be possible

to construct an alternative argument for the extent of cereal agriculture by considering the finds of sickles (McGregor, M. and Simpson, 1963). These occur more widely than any storage pits and are known on sites in the Welsh borderland (fig. 3:2). A number of these sites also include burnt cereals. Pits, on the other hand, are extremely rare and the distribution of sickles agrees far more closely with the distribution of four- and six-post structures (fig. 3:2).

These buildings have traditionally been claimed as granaries, mainly on the basis of ethnographic analogy (Bersu, 1940, pp. 97 ff.), but other possibilities have been suggested. Among the alternative explanations for certain of these structures are watchtowers, exposure platforms, houses, stables, fodder barns, shrines and sheds (cf. Ellison and Drewett, 1971). There is little that can profitably be said to solve this confusion. Only occasionally have carbonised cereals been found with structures of this type (Wainwright, 1968, p. 116) and only once has phosphate analysis been attempted. This in fact suggested some association with organic matter (Clydesdale in Bradley and Ellison, 1975, p. 129). At Meare there was a clear connection between these buildings and finds of waterlogged grain (Gray, H. St G. and Bulleid, 1953), yet at Glastonbury Tratman preferred to see similar structures as the houses of an initial phase (1970). If some of these buildings were prefabricated the limited range of ground-plans need not imply one function. As on the Continent, these buildings may have been subsidiary structures of various kinds. Although they are usually treated as a novelty of Iron Age agriculture, small structures of this kind are known from the later Neolithic onwards (Bradley and Ellison, 1975, pp. 164–5).

'Working hollows' have been regarded as

3:2 The distributions of four-posters and related structures in England and Wales (shaded) and of Iron Age sickles and related artefacts. Data from McGregor and Simpson (1963) with additions.

another aspect of cereal agriculture. They were interpreted by Bersu as threshing floors (1940, pp. 64 ff.), but there is no positive evidence for this view. Their distribution is apparently limited to the chalk, and sometimes to areas including clay with flints. If this continues to be the case, a simpler explanation might be that these were mainly quarries. This suggests that some might be connected with marling and others may be borrow pits for material used in cob construction. If the first suggestion were right, a connection with cereal farming could be maintained, and any of these features could still have seen secondary use of the kind that Bersu envisaged. Some could also have held silage and without some additional function they would be better placed outside the settlement. Whatever their final explanation, they first occur with any regularity in the early Iron Age, although a possible example was found in the Middle Bronze Age settlement at Shearplace Hill (Rahtz and ApSimon, 1962, p. 305).

'Two-post structures' were also integrated by Bersu into his interpretation of Iron Age farming (1940, pp. 94 ff.), but there seems little reason

to accept these all as grain-drying racks. Guilbert has argued most persuasively that some could be the porches of eroded stake-built houses (1975). They are known from the early second millennium onwards. Finally, grain-drying ovens must be considered. These are especially necessary with spelt, which in Helbaek's opinion should be dried before threshing, and fragmentary ovens are known in Late Bronze Age and Iron Age contexts. Burnt areas at Itford Hill, Plumpton Plain and New Barn Down, Sussex, may be precursors of this practice (Burstow and Holleyman, 1957, pp. 172–3).

These, then, are the main classes of evidence for cereal farming. They are certainly not sufficient to construct any regional schemes, but do at any rate show that the simpler outlines described at the beginning of this chapter are more than likely misleading. There is some chronological patterning at a national level, although it must be emphasised that there have been more published excavations in southern England than in the north. Figure 3:3 is an attempt to sketch the chronological range of sixteen types of evidence which are apparently connected

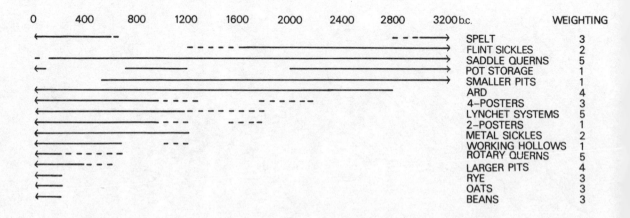

3:3   The chronological distribution of evidence for arable farming. Numbers indicate suggested weighting.

with cereal growing. Where appropriate this makes a distinction between the period in which each is a normal component of the archaeological record, and the period in which their presence is occasional or contentious. Their reliability is also indicated on a scale from 1 (low) to 5 (high). For all these uncertainties, a fairly clear pattern appears, in which the first real increase in cereal farming was in the Middle Bronze Age, with later periods merely representing a gradual intensification through to the Roman conquest. There may also be some decline in cereal growing between the later Neolithic and the Middle Bronze Age. It is this very general pattern which must now be compared with the evidence for pastoral farming.

Pastoral farming

Artefacts and pastoralism The artefacts related to pastoralism can be divided into three groups: those probably connected with leatherworking; those associated with wool products; and those used in dairy farming. The first group are the most difficult to assess, since so few of the tool types are free from ambiguity. Flint scrapers are ubiquitous and, on the evidence of edge-wear analysis, may be used for a whole variety of tasks apart from preparing skins. These in-clude butchery, bone-working and woodworking, and without supporting evidence a straightforward connection with livestock cannot always be assumed. One case in which there is such evidence is at Broome Heath, where the changing proportion of these tools matches environmental evidence for overall land use (Table 2).

These problems become especially acute when one considers a distinctive group of sites on which scrapers are the dominant and, at times, the only tool type (cf. pp. 56–7). Other problems stem from the gradual decrease in the number of flint scrapers from the Early Bronze Age, since it is not clear which metal implements were suited for quite the same uses. Bone scrapers have been claimed in the Iron Age, particularly in Scotland. Early Neolithic antler combs may also have been used on skins.

Awls pose rather similar problems. Flint awls or borers are a very generalised type and could have been used in working bone or wood. The copper and bronze awls, which have been used as evidence of pastoralism, might also be metal-working or modelling tools (Rowlands in Bradley and Ellison, 1975, p. 88). Further ambiguities arise with the recognition that Late Bronze Age 'chisels' were probably leatherworkers' knives (Roth, 1974). A more distinctive series of artefacts are the bone and antler tools discussed

TABLE 2: *The relationship between land use and the deposition of flint scrapers at Broome Heath*

Environment and land use	Scrapers as % of all implements	Radiocarbon dates
Forest clearance ? open woodland	? 80	3474 ± 117 BC (BM 679)
Cultivation	47	{ 2573 ± 67 BC (BM 756) { 2629 ± 65 BC (BM 757)
Pasture and over-grazing	80	—
Building of enclosure	83	2217 ± 78 BC (BM 755)
? heathland and barrows ?	97	—

Data from Wainwright (1972).

by I. F. Smith and Simpson in 1966. The main types are bone or antler spatulae and the so-called 'sponge finger stones'. These are usually found in Beaker contexts and these authors have argued that they might have been used in working leather. Such an interpretation is supported by wear patterns on these tools. They were associated with awls at Overton Hill and four other sites, and are also found with flint scrapers or knives. At Wetton Mill in Staffordshire they are also associated with bone needles, and in his discussion of this site Stephen Green has suggested that a distinctive group of burials with this type of material reflects the importance of the leatherworker in contemporary society (in Kelly, J., 1976, pp. 68–9). The main period in which all these classes of evidence are found is in the early second millennium b.c.

The major evidence for leatherworking is earlier than that for weaving. To some extent this may reflect the development of sheep husbandry, but it also relates to changes in the predominant mode of dress. As Green has pointed out, leather garments would be fastened by toggles or buttons (in Kelly, J., 1976, pp. 68–9), and jet and shale buttons are best known at the same date as the evidence already described. This argument may also apply to Early Bronze Age toggles and to the belt fittings of the later Neolithic. Gerloff has made the valuable point that within the Wessex Early Bronze Age there was a growing preference for pins instead of buttons (1975, p. 112). These would obviously be better suited to woven garments. This is not to deny the existence of some bone pins in Grooved Ware and Beaker contexts.

It is reassuring that there is little evidence for the extensive use of wool products before the general adoption of pins. There are very few finds either of loom weights or of spindle whorls which could date from before the Middle Bronze Age, although these need not have taken forms which would survive. Their first appearance in durable form could overlap the late Wessex graves and they then remain a common feature of later Bronze Age and Iron Age occupations (Henshall, 1950, pp. 144 ff.). 'Weaving combs', whatever their precise function or functions, are

not known before the later Bronze Age and there is no agreement on the extent to which they are found before the Iron Age. It is possible that the evidence from Shearplace Hill, Ogof-yr-Esgyrn and Lower Garth Cave could take their history into the second millennium b.c. (Rahtz and ApSimon, 1962, p. 323; Mason, 1968, p. 37). Weaving tablets are too infrequent to be of much assistance, but were certainly used by the Roman Iron Age (Henshall, 1950, pp. 148 ff.). However, like bone 'pin beaters' and 'bobbins' they will not allow for useful discussion here. Actual finds of fabric do support this outline and the earliest published examples are all from Early Bronze Age, rather than Beaker, contexts (Henshall, 1950, pp. 158–9). The evidence remains very slight but it is consistent with a movement away from intensive leatherworking to a greater emphasis on wool and its products. Of course this does not imply any overall change or replacement; it merely suggests a widening range of options.

There is slighter evidence for dairy farming. Occasional pots have been claimed as cheese strainers, notably one from a later Bronze Age settlement in West Sussex, whilst wooden vessels of the same period could have been used for milk products (Curwen, E. C., 1954, pp. 183–4). A number of these vessels from Ireland mirror the traditional forms of casks and churns and occasionally contain traces of butter (pp. 58–9). At least two such finds from Scotland are of prehistoric date (cf. p. 58). Vessels of this kind came from the Late Bronze Age site at Balinderry where between 70 and 90 per cent of the bones were of cattle (Hencken, 1942). A point of some interest is how the domestic pottery of the later Bronze Age can resemble these wooden forms, and some of these pots could be directly skeuomorphic. This is not an argument which should be taken too far, but it is particularly interesting to see how these larger vessels became less common at Eldon's Seat with an increasing emphasis on sheep rather than cattle (Cunliffe and Phillipson, 1968).

Field Evidence   There are also a number of specific features or structures within settlements which, with varying degrees of confidence, can be connected with stock management. These come under several broad headings: stock sorting and enclosure; pastoral boundaries; the provisioning of livestock and, finally, livestock products. This section will consider the first two of these categories.

A large number of individual sites have at different times been attributed to a pastoral function, although the detailed morphological and economic evidence is generally rather slender. This tendency reached its full extension with the appearance of a distribution map of 'Iron Age pastoralism' in Wales (Savory, 1976, fig. 13). The most significant elements in this argument are normally linear ditches.

The role of these particular boundaries has given many difficulties since they seem to be almost peculiar to Britain. This discussion has probably been too restricted. There has been a temptation to seek one explanation for the whole phenomenon, and too little attention has been paid to the actual circumstances in which the boundaries were built (cf. pp. 117 ff.). They have been seen as one element in a mixed farming economy, constructed in an attempt to secure the best integration of arable and pasture; but they have also been viewed as boundaries between the lands of quite separate communities. If the first point is developed uncritically, it is easy to suggest that wherever such boundaries cut across earlier fields there was a shift towards a pastoral economy. If the second point is expanded, they become a symptom of social change.

It is important to be clear that the building of linear earthworks, on whatever scale, occurred over a wide area and a very long period. There is no reason to expect a connection between all these groups, many of which belong to quite different phases, from the Middle Bronze Age to the Late Iron Age. In fact the most convincing connection appears to be between the 'ranch boundaries' of the Wessex downland and the Dartmoor reaves (Bowen, H. C., 1975; Fleming, 1977).

Where such boundaries come into contact with field systems, two main relationships are found.

In some cases the ditches actually flank the edge of the fields, and here it *is* possible to suggest that their function was to define areas of pasture. On some sites in Wessex, however, they override the fields altogether (Bowen, H. C., 1975). It is important to set the problem in perspective. This is evidence for local adjustments, albeit often on a considerable scale. In some cases this could be a response to over-exploitation, but it is not safe to postulate a wholesale change of economy, especially since these linear ditches have a relatively restricted distribution. One analogy, perhaps a distant one, is with the large fenced enclosures which can override Iron Age field systems in Sweden. This is not a sign of complete economic change but probably resulted from a system of infield/outfield agriculture in which the manuring of arable land was increasingly strictly controlled (Lindquist, 1974, pp. 29–32). This is reminiscent of Appelbaum's interpretation of Iron Age agriculture in southern England (1954), even though the field evidence on which he relied has rightly been discredited (Bowen, H. C., 1972, p. 48). This use of linear earthworks recalls the later 'head dykes' of highland areas (Whittington, 1973, p. 535) and is a reminder that such earthworks may have both a territorial and an economic role. This is particularly important when the ditched areas and the fields were set some way apart, so that any connection with stock management could involve the movement of animals from the main settled area.

Two aspects of the problem need more discussion. First, it must be accepted that the construction of land boundaries, some of considerable length, would have made real claims on the time and labour of prehistoric communities. Their construction may be one sign of pressure. Moreover it can now be seen that some of the distinctive subrectangular enclosures which accompany the ditches, far from all being specialised sites, might owe their size and shape to the re-use of individual fields which were taken out of cultivation and reserved for settlement (e.g. Angle Ditch and South Lodge Camp; see Toms, 1925). Even though their building involved the loss of some arable land, it is clear that this was kept to a minimum. Only where fields are evidently absent and enclosures are directly integrated with boundary ditches, as at Boscombe Down in Wiltshire (Stone, 1936), should the traditional view be retained. It is also clear that the lack of internal buildings on these sites may be more apparent than real (cf. Piggott, S., 1973, p. 397).

The second point emerges if the detailed relationship of fields and ditches is set aside and these earthworks are considered on a larger scale. One tendency which can emerge is for the land blocks defined by these boundaries to incorporate a variety of different natural zones. Stuart Piggott has drawn attention to earthworks on the Hampshire–Wiltshire border which form long narrow land blocks running down from the chalk into a river valley in much the same way as the Saxon strip parishes of the area (1973, p. 403). The Saxon pattern was the product of a mixed economy and was an attempt by different communities to secure the optimum variety of land at a time of severe competition. A similar pattern of ditches can be traced on the Berkshire Downs (Bradley and Ellison, 1975, fig. 6:3).

Not all 'pastoral enclosures' were integrated with linear ditches. A number of other classes of monuments have been included in the argument with varying degrees of confidence. Among the more convincing are the so-called 'banjo' enclosures, which have a quite limited distribution in Wessex, although vaguely reminiscent forms are known as far afield as Kent, the Upper Thames and the Mendips (Perry, 1972). These are small rounded enclosures approached by clear ditched droveways. They date from the later Iron Age, but excavation has shown that, like other sites, they contained not only houses but pits (Perry, 1972). This being so, it may be unwise to allow them an exclusively pastoral role. The banjo enclosure at Bramdean, Hampshire, perhaps had an unusual entrance in which the gate could be raised and lowered to control the movement of animals (Reynolds, 1972, fig. 4). Other types of compound may have made use of movable hurdling, and in certain cases the doubling of gates could even have created a pen

in the entrance. A good but little-known example is on the later Bronze Age site at Cock Hill, Sussex (Ratcliffe-Densham, 1961). A further alternative is the siting of entrances in the corners of earthwork enclosures. This arrangement could be designed to funnel the livestock towards the gate and is characteristic not only. of later Bronze Age enclosures on the downland but also of the Neolithic and Bronze Age field systems at Fengate (Pryor, 1976a). On the latter site these entrances were integrated with droveways in both of these periods. The same entrance type is also found in some enclosures of the late Iron Age, in particular Casterley Camp in Wiltshire, which is one of Ritchie's 'multiple enclosures' (Cunnington, 1913; Ritchie, A., 1971). A related trend may be towards the building of annexes to hill forts in western England, a number of which enclose a water supply (Fox, A., 1961; distribution in Forde-Johnston, 1976, fig. 152). Their distribution corresponds quite closely to the main area of cattle farming today, but in no case can these morphological arguments be adopted without supporting evidence.

'*Facilities*' Arrangements for housing livestock are scarcely known before the Roman period, and there is considerable evidence that, even today, stock can be wintered in the open in areas of lowland Britain (Grundy, 1970). There is also some correlation between modern stock housing in north and west Wales and very similar evidence from the Roman period (Smith, C., 1974). But the evidence for special arrangements is not particularly widespread, a feature which Addyman has also noted for the Saxon period (1972, pp. 278–9). It may be that the use of byres and similar buildings is mainly a Roman and medieval phenomenon. If this is true, it may be less remarkable that long houses were rarely adopted in British prehistory. If these were really intended to include stalls for animals, their distribution need have little bearing on the merits of the invasion hypothesis.

Byres are not known for certain until the Iron Age, although there are rectangular buildings of some kind on several waterlogged sites of the Late Bronze Age (e.g. Hencken, 1942; Davies, O., 1950). The most convincing of the later structures are in remote areas of north and west Scotland. Despite the arguments of Euan McKie, who would relate their rectangular shape to continental traditions (1972a, p. 16), they are found with circular buildings of domestic character and bear little relation to long houses. Among the types of site on which they occur are a series of enclosures, which Curle specifically associated with livestock (1948). In a valuable analysis of Roman native settlement plans in Wales, Christopher Smith has argued that a major variable is the relative proportion of space given to houses and to similar structures. He equates a higher proportion of ancillary buildings with greater communal wealth (1974, pp. 164–8). Apart from this evidence from Wales and Scotland, there have been few claims for byres. ApSimon and Greenfield have viewed a damaged rectangular building at Trevisker as one possible example (1972, pp. 353–4). This was defined by two parallel side walls and resembles a wooden building of later Bronze Age date at Poundbury, Dorset (Green, C., 1971). In neither case is there definite supporting evidence, but at Fengate in the Iron Age small rectangular structures suitable as byres were associated with concentrations of phosphate (F. Pryor, pers. com.). Here again round houses were also represented.

The rarity of byres like those in northern Europe raises the question of whether other types of building could have housed livestock. In a recent discussion of the continental evidence, Waterbolk has argued that no British round houses were used for this purpose (1975, p. 393). But there is some evidence for the contrary view. At Fengate in the Late Iron Age one distinctive feature of a recently excavated settlement is the pairing of circular buildings, one of which was associated with high phosphate values (F. Pryor, pers. com.). This recalls D. L. Clarke's suggestion that the Iron Age settlement at Glastonbury was composed of a group of consistent modules (1972). A variant of this might be the courtyard house, where a range of separate rooms surrounds a pen suitable for animals. This

could explain the careful provision of drainage. Otherwise it is certainly true that pairs of circular or oval buildings are a common feature of settlement sites from the Middle Bronze Age onwards (Bradley and Ellison, 1975, p. 164), and in some cases there is evidence that one major structure was for occupation and that the other was in some way subsidiary. ApSimon and Greenfield took this view of Trevisker, where they felt that one hut, with signs of rebuilding, was for domestic use and that the other was for weaving or for animals. They based this second suggestion on its trampled floor area. It is less clear whether stock could be kept inside the larger round houses of the Iron Age. The best evidence is from Alnham in Northumberland, where the area between the rings of posts supporting the roof seems to have served as a series of compartments, each with a very worn floor (Jobey, 1966, fig. 4). It is not necessary to assume that animals were responsible, and drainage would have been a problem. There is already ethnographic evidence that buildings can undergo a devolutionary cycle of uses, when they are no longer lived in, and this could explain such evidence (cf. David, 1971). This was in fact one interpretation considered at Trevisker.

There is little evidence for the provision of fodder and of water, an area which, more than most, requires specific research. The collection of hay and straw are two of the major issues. The small sickles of the later Bronze Age and Iron Age may have cut the crop close to the heads, leaving the residue to be consumed in the fields. This was mainly because the scythe was not yet in use. On the other hand, Peter Reynolds has shown that simple four-post structures of the type so common in later prehistory can be reconstructed as fodder barns (1972). A building with a ground plan measuring only 1·9 by 2·4 m might have taken the straw from 1,000 sq. m of wheat. Later evidence from northern Scotland raises the possibility that the positions of ricks might leave an archaeological trace, and on a medieval site in Cornwall Beresford interpreted a ring of post holes, much like a prehistoric round house, as a shed for unthreshed corn (1974, pp. 125–6). Stack stands offer in-teresting possibilities. These were slightly raised platforms, with an unbroken surrounding ditch designed to keep moisture away from the rick (Ramm, McDowall and Mercer, 1970, pp. 54–6). Some of these bear a disquieting resemblance to prehistoric ring ditches, or the stormwater gullies around Iron Age houses. Two sites may be relevant here: an Iron Age ring ditch in Port Meadow, Oxford, which showed clear evidence of having been flooded (Atkinson, 1942, pp. 30–35); and a series of comparable enclosures at Parwich in Derbyshire. There was no evidence for a domestic or ritual function on this second site, but pollen analysis suggested the likelihood of pastoral land use (Lomas, 1962).

These speculations apart, the problems of water supply remain. Livestock have different needs and Cunliffe has suggested that some hill forts were located around the junction of cattle and sheep pastures (1976a, fig. 2). Cattle need a con-siderable amount of water and could have been driven some distance to obtain it. But there is some evidence for water management from an early date and excavation has revealed both ponds and wells.

The evidence for ponds probably begins in the Middle Bronze Age, when a number of artificial hollows were constructed inside domestic enclosures. One example, at Shearplace Hill, seems to have possessed a clay lining (Rahtz and ApSimon, 1962, p. 305), and this may also apply to Late Bronze Age examples on the Ken-net and Surrey gravels (Bradley, 1978b; Turner, D. (ed.), 1975). A more formal cistern is known inside the hill fort at the Breiddin and appears to belong in the Iron Age (Musson, Smith and Girling, 1977). A similar rock-cut example has been claimed from the south Welsh hill fort of High Penard (Williams, A., 1941, p. 26), and there was apparently another water-hole inside Traprain Law (Jobey, 1976). This leads one to consider whether the artificial 'pool' inside the hill fort of Dinas Emrys could have a pre-historic origin (Savory, 1960, pp. 28 ff.). Wells may begin at an earlier date, although their identification is made more difficult by claims for a ritual importance, which are not always

justified. There is evidence from sediment analy-sis that a series of Neolithic shafts at Maiden-head, Berkshire, were dug in an area of fluctuating water table (Bradley, Over, Startin and Weng, 1978), and the same interpretation could be applied to a comparable series of pits at Eaton Heath, Norwich, which possibly belonged to a domestic settlement (Wainwright, 1973). In the late Neolithic a number of similar shafts are now known, but there is the additional compli-cation that not all of these can be interpreted as wells. At Maumbury Rings, for example, the circle of forty-four rock-cut shafts can only be seen in ritual terms (Bradley, 1975a). The same applies to the Middle Bronze Age shaft at Swanwick, which included a wooden upright with traces of animal blood (Fox, C. F., 1928 and 1930), and to another shaft of this date which accompanied the urnfield at Kimpton (Dacre, 1970, p. 16). The Wilsford Shaft, on the other hand, contained ropes and a bucket. Pending complete publication, there seems no evidence that this site was more than a well (Ashbee, 1963). A third peak of shaft-digging came in the Iron Age, and these have also been taken for evidence of ritual (Ross, 1968). Whilst veneration of wells is known from many periods, it is not a full explanation, and smaller wood-lined water-holes of this date have also been excavated. They complement the main periods of activity shown by the other sites. Three groups at Fengate, in the later Neolithic, the Middle Bronze Age and the Iron Age, are representa-tive of a variety of examples, with some suggestion that these are generally most frequent in the last of these phases (Pryor, 1974a and 1976a).

Evidence for the treatment of stock products is hardly more extensive. One important aspect is the production of salt for preserving meat. Without doubt, salt had been extracted since earliest prehistory, but the first process to leave an archaeological trace occurs in the Middle Bronze Age, when briquetage from salt extraction was deposited in the ditches at Fengate (Pryor, 1976a). There are hints of a few other finds from the later Bronze Age, perhaps including the fragments carried inland to Almondbury hill fort (Varley, 1976, p. 128), and more evidence from Iron Age contexts. There was a steady, if local, increase in salt making throughout this period, with regional peaks in the middle and late phases. In some cases salt production may be connected with summer grazing (p. 68).

Another method of preserving meat is by curing or smoking. This was discussed by Sir Lindsay Scott in publishing the Iron Age site at Clettraval (1948). He employed recent ethnographic evidence to suggest that special stone-built rooms, or even whole structures, could have been used for this purpose. Some of the detached huts on Scottish Iron Age sites certainly recall the smoking houses used in recent years, but this connection is unproven. His explanation might even extend, as Scott suggested, to the smaller rooms, and mural passages, within the structure of stone-built houses. It might also apply to the small annexes or 'storage chambers' attached to some of the larger stone houses on Dartmoor (cf. Worth, 1945); but in every case, supporting evidence is needed.

Scott himself extended this interpretation to souterrains, some of which include evidence of fire. But discussion of analogous structures built in recent years has generally favoured their use as stores for dairy produce. This was the main purpose of Cornish 'hulls' (Tangye, 1973) and reflects Irish evidence for similar structures employed in summer transhumance. Irish literary evidence suggests that they might also have stored grain, but the main groups of sites in Cornwall and in north-east Scotland are in areas of modern dairy production (cf. Gilchrist-Shirlaw, 1966, pp. 73 and 139 ff.). It is not likely that all these sites were confined to one activity and, as Charles Thomas has pointed out, they may not be a unified phenomenon (1972). Most prehistoric examples were Iron Age, but there was a Late Bronze Age souterrain at Jarlshof (Hamilton, 1956, pp. 34 ff.).

Finally, there is very limited evidence for tanning. It seems that oak galls were being collected by the Iron Age (Cunliffe, 1976b, p. 47), and two pits of earlier date, at Stockbridge Down and at Havant, Hampshire, resemble the 'hide pits' of the European Neolithic (Stone and Gray-Hill, 1938; Bradley and Lewis, 1974, pp. 10, 16; cf. Van der Velde, 1973). These sites may belong to the Early Bronze Age. The pit at Stockbridge Down contained a series of flint scrapers, but this should not be over-emphasised. A series of interrelated gullies in a late Iron Age site at Puddlehill have also been interpreted as a tanning establishment, but the argument is rather tenuous (Mathews, 1976, pp. 165–6 and 175–6). All this scattered information can do is remind excavators of a neglected problem.

CONCLUSIONS

As with the evidence for arable farming, the limitations of this information should be firmly understood. Here the evidence is even more scattered, forming an uneasy alliance between the extreme south and the extreme north, but still permitting no distinct regional schemes. The range of information is rather wider than it was with arable farming, but the argument which links these different elements is correspondingly more tenuous. Figure 3:4 is an attempt to sketch the time-range of each type of evidence. The basic scheme is the same as in the previous diagram. To some extent the two patterns *are* comparable, partly by the fortunate accident that the number of variables is roughly the same in each case. At first sight it might appear that both patterns are really the same: each shows an increasing elaboration which culminates in the full Iron Age. There are, however, two major differences: the cumulative pattern from the evidence for stock raising shows a major increase in the Early Bronze Age, but this has no counterpart in the other diagram. Stock raising also gives an impression of three distinct phases of innovation, in contrast to the fairly even growth of the arable evidence. These three phases were at the start of the Bronze Age, again around 1200 b.c. and finally in the mature Iron Age. The last two peaks do correspond to developments in arable farming and suggest the integrated patterns discussed in the introduction to this chapter. The Early Bronze Age evidence suggests a real contrast. If it is possible to press this information one stage further, it is worth observing a series of troughs in the pastoral evidence which find no counterpart in the arable data. These centre upon 1400 and 400 b.c. and could show further changes of emphasis. Otherwise, the agreement between these two patterns rules out inflexible schemes of economic change.

Such evidence is insubstantial in itself, but can be tested against another type of information. Since an important study by Judith Turner was published in 1965, pollen analysts have been concerned to distinguish arable and pastoral land use within humanly created clearings. Turner in fact developed an arable/pastoral ratio based

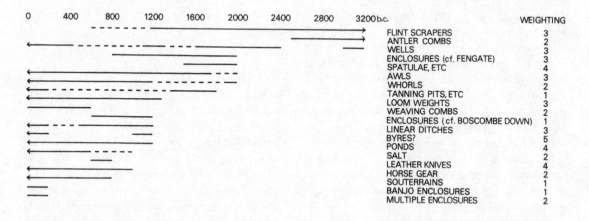

3:4   The chronological distribution of evidence for pastoral farming. Numbers indicate suggested weighting.

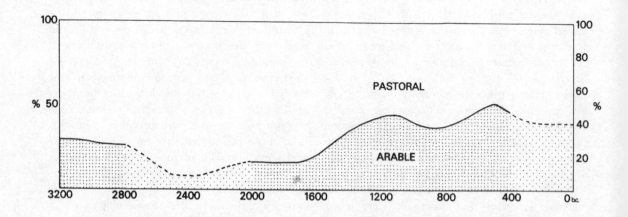

3:5   The arable/pastoral ratio in dated clearance horizons, plotted on a 200-year moving average. Dates were originally plotted at two standard deviations.

on the proportions of different weeds. This she compared directly with the study of modern surface samples and with pollen evidence from historically documented clearings. Godwin subsequently elaborated this arable/pastoral ratio in his study of Old Buckenham Mere (1968) and Turner has used his version in a later study of her own (Roberts, Turner and Ward, 1973). In the previous chapter there was some suggestion of the changing landscape from the percentage of arboreal pollen in all the firmly dated prehistoric clearings in England, Scotland and Wales. The results were plotted on a 400-year moving average. Figure 3:5 makes use of exactly the same group of clearings, but in this case Godwin's arable/pastoral ratio is recorded on a 200-year moving average. Again there is too little information for the later Neolithic, but otherwise the cereal curve shows a remarkable agreement with the scheme developed in this chapter, with the major increase in arable farming at about 1200 b.c. But there is also some support for the pastoral curve, since the two most distinct fluctuations in the pollen evidence are in the Early and Late Bronze Ages, both periods with some archaeological evidence for pastoral activity. The change is far slighter in 800 b.c. than it was in 1200 b.c., but it is persistent enough to need comment. All told, the agreement of these different schemes suggests that this well-worked data does contain some patterning. There is still the serious objection that the sample is far too small to treat highland and lowland zones separately. All that can be done until more analyses are available is to compare the average ratios irrespective of detailed chronology. In lowland Britain arable weeds formed 41 per cent of all the weeds considered; in the highland zone the figure was 33 per cent. The fact that these figures are not dramatically different raises problems that still need an answer.

Rigidly Liturgical Movements   *Chapter 4*
Transhumance and Nomadism

And I wondered, as I pottered upon those serene and sunny streets or sat drowsily in the Casino Gardens, at that provision of destiny which has made rich people so rigidly liturgical in their movements that they will come to Monte Carlo in the snow because that is the time ordained for their arrival in rubric and calendar, and will leave as soon as it becomes habitable for their grubby great shambling cities in the north.
Evelyn Waugh,
When the Going Was Good, *1946*

In your trade, is the work seasonal, or is it, in normal times, spread more or less evenly over the year? If your work is seasonal, how do you live in the periods between working?
Karl Marx,
Enquête Ouvrière, *1880*

Karl Marx was addressing his question to Paris factory workers, but it raises a problem which every excavator must face. Not all sites were in continuous use, and many activities on them would have been limited by the seasons. Is there sufficient evidence to consider these activities as part of a regular cycle of movement, or are there social and economic nuances which indicate a less predictable pattern?

Transhumance is the regular movement of all or part of a farming community from one economic environment into another. The movement must be regular and take place at a particular time or times of year, and it should be determined by seasonal changes of resources. It is frequently carried out by only part of a community, often by specific sex or age groups, and involves a prolonged shift of location rather than movement on a day-to-day basis. If movement is so irregular that there is no predictable cycle, what is being discussed is probably nomadism. The archaeologist must be able to show that the home territory and the seasonal territory were in some sense complementary. What is *not* implied by this statement – but is at times assumed in the literature – is that transhumance always takes place between lowland and highland areas and that it is exclusively concerned with animals. Where the basic requirements are not fulfilled, there are other forms of mobility to consider.

The British evidence suggests five types of movement: the seasonal use of intermittently waterlogged areas; the use of woodland from a more open environment; intermittent use of the shoreline; the occasional use of small islands; and seasonal use of the uplands. These will now be considered.

The first group of material is taken from two kinds of environment: the floodplains of some major rivers and more extensive areas of fenland. In the first instance it may be easier to establish intermittent use than to prove transhumance. Case was among the first to discuss this zone, and he observed that in the Upper Thames Valley ring ditches tend to cluster towards areas of land which would have been too damp for continuous use (1963, p. 51). As he pointed out, some of these monuments could have had a domestic function.

This pattern does not apply in all areas. In the

Great Ouse valley the ring ditches were located on rather higher ground away from the rivers, although Stephen Green's excavations at Milton Keynes have certainly shown evidence for a grassland environment (1974, pp. 128 and 129). Fieldwork elsewhere in this valley suggests that the main scatters of artefacts may not be found upon these sites but on the higher gravel terraces, close to the interface with heavier soils (P. Woodward, pers. com.). The sites in the Upper Thames show a rather similar pattern, and it would appear that pits with domestic material are usually on higher ground than the ring ditches and are sometimes found towards the upper limit of the gravels. This suggests an alternative hypothesis, that the ring ditches were placed where they were to avoid taking up better land. This is a pattern often seen in the location of barrows (cf. Dunn, 1975, p. 64).

In some instances, however, the flint industries which come from these areas show characteristics which set them apart from normal occupations. If it is accepted that in the Neolithic the more lasting sites were those with pits or houses, it is instructive to consider the proportions in which the associated tools are found. One characteristic feature of all the settlement sites is that the ratio of scrapers to other types is between 1:1 and 4:1. Many uses have been suggested for these tools, but some relationship with livestock still seems likely. At Broome Heath, for example, the proportion of scrapers in each phase varied with changes in the basic economy (p. 45). These tools were probably associated with butchery, skinworking and boneworking, and the sites on which they are most abundant are usually dominated by cattle bones. Flint industries in which scrapers are particularly prominent are known in riverside areas, and fieldwork in the Great Ouse valley even suggests that these items increase in number towards the floodplain (P. Woodward, pers. com.). Scraper-dominated industries are known along the River Wey in Surrey (Oakley, Rankine and Lowther, 1939) and are frequent in the drowned valleys of Portsmouth and Langstone harbours, where they may reflect use of the floodplain before this area was inundated by the sea (Bradley and Hooper, 1974). In nine cases

here the ratio of scrapers to other types is outside the range from settlement sites and averages 7:1. This evidence is of particular interest because coastal erosion has provided an opportunity for prolonged field observation. This seems to suggest that the area was without querns or pits; in fact, the only features found were hearths and a burial. Settlements on a chalk ridge overlooking these sites showed a normal proportion of scrapers (J. Johnston, pers. com.). The same pattern occurs along the River Thet, where a series of hearths associated with Beaker pottery were carefully recorded by Apling (1931). He showed that these were clustered in areas which would have been flooded in winter, and which were overlooked by round barrows located on slightly higher ground. Scraper-dominated industries are a feature of the later Neolithic and earlier Bronze Age (Holden and Bradley, 1975), and it is likely that increased use of the floodplain is related to the making of dugout canoes in this period (McGrail and Switsur, 1975).

So far none of this evidence has been sufficiently specific to imply transhumance. There are two additional arguments. Case has suggested that the alignments of ring ditch complexes in the Upper Thames mark long-distance routes linking the floodplain to the chalk and limestone uplands (in Case *et al.*, 1964, p. 50). This would resemble medieval intercommoning over this area. A similar approach might be to examine the ditched droveways running down to the rivers. Not all of these seem to lead into settlements and Collin Bowen has suggested that the wider droveways might have been used to move livestock onto the floodplain (pers. com.). Evidence from preserved plants and insects in the Upper Thames shows that some of the Iron Age sites in this zone were only briefly and occasionally used, perhaps on a seasonal basis (M. Robinson, pers. com.). Some of these are certainly connected with droveways and are dominated by cattle bones. It is possible that rich Late Bronze Age settlements had been located in similar areas. An obvious comparison is with the East Anglian fens (Pryor, 1976a).

Stephen Green has also emphasised the sex of the burials in his ring ditches at Milton Keynes

(1974, p. 130). These were all of females or infants. He felt that this might suggest that they were located in the home area of a transhumance cycle, and that the men could have been buried elsewhere. Pryor used the same argument in considering the human burials at Fengate (1976a, p. 41). There may well be patterns of this type within the evidence, but the problem is to establish whether they are related to transhumance. The barrow cemeteries in Wessex which Fleming (1971b) considers were in summer pasture contained male, female and infant burials. Male burials were particularly common in the peripheral areas between these groups. On a smaller scale the flat cemeteries at Eynsham and Cassington indicate some separation of male burials from the rest (Leeds, 1934, 1938; Case, 1977).

A comparable approach to land use in the East Anglian fens was first suggested by Lethbridge in connection with the Beaker occupations of two Cambridgeshire sandhills (in Leaf, 1935). He argued that parts of the fens dried out sufficiently in summer to allow their use for seasonal grazing and that each of these sites had been employed in this process. On each site there was stratigraphic evidence for 'two short occupations' but neither showed any sign of durable structures. Fifty Farm included cattle, sheep and pig bones, as well as deer and human remains. One point of interest is that the scrapers on this site outnumbered the other tools by a ratio of 15:1. Similar industries are known from other sand islands in the Fenland and include knives, awls and bone spatulae. Again, a specialised range of activities can be envisaged. Characteristic of some of these sites is the rechipping of flints after patination. This could also suggest intermittent use of one location. Such evidence is further supported by other sites at Mildenhall (Kelley, T., 1967). One of these included eighty-eight flint scrapers and a later Bronze Age knife, together with six needles and some animal bones. Analysis of these bones suggested that the site could represent one seasonal occupation, associated mainly with cattle. It is possible that the animals were butchered on this site and that the meat was then taken elsewhere. Clark's better-known site at Mildenhall Fen amplifies this information and also included flint borers and a series of bone awls (1936).

The complementary aspect of this pattern appears on the fen edge. At Fengate a complex series of droveways, paddocks and water-holes is at present under excavation. This appears to be connected with intensive management of livestock at a time when feed was scarce in the winter months and the fens could not be used (Pryor, 1976a). Phosphate analysis has confirmed the use of this complex by livestock, and the faunal remains seem to indicate a predominance of cattle raised for pastoral produce. Two systems have now been recovered, one later Neolithic and the other Middle Bronze Age, if not earlier. The excavator has argued that no hiatus occurred. The late Neolithic complex is reminiscent of a ring ditch settlement at Playden overlooking Romney Marsh, which is again dominated by scrapers (Bradley, 1978b).

Flint implements are not the only evidence from the fens themselves. Increasing attention is now being paid to the wooden trackways preserved by the peat in these areas. At least one example from the East Anglian fens may belong to the later Bronze Age (Lethbridge, 1934), whilst other areas in which they have been found include the Somerset Levels, the Essex marshes, the Humberside estuary, Lancashire and Ireland. The main work so far has been in Somerset, and here Coles and his colleagues have again suggested seasonal exploitation of the levels between periods of winter inundation, a pattern rather similar to medieval use of this area (Coles and Hibbert, 1975). It is not suggested that the tracks themselves were intended for animals but they do clearly show use of the lowlying areas and traffic between settlements located on the higher land. The primary use of the trackways was perhaps in hunting and fowling. The main groups of sites in Somerset are earlier Neolithic, late Neolithic and late Bronze Age, but it was in the Iron Age that the famous settlements of Meare and Glastonbury developed on the edge of these levels. David Clarke has argued that their economy depended upon summer grazing of the peat (1972). Of the animals at Glastonbury 92 per cent were sheep which had been raised mainly for their wool, whilst the cattle bones can be divided into two groups, one indicating animals culled for meat and a larger one suggesting dairy production (Bulleid and Gray, 1917, pp. 648 ff.).

Additional evidence for this use of lowlying areas comes mainly from Ireland. Here a number of hearths, some incorporating imported materials, have been recovered in the peat, for example at Beaghmore (May, A., 1953) or Rockbarton (Mitchell and O'Riordain, 1942), and occasional finds of burnt plants seem to indicate activity at least in summer or autumn. A wooden platform was built at Rathjordan at this time of year (O'Riordain and Lucas, 1947). These finds are mainly of later Neolithic date. Although not all these sites can be associated with farming, a number of items from later periods seem to indicate the pattern already noticed in East Anglia. Among the more frequent discoveries in the Irish peats are wooden tubs or stave-built vessels. Most of these cannot be dated, although Grahame Clark did point out their resemblance to a wooden vessel containing the Late Bronze Age hoard at Stuntney Fen in East Anglia (in Clark and Godwin, 1940). There is some evidence that these casks were used to store butter, which could be preserved by burial in peat. This is quite a widespread phenomenon and finds of 'mor butter' in Europe have been discussed by Dieck (1961). There seem to be two reasons for these deposits. In some cases butter was stored for up to seven years in order to improve its flavour, but this practice is also an important method of conserving surplus dairy produce in summer (cf. Williams, J., 1966). Two well-published finds from Scotland confirm the antiquity of this practice. In each case the butter itself survived for specialist examination and at Kilmaluag it even included recognisable cattle hairs (Ritchie, J., 1940). Pollen analysis could allow a late prehistoric date. The other example is also from the Island of Skye, where a group of these vessels at Kyleakin were found in direct association with a cauldron of Iron Age type (Anderson, 1885). A piece of bog butter was also recovered from the famous Irish site of Lisnacroghera, but it is not clear whether this belongs to the early occupation or to use of the site in the post-Roman period (Munro, 1890, p. 386).

More doubt must attach to the larger structures recovered in peat bogs, especially if a ritual explanation is adopted for some of the metalwork found there. There is, however, some evidence that sites in this zone might have possessed a special status. Some of the sites with fine metalwork perhaps served as hunting camps, but the finding of bog butter in the same deposit as a cauldron suggests that pastoralism could also be connected with rank. Two contrasting sites, both with palisades and internal buildings, serve to illustrate this difficulty. The first, at Cullyhanna Lough, dates from the second millennium b.c. but produced so few finds on excavation that it was originally identified as a 'hunting lodge' from the medieval period (Hodges, 1958; Hillam, 1976). The second site at Balinderry, however, preserved a range of animal bones, only 3 per cent of which were game (Hencken, 1942). In fact 70 to 90 per cent of the animals were cattle. The social eminence of this second site can hardly be doubted. It produced a quantity of metalwork, including a flesh hook and personal ornaments of bronze and amber. There was little evidence for cereal farming, and preserved fruits and nuts show that the site was used at least in summer and autumn. It is not certain whether occupation was maintained throughout the year and so its real status remains in doubt. Sites of this type may well have been economically specialised, but it is important to remember that they were being used at the same time as the earliest crannogs. They were specifically adopted as remote defensible positions. Their social eminence has never been questioned, and for this reason it is possible that the choice of such locations was not economically determined.

A related topic is the grazing of small islands for part of the year. Case has suggested that this was one method by which new areas might be settled, and it is more than likely that it was integrated with other activities, like fowling and the collection of birds' eggs. Much depends on the nature of contemporary boats and their capacity to carry livestock (cf. McGrail, 1976).

The main argument for this practice is that certain islands were too limited in extent and resources to support year-round occupation. Their resemblance to crannogs again leads to problems. Dalkey Island, where occupation was probably of limited duration, included several Late Bronze Age moulds (Liversage, 1968, p. 184), and Island MacHugh, which really defies analysis, apparently produced crucibles and bronzes (Davies, O., 1950, p. 37). The Neolithic evidence is less complicated and recalls the placing of chambered tombs in this type of location. The excavator of Rough Island found 'a meandering series of shallow pits' with just a few cattle and pig bones (Movius, 1940), and Geroid Island, near the better-known sites at Knockadoon, was also occupied in this period (Liversage, 1958). High oak pollen seems to suggest that it was largely uncleared. The small faunal assemblage here included cattle and sheep but the higher proportion of pig led the excavator to believe that the site was really the refuge of a community which had lost its cattle in war. Remembering that pig is a woodland animal, the island may have been used in seasonal grazing.

On the mainland, the grazing of woodland from more open country is another form which transhumance might have taken. Most discussion of woodland grazing has been in an early Neolithic context and has usually amounted to a commentary on the evidence of pollen analysis. These rather general considerations have already been discussed, and apart from the molluscan evidence from Knap Hill – a site of unusual status – there is little direct evidence of activity in a wooded environment (Evans, J. G., 1969, p. 246). In fact it now seems likely that some clearings could have been rather larger than was originally envisaged (Evans, J. G., 1975, p. 116). If this were the case in lowland England, any seasonal movement might have been from sites where cereals were grown into the areas of grassland in which large monuments were built.

At present it seems that it was with the expansion of settlement in the late Neolithic that woodland was used on a seasonal basis.

Apart from Geroid Island, there are two sites of a certain interest. One is a settlement at Stacey Bushes, Milton Keynes, which the excavator suggests was occupied in autumn or winter, since the occupants evidently took care to drain the site, which is situated on rather damp ground (Green, H. S., 1976). There were no signs of permanent buildings, and some of the excavated features could have been dug for potting clay. The molluscan evidence seemed to indicate a wooded environment and Green suggests that this site was used for hunting and grazing.

The other site is at Rackham in the Weald (Holden and Bradley, 1975). Here, rescue excavation disclosed a series of hearths and a stake-built windbreak, but no sign of more permanent structures. The site was dominated by a large quantity of scrapers, which greatly outnumbered the other tools, mainly knives. All of these had been made and used on the spot. This flint industry resembles those already discussed from the East Anglian fens, but with the essential difference that in this case pollen analysis suggests that they were used in the first small clearing of the forest. Similar but less extensive sites in the same area have produced cattle and pig bones. Some seem to have made exclusive use of flint from the downland chalk, even though adequate raw material was available nearer to hand. The limited character of these sites, with their continued dependence on another area, might again represent the earliest use of this region (Dimbleby and Bradley, 1975). If so, they would recall the Saxon colonisation of the Weald through the development of seasonal swine pasture (Brandon, 1974, p. 71). A second, more extensive, clearance at Rackham included evidence of cultivation and it may be to this phase of settlement that the flint sickles from the Weald belong.

The final development in these areas might be towards over-use and podsolisation, a process well documented at Rackham (Dimbleby and Bradley, 1975). Such changes are not irreversible, and can be partly controlled by grazing and burning. This is of course speculation, but at Broome Heath there is certainly evidence for the deposition of a flint industry, consisting almost entirely of scrapers, after overgrazing had led to the appearance of heathland (Wainwright, 1972, pp. 20 and 61 ff.). In the same way, ivy pollen beneath the Portesham round barrow in Dorset suggests that heathland resources could have been supplemented by the introduction of fodder (Thompson and Ashbee, 1957, cf. Dimbleby and Simmons, 1974).

In the case of upland grazing there is a body of information on recent practice which can be employed in establishing preliminary hypotheses. Among the best-documented regions are central Wales, the Scottish borderland, the Scottish Highlands and south-west Ireland (Crampton, 1966; Ramm, McDowall and Mercer, 1970; Millar, 1967; Aalen, 1964). These studies are particularly valuable since they suggest a number of the characteristics which might distinguish permanent settlements from shielings. Among these are the limited floor areas of seasonally occupied shelters; the provision of storage for dairy produce; distinctive building materials; and occasionally the absence of hearths. Some of these points require elaboration. There is great variation in the size of individual shielings, but in most circumstances they would house a smaller social unit than the settlement used throughout the year. The floor areas of recorded examples range from about 8 sq. m for some Irish structures (Aalen, 1964) to about 35 sq. m for examples on the Scottish border (Ramm, McDowall and Mercer, 1970). In the west of Ireland buildings of different sizes could be found in clusters, with the smallest structures as little as 2 m in diameter (Aalen, 1964). Some of these buildings were used as stores or had stores attached to them. Some of the Irish *clochans* which were also used as shielings had sunken dairy compartments, the description of which is reminiscent of souterrains (Aalen, 1964). Others were less substantially built, quite often in turf. These would not last long unless a fire were kept burning inside them, and on collapse would resemble robbed barrows. A further complication is that soot-caked turves might be taken from abandoned buildings and used to nourish garden plots. In some cases where the roof was more substantially

built it could be dismantled before the winter and the rafters used as a slide car to transport equipment to the main settlement (M. Campbell, pers. com.). There have been few studies of the locations of shielings but classic positions seem to be at the headwaters of rivers and streams and at heights of between 300 and 500 m. Most transhumance in this range was based on sheep, but this was not always the case and dairy cattle were also important. They would require greater management (Crampton, 1966) and dairy stores would be needed.

Most of these characteristics can be recognised in the archaeological evidence from marginally situated areas. Some correlation has been shown between elevation and the size of structures. In north-west Wales a series of studies suggests such a pattern. The most sensible analysis of this evidence was published by Griffiths, who pointed out that groups of huts or single buildings occurred very widely on the higher ground, either in complete isolation or accompanied by quite limited plots (1950). These were found at heights of up to 520 m. The huts in his sample had an average diameter of only 3 m. The total range was from 2 to 5 m and 70 per cent of these sites were at 320 m or higher. Griffiths contrasted these sites with those on the lower ground, whether they were enclosed or not. The huts in this second area were usually 7 or 8 m in diameter but could sometimes be larger. They were normally better constructed than the other buildings and were sometimes associated with field systems. Hemp and Gresham examined the latter sites in rather more detail and suggested that the groups of enclosed and unenclosed sites might show some patterning of their own (1953). One possibility is that the open sites represent what is left of an early settlement pattern removed by more intensive agriculture on the lower ground (Gresham, 1963). This scheme gives the enclosed sites an average elevation of 130 m and the open sites one of 270 m. It may well represent a distinction between two economic zones, but there is no evidence to imply any specific arrangement. The Royal Commission adopt Griffiths's scheme and consider the cleared plots which accompany the upland sites as paddocks rather than arable fields (RCAM (Wales), 1964, pp. LXXXVII ff.). In the old county of Merionethshire there is an equally regular relationship between hut size and elevation. Figure 4:1 illustrates this point using data assembled by E. G. Bowen and Gresham (1967, pp. 176 ff.).

On Dartmoor a similar pattern may be seen, but in this case other classes of evidence can also be taken into account. Lady Aileen Fox distinguishes two main types of later Bronze Age settlement here: those with small arable fields; and sites where the absence of fields might suggest a pastoral economy (1954; 1973, ch. 6; but cf. Price, D. G. and Tinsley, 1976). Her 'arable' and 'pastoral' settlements usually occupy distinct areas of moorland, with most members of the pastoral group in the parts with the higher

rainfall. In her basic statement Lady Fox noticed two other features of these settlements. The huts on her arable sites were both larger and more sturdily built than those in the other group. She in fact suggested a range of 7 to 10 m, or even 13 m, for the hut diameters on her arable sites, and of 3 to 8 m for those in the pastoral group. Worth (1945, fig. 2) has provided a useful summary of hut sizes on some of these sites and their bimodal distribution strongly supports Fox's outline (fig. 4:2).

If this basic distinction does mirror the traditional division between permanent houses and shielings, can it be supported by other types of evidence? In fact one feature of some of the huts is a series of stone-based beds. These show some tendency to occur in the smaller huts and are apparently more frequent on sites where

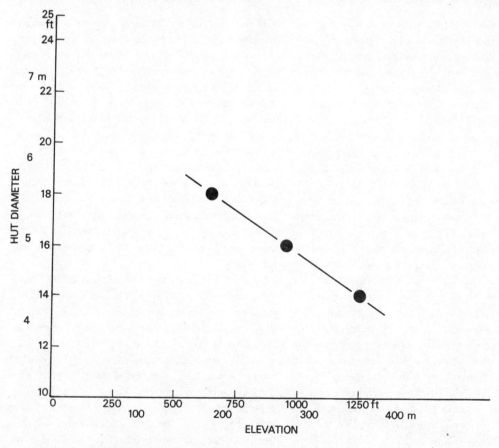

4:1 The relationship between average hut diameter and elevation in the uplands of Merionethshire. Data from Bowen, E. and Gresham (1967).

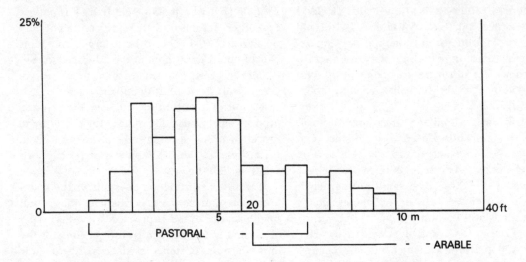

4:2 Hut diameters of stone-built huts on Dartmoor compared with Lady Aileen Fox's interpretation. Sample from Worth, 1945. Interpretation after Fox, A., 1973.

there are no fields. Since there is only one small bed to each hut, this could, but need not, reflect the smaller unit of the transhumance cycle. Some buildings also possess annexes which could be used for storage, but their precise purpose is uncertain and they are not limited to one class of hut. Cunliffe has already suggested transhumance as an explanation for this settlement pattern (1974, p. 19) but a fuller assessment must await the completion of fieldwork on contemporary land boundaries (Fleming, 1977).

In north-west Wales and on Dartmoor, then, there seems to be some relationship between hut size and elevation. This has also been observed in a recent study of sites on the North Yorkshire Moors (Fleming, 1976). In this area, however, the huts are usually found with small plots of cleared land, and a study of their detailed siting in relation to climate, vegetation and topography suggests that crops were being grown despite the high altitude. The best evidence for grazing, on the other hand, comes from lower ground overlooked by the settlements. It is possible to see the sites as permanent farms forced into extreme locations by pressures on more suitable land. But an alternative view is just as attractive. These sites occupy positions which would be more satisfactory in summer than in winter, and Millar has produced useful

evidence for arable farming on some Scottish shielings (1967). In certain cases the penning of livestock brought such an improvement of the soil that the occupants turned to arable farming. The same pattern is known in Wales, where sites which began as shielings even developed into permanent settlements. In the Black Mountains farmers retained one element of seasonal land use and the stock would be sent to winter in lowland areas, almost inverting the original cycle (Crampton, 1966 and 1968). This last example suggests that the Yorkshire sites could still belong to a complex annual pattern, even when crops were being grown. The same could apply to those plots in north Wales where tillage could be represented.

Almost the opposite relationship has been seen with some enclosed sites. This problem has been discussed by Alcock (1965) who has pointed out that in north Wales the largest Iron Age hill forts can be found on the highest ground (fig. 4:3). Although Hogg considers that these sites were permanently settled (1962), their immediate surroundings could not have supported a large and stable population. It seems rather more likely that the main settlements of this period were on the productive lowland soils and have been destroyed in later agriculture. A number of these sites, notably Tre'r Ceiri, include

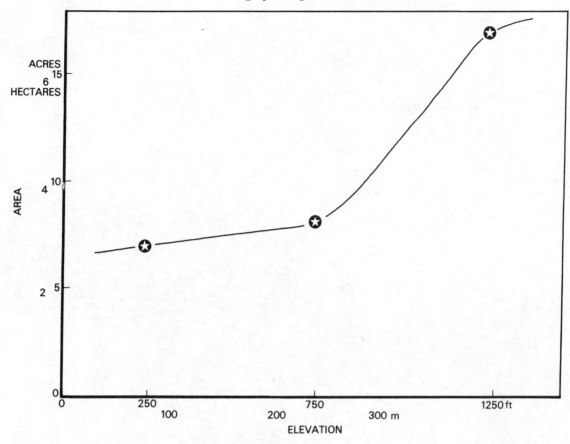

4:3   The relationship between average hill fort area and elevation in the north Welsh Marches. Data from Alcock (1965).

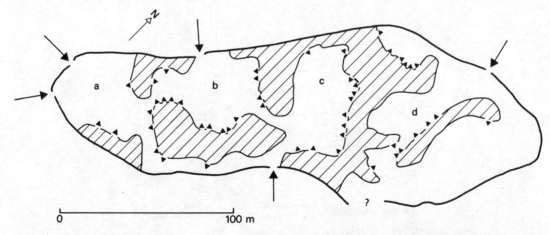

4:4   Outline plan of Tre'r Ceiri interpreted as four self-contained compounds approached by separate entrances through the defences. Building areas are shaded and large arrows mark the gateways to the site. Small arrows represent external doors to the buildings.

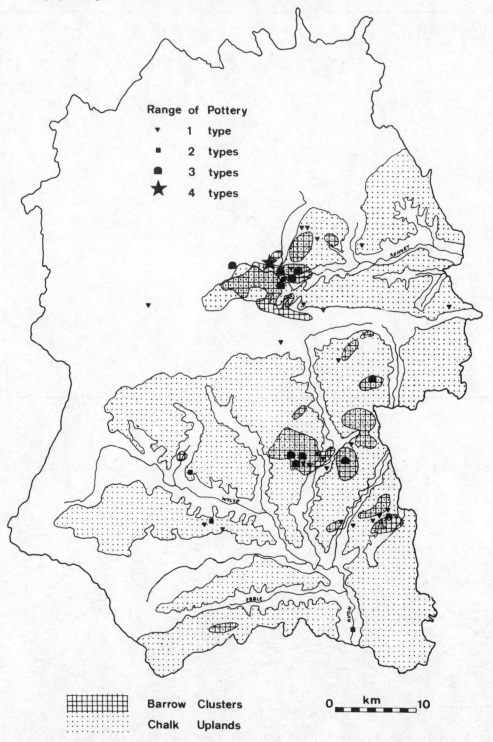

4:5   The range of potentially contemporary pottery beneath Bronze Age barrows on the Wiltshire downs. Source: Bradley (1977).

small cleared plots and a large number of huts. Almost certainly the plots themselves could have fed very few people. As Alcock has pointed out, querns are rare or absent on these sites, although spindle whorls are frequently found. Tre'r Ceiri can in fact be interpreted as a series of conjoined enclosures, each surrounded by its own huts and ancillary buildings, and possibly approached by a separate entrance through the defences (fig. 4:4). This would be explained if the site had met the needs of several different settlements. Although the relationship between size and elevation is clearest in Wales, it may also appear in the earliest Iron Age of southern England (Bradley, 1971).

A rather similar approach has been taken by Andrew Fleming in an interesting study of Early Bronze Age cemeteries in Wessex (1971b). He considers that these occur in such well-marked clusters that they are not likely to represent the burial places of a resident population, particularly considering the areas of productive land between them. There is some evidence that these cemeteries were constructed in grassland, and Fleming has suggested that they were built in summer pasture by groups who were practising transhumance. One concentration of mounds is in the headwaters of the Lambourn River, which flows only between March and October (Bradley and Ellison, 1975, p. 193).

There are good reasons for accepting this outline, at least in Wiltshire where most data is available (Bradley, 1978a). The best evidence for contemporary settlements is from the river valleys which were cultivated throughout the historical period, and some of the barrows in these areas may have started as cairns of field-gathered stones. Others on the higher ground were built around a core of turves. The central areas evidently possessed a focal attraction and the mounds have a variety of different sherds in their buried soils. It is not clear whether these are an index of social, economic, cultural or commercial contacts, but it is obvious that the range of pottery styles is greater beneath these barrows than it is on sites closer to the rivers (fig. 4:5). A comparable argument was applied to the later Bronze Age pottery from Rams Hill, which lies only 5 km from the Lambourn cemetery. Here the range of ceramic fabrics was far wider than on excavated farms of the same period (Bradley and Ellison, 1975). The problem in both cases is that this evidence could be limited to a social elite.

A weakness of arguments based on sites like Rams Hill is the very limited amount of artefact and faunal evidence which they provide. The problem is greatest in highland Britain because of the hostile environment in which shielings may be found. Fortunately these areas sometimes include another type of site on which preservation is better. Caves were used in most periods of prehistory and could well have been occupied in summer or winter land use. Their cool conditions would make them ideal stores, but they should not be treated as a distinct form of site just because they allow so much material to survive. Their importance should not be exaggerated in comparison with stone- or turf-built huts.

Caves were certainly in use into the historical period but there are few examples with occupation in the earlier Neolithic and not many with later Bronze Age activity. Only in the Iron Age could the quantity of artefacts suggest that caves were used as ordinary domestic sites, and in this period some may in fact have been specialised parts of large open settlements (Raistrick, 1939). Otherwise caves were mainly used for burial or as occasional shelters in hunting and pastoralism. The earlier Neolithic evidence is very limited and its dating depends entirely upon pottery typology. It suggests that caves were mainly used for the storage or burial of corpses. Only at the end of this period did the main use of these sites begin. Despite unambiguous evidence that many were still used or adapted for burial (Gilks, 1973), they now include artefacts, hearths and animal bones in enough variety to suggest an economic role. Apart from coarse pottery, common finds include flint scrapers, axes, knives and borers; bone gouges, pins, needles and spatulae, and occasional metal awls. These items rarely appear in quantity, but the variety of bone tools is of particular interest considering their comparative rarity in other contexts. The majority of these types are conventionally associated with leatherworking (Smith, I. F. and Simpson, 1966, pp. 134 ff.). Among the more varied groups of this kind are those from Merlin's Cave, Sun Hole and Wetton Mill (Hewer, 1925; Tratman and Henderson, 1926; Kelly, J., 1976). The latter site contained needles, spatulae and a sponge-finger stone, scrapers, knives and an awl. It seems likely that these items were originally the grave goods with a Beaker burial. In Green's view such burials 'may indicate an important social position for the leatherworker in Bronze Age society' (in Kelly, J., 1976, p. 68). There were no human remains in Sun Hole, and if all this equipment was originally deposited with burials it would still be a problem why such a specialised tool kit should accompany burials in such an unusual location. The evidence from such burials does not show any patterning by sex, and male, female and infant burials have all been found. If these sites were in seasonal use, perhaps the basic distinction could have been a social one, by kin group rather than age or sex. It is at least as likely that these occupations were associated with more specialised pastoralism.

The best evidence that the finds were partly of domestic character is provided by the animal bones in these deposits. Normally the species can only be assessed on a presence or absence basis, since precise figures are not provided in the literature. It appears that sheep and cattle are the most common animals in upland caves, followed rather surprisingly by dog. Since there are relatively few game bones on these sites, the natural inference is that the dogs were used to control the other animals. Horse is present in this group but is rather rare.

Later Bronze Age caves show few developments of these patterns. Human burials were still deposited and bone tools and awls remain quite common types. A single weaving comb was found with later Bronze Age metalwork at Ogof-yr-Esgyrn (Mason, 1968). Querns and cereals, on the other hand, remain elusive. The sample of animal bones is very small and has no novel features, except possibly an increasing number of associations between horse and the main domesticates. Heathery Burn Cave contained artefacts associated with riding (Greenwell, 1894). Only one element is new. This is the deposition of fine metalwork in caves of this general period. Apart from Heathery Burn, a variety of sites have now given this evidence and characteristic items include weaponry, craft tools, awls, bracelets and beads both of gold and of amber. The circumstances of these deposits are rather interesting. At least three of the sites included human remains, but not all these metal types are standard grave goods and some are rarely found in hoards (cf. Burgess, 1976c). In at least four cases there is evidence for domestic activity. While such a small sample proves nothing, this could be some indication of the status of those making use of these caves. The fact that the burials are not limited to one age or sex group may suggest the same interpretation.

The Iron Age developments are more clear-cut. Since many of these caves are in remote areas, some 'Roman Iron Age' sites are included in this discussion. This period certainly saw a

TABLE 3: *Frequency of association between domestic and game animals in major inland caves occupied in the Late Neolithic to Early Bronze Age*

	Cattle	Sheep/goat	Pig	Dog	Horse	Red deer	Roe deer
Cattle	.	11	7	10	3	2	1
Sheep/goat	11	.	7	10	3	3	1
Pig	7	7	.	10	2	1	–
Dog	10	10	10	.	3	2	1
Horse	3	3	2	3	.	1	1
Red deer	2	3	3	2	1	.	1
Roe deer	1	1	–	1	1	1	.

greater amount of material deposited in caves and some increase in the number of sites which were used. Some of the caves themselves were modified. For instance, Read's Cavern contained three iron keys (Tratman, 1931) and Roman occupation at Old Woman's Cave was associated with a laid floor (Storrs-Fox, 1911). These caves were sometimes on the edge of contemporary settlements and served as occasional shelters, particularly in Derbyshire and Yorkshire (Raistrick, 1939), but more often their contents and their position indicate a quite restricted use. The majority of these sites no longer contain any burials, although some scattered bones occur, just as they do in settlements. The majority of the formal inhumations are Roman.

As in earlier periods bone tools are frequent finds, especially those connected with leather-working or weaving. The most common bone tools are points, needles, gouges, scrapers, knives, pins, awls, burnishers and weaving combs; hones, spindle whorls, pottery and personal ornaments are also represented. Weaving combs and spindle whorls are commonly found together but loom weights are rather rare, perhaps implying that only the preliminary processing of wool was carried out on these sites. Very few caves had any items which might suggest the nearness of cultivated land. The main exception was Wookey Hole, which had a field system nearby (Balch, 1914). Like Rowbarrow Cave, again in the Mendips, it preserved a deposit of organic material which was interpreted as 'stable bedding' (Taylor, H., 1925). The animal bones from Iron Age sites are quite informative. Sheep and cattle are the most common animals, with sheep dominating the sample in several caves. On a few sites, lamb is prominently represented, but there is little to show one period of killing. Pig is present on most sites, but is not particularly important. Dogs are virtually absent and might have been replaced by horses. A whole series of artefacts from these sites are connected with riding, in particular bone cheek pieces. Taken together this evidence would seem to imply that the development of horsemanship from the later Bronze Age had allowed mounted pastoralism to develop in the uplands and to take over from stock management with the aid of dogs. It does not seem that this pattern extends to other sites.

On the coast there are three types of environment to consider: areas of salt marsh which would have been subject to the same limitations as fenland; areas of unstable dune pasture; and generally more productive zones of stabilised shell sand. Since coastal sand deposits are so notoriously volatile, the distinction between the last two areas is not rigid, and alterations in the coastal environment would bring changes in the likely duration and scope of settlement. A number of lowlying sites, not directly on the shoreline, will also be considered in this section, provided they were within easy reach of this zone.

The information from salt marshes is extremely limited, and can only be interpreted if the contemporary shoreline is known. It is not possible to establish transhumance with any certainty. Again all that can be done is to point to features which might limit the period over which domestic activity was profitable. In this

TABLE 4: *Frequency of association between domestic and game animals in major inland caves occupied in the Iron Age*

	Cattle	Sheep/goat	Pig	Dog	Horse	Red deer	Roe deer	Wild pig
Cattle	.	9	6	–	2	2	1	1
Sheep/goat	9	.	7	–	3	2	1	1
Pig	6	7	.	–	2	2	1	1
Dog	–	–	–	.	1	–	–	–
Horse	2	3	3	1	.	–	1	1
Red deer	2	2	1	–	–	.	1	1
Roe deer	1	1	1	–	–	1	.	1
Wild pig	1	1	1	–	–	1	1	.

case, however, evidence of Iron Age salt production will allow a more accurate assessment
of season (Bradley, 1975b). There are definite
constraints on the period in which this activity
is feasible in the British climate, in particular
sea temperature, air temperature and rainfall.
Taken together these delimit a period for efficient
production between about May and August, the
slack months of the agricultural cycle and the
period in which these areas could be used for
grazing (fig. 4:6). There is evidence that some
of the distinctive briquetage used in salt production was made on inland settlements while the
spelt crop was ripening (Bradley, 1975b, p. 23).
Briquetage is only needed in the later stages of
salt making, and it may be that by then activity on the coast was coming to an end.
Scattered animal bones and hearths are often
found near these sites, and at Ingoldmells

in Lincolnshire there were small waterlogged
structures which could have served as temporary shelters (Warren, 1932). One might well
envisage a sequence of industrial and domestic
activity in which animals were fattened and
killed on the shoreline and their salted carcases
traded inland. The faunal remains on one of the
Essex Red Hills may support this view (Wilmer
and Reader, 1907). There is a timber trackway
in the Southchurch Marshes dating to the
Bronze Age/Iron Age transition (Francis, 1931).
Flint scrapers are also common in these environments.

Scraper-dominated industries of the later
Neolithic to Early Bronze Age are known from
several coastal dunes. These include a series of
sites in Ireland (Hewson, 1935) and Walney
Island in Cumbria (Cross, 1938). This pattern
can be suspected far more widely, although it

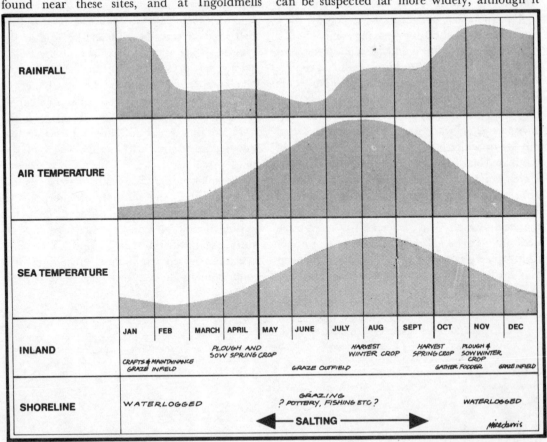

4:6 Outline interpretation of the place of salt working in the Iron Age agricultural cycle. Source:
Bradley (1975b).

cannot be proved. Many of these occupations were on a very limited scale, and several included bone pins, points and spatulae. A tool kit perhaps connected with leatherworking comes from the Beaker site at Northton, which also produced a mass of animal bones, but showed no sign of cereal farming (Simpson, 1976).

The main use of the coastal dunes was in this period and again in the Iron Age. As the Irish term 'Sandhills Ware' implies, there was considerable use of these environments in the later third millennium b.c. Apart from these distinctive flint and bone industries, a number of sites have produced human burials. These may be represented by scattered bones, but can include small cairns, cists or urned cremations. There is no particular evidence that they were only related to the full settlements established in this zone. There is not enough information to discuss their age or sex structure.

Despite their limited extent, these sites show a surprising range of activities, a number of which are traditionally undertaken in summer. Potting is one activity which needs more attention. This was probably undertaken at Ross Links in Northumberland, where clay lumps were found together with a series of stone implements (Brewis and Buckley, 1928), and has also been suggested for the Luce Sands (McInnes, 1964, p. 41). Bone combs, suitable for decorating pots, are known from coastal sites at Gwithian and at Northton (Megaw, 1976, p. 61). The use of crushed shell as a tempering material may also be relevant to this argument (cf. Coles, J. and Taylor, 1970). There is evidence that pottery and salt were produced together in later periods (Bradley, 1975b). Colin Renfrew has pointed out how there is a concentration of faience beads on some Scottish sand dunes and it is possible that they were actually made there (Newton and Renfrew, 1970, p. 204). Most of the evidence for ironworking comes from permanent sites where the more stable subsoils could be farmed. One notable exception was at Merthyr Mawr in South Wales where metalworking debris was recovered together with a La Tène 1 brooch (Fox, C., 1927). This site is rather unusual and the increasing frequency of

querns, slag and stone buildings in the Iron Age suggests that by this stage the shoreline was coming into more intensive use.

The evidence for early buildings is not very informative. Structures resembling 'tent rings' have been described from Walney Island, perhaps in the Bronze Age, and from Valtos in the Iron Age (Cross, 1946, p. 76; Lacaille, 1937). Rather limited post-built shelters are also known on the Dundrum and Culbin Sands (Collins, 1952; Coles, J. and Taylor, 1970). No definite post structures are known at Dalkey Island, although some stake holes were found and a number of large nodules had been introduced from the beach (Liversage, 1968). It is not clear whether the Beaker structures at Northton were used all year round, and the excavator, Simpson, suggests 'sporadic' occupation of the site (1976). He has made the interesting suggestion that the oval building, Structure 2, might have been roofed with an upturned boat, a practice for which there is recent precedent. A series of late Neolithic huts is known at Whitepark Bay, Co. Antrim (Herity and Eogan, 1976, pp. 99 and 102), as well as the better known sites of the Orkneys.

In addition to these sites, a number of caves on or near the coast show evidence of occupation. Once again their significance should not be exaggerated. They show almost the same trends as the inland sites. There are few earlier Neolithic examples and the majority of caves include Beaker or Early Bronze Age material. Among these are human burials, scrapers, borers, spatulae and pins. The bones show no specific grouping by age or sex, and the artefacts completely lack the mass of scrapers found on the open sites. There is some fall in the frequency of later Bronze Age examples, although the Potter's Cave, Covesea, contained fine metalwork, needles and awls, as well as human remains (Benton, 1931). There is then a marked increase in sites of Iron Age date. A proportion of these may well have been near to permanent settlements. This was specifically suggested for Ruidh' an Dunain which included slag and burnt grain (Scott, L., 1934). The evidence for metalworking from several other sites might carry the same implications. Otherwise the principal finds in these caves were weaving equipment, pins, needles and cheek pieces. Again it would appear that some of these artefacts represent a specialised tool kit for processing animal products.

The bones shed a little light on the relationship of coastal and inland settlement. In several cases the association of coastal sites with other activities, notably pottery and salt production, implies that at least part of the occupation would have been in summer. It will be seen in the next chapter that associated shells, fish and bird bones suggest the same arrangement. On the other hand there are definite contrasts between the evidence from these two groups of sites. In the later Neolithic the basic association between dog and the other domesticates was the same and this continued unchanged into the Bronze Age. In the Iron Age, however, the two areas show contrasting patterns. There is a clear association between horse and other domestic animals on the coast but the representation of dog is sustained where it falls in the inland caves. On the coast it could be associated with game, which shows a major increase in this period. If so, it might suggest that the development of riding had most impact in inland areas, where stock movements were controlled from horseback, and that dogs were kept on the shoreline for their use in hunting.

There are other contrasts between coastal and inland sites. Potentially the most important is the higher number of coastal groups with specifically young animals. This applies to cattle, sheep and pig. A few lowland caves also contain unshed antler. This might suggest that some occupation was maintained into winter. The relative frequency of red deer bones from coastal areas could also indicate that occupation sometimes lasted into winter when these animals came down to lower ground. There is some reason to envisage a growing number of permanent settlements on the shoreline, especially by the Iron Age, and this evidence could be related to the activities based upon them.

TABLE 5: *Age distribution of animal bones on minor Iron Age sites, by number of separate occurrences*

	Coastal caves and sand dunes	Upland caves
'Young' cattle	5	1
sheep	9	3
pig	5	2
Shed antler	–	1
Unshed antler	2	1

The contrasting age distributions of the animals might be explained in several ways. Noddle, discussing the evidence from Dun Mor Vaul, observed that 'juveniles would not make good carcases and one would not expect them to have been slaughtered except in the face of fodder shortage or possibly for their hides' (in McKie, 1974, p. 187; cf. p. 87 below). In fact there is evidence for skinworking in both coastal and inland areas. Her first suggestion has more to commend it. It is clear that aging criteria for domestic animals are too flexible to support the hypothesis of an autumn slaughter and it would be wrong to use these bones to determine when the sites were occupied (Higgs and White, 1963). But the fact that autumn slaughter cannot be proved does not eliminate it from the argument. One alternative approach would be to relate this evidence to the practice of inverse transhumance in which the more vulnerable animals were taken off the high ground in winter (Carrier, 1932). This was widely practised in highland Britain and it is interesting that Walney Island, which was so much used in the Bronze Age, was one area to which the *young* hill sheep of the Lake District were taken at this time of year.

The previous chapter suggested that at no time in British prehistory was an exclusive emphasis on pastoralism either likely or feasible, but this did not imply a fixed balance between the two regimes. To a certain extent the practices discussed in this chapter overlapped the main periods in which stock farming was important, but one notable contrast is that there is increased use of upland and coastal locations in the later Bronze and Iron Ages when the pollen evidence shows an added dependence on cereal farming. It has been in these periods that the criteria for distinguishing transhumance have really been met and in a few instances it has been possible to suggest the full annual cycle. Examples may be found in north Wales, in East Anglia and on Dartmoor. In other cases, the evidence may simply show mobile pastoralism. It can be demonstrated that certain sites were not suited to year-round occupation and at times that their economy was specialised. In some cases the season of occupation can be decided with a certain confidence. But because the full pattern of activity over the year is not available, it is not clear how far these represent the optimum use of resources by a nomadic community and how far these sites belonged to a regular annual cycle with a fixed home base. To some extent the pattern is confused by the occurrence of burials, for only at Fengate is there very much evidence that seasonal stock raising was confined to one section of the community. In other areas it seems that complete families were on the move. If transhumance is the correct explanation, it would have been a kin-based activity. But here the occasional evidence for the high status of some temporary sites must bring in another problem. In Ireland and in Scotland some of these sites include cauldrons and fine metalwork, whilst in Wessex the graves on the chalk plateau contain the elite of the Early Bronze Age community. In other areas there is fine metalwork from caves, and even the evidence for horse riding could have its social aspect, in the Late Bronze Age at any rate. In his discussion of the Wessex graves, Andrew Fleming suggested that the uplands were used by an elite of warrior pastoralists and that cereal farming was the task of a less mobile peasantry (1971b). It may be that this type of scheme has a wider application, beginning with the appearance of Beakers and only really ending, if it ended at all, with the close of the Bronze Age. It is for future workers to separate these strands.

The Healing of the Woods   *Chapter 5*
Hunting and Gathering

And like a stricken numen of the woods
he rode
with the trophies of the woods
upon him
who rode
for the healing of the woods
and because of the hog.
                        David Jones,
            'The Hunt', c. 1954 and 1960

The distribution of barbed and fanged
arrowheads . . . may also be interpreted as
the summer hunting and pastoral tracks of
those peoples.   Misprint, *1976*

That passage from David Jones is based on an early Welsh tale and presents hunting in its less familiar aspect, as a social and even ritual activity. Most archaeologists see it in terms of subsistence. One theme of this chapter will be the way in which hunting has changed its nature and its purpose through time. In its simplest outline this has been a progression from subsistence to sport.

Most discussions of hunting and gathering have been restricted to Mesolithic practice. But it has yet to be discovered how long such practices outlasted the appearance of agriculture. In many farming communities, hunting guards against the failure of other resources, and the traditional literature, even of the British Isles, has an emphasis more in keeping with the David Jones poem. For these reasons it is wrong to see such basic activities as in any way culturally distinctive, and the question of Mesolithic survival must still be treated in typological terms. There is also some evidence for fishing and the gathering of food plants, but here the evidence has been so slight that the cultural model has been rarely used. If the account that follows is deflected away from Mesolithic evidence, this is a deliberate reaction to the literature, in which this period has been considered more fully than others.

There remain some important distinctions. The major one is between hunting and gathering as a complete economic system and their adoption on an occasional or seasonal basis. The latter arrangement would offer less scope for complicated relationships, like herd following, and would involve a smaller range of sites. Here, hunting, gathering and fishing might be combined with varieties of seasonal land use, and were possibly eased into the slack intervals of the farming year. It may have been these *less cautious* practices which did most to upset the feasibility of a long Mesolithic survival.

A further consideration is that in communities based on agriculture animals can more easily be hunted for non-economic reasons. On the Neolithic ritual site at Maumbury Rings, where most of the animals were red deer, meat bones were completely absent and all the fragments were skull and unused antler (Bradley, 1975a, p. 35). The Devil's Quoits in the Upper Thames shows a similar emphasis on red deer (Gray, 1974, and pers. com.). The pattern also extends to funerary monuments. Of the bones at Nutbane long barrow 37 per cent were of red deer (Morgan, 1959, pp. 47–9), whilst in highland Britain the bones of wild pig are more frequent in chambered tombs than those of the domesticated variety (Murray, 1970, table 145). The opposite is the case on settlements. In the Iron Age, literary evidence raises further problems, since it appears that game animals might be adopted as tribal totems (Ross, 1967, ch. 7). Some birds were not eaten at all for ritual reasons (Caesar, *Bello Gallico*, v, 12).

The most persuasive model for Mesolithic hunting is of seasonal movement from highland into lowland areas, matching the migratory cycles of red deer (Clark, 1972). However, this model may not be appropriate in a less varied topography, and in any event modern understanding of red deer movements is based on observations from a period in which farming communities have competed for the same resources. An area like the Pennines, the region studied by Clark, is now of limited agricultural value, but it was once more extensively and less efficiently used. Any cycle of this type could have been distorted or *truncated* by the activity of early farmers, and it is recorded that in sixteenth-century Wales the enclosure of major sheep walks had this precise effect, confining the animals to the uplands and hastening their local extinction (Pearsall, 1970, p. 344). There is the further possibility that where such conflicts arose, hunting could have been a method of controlling a natural competitor (Uerpmann, 1976). This model also ignores the availability of fish (Jochim, 1975).

Mesolithic hunting and gathering are both adaptations to quite specific circumstances, and their internal structure and balance may both have undergone alteration. Lee has shown from ethnographic evidence that the balance of meat and plants in the diet will vary with differences of climate (1968, p. 42). Taking into account such changes between the Late Glacial and the Elm Decline, this balance would probably have shifted in favour of plant foods, not only with the passage of time but also from one area to another. Unfortunately, floral remains rarely survive, and at present the artefact evidence is probably biased towards hunting.

The internal balance of the economy changed in other ways. With the afforestation of north-west Europe the range of potential game was radically altered and it has been suggested that in the later Mesolithic there was an increasing emphasis on the coast. Roger Jacobi has shown that a group of inland sites of this date are located to allow access to the shoreline (1973, p. 249). There have also been suggestions that Mesolithic man was modifying the forest in limited areas, partly in the course of fire-drives, but also to improve the plant cover for human and animal consumption (Mellars, 1976a). The creation of artificial clearings would have been a direct aid to hunting. This apparent increase in the use of forest and coastal resources may be explained by population growth (Jacobi, 1973, p. 246). More elaborate adaptations may also have been needed when the North Sea and the English Channel were formed, and the later Mesolithic settlement of the north and west could show a greater familiarity with marine resources (Jacobi, 1973, p. 252).

There have been various attempts to construct a hierarchy of Mesolithic sites, and even the crudest quantitative data can show some patterning. There are two permissible approaches: the use of ethnography to define the activities which could appear in the archaeological record; or the detailed analysis of living floors to devise a purely archaeological scheme which other disciplines may then illuminate. The first approach is best seen in two speculative models for the European Mesolithic (Price, T. D., 1973; Clarke, D. L., 1976a). The second has been pursued with particular success in studies by both R. R. Newall (1973) and Mellars (1976b).

Newall, working in north-west Europe, recognises three types of Mesolithic site, basing his analysis on floor area and contents. The first of these is roughly trapezoidal and varies from 265 sq. m to 1,040 sq. m in area. It includes 150 to 400 tools. He sees this as a base or maintenance camp, in which the 'primary subsistence group' carried out the complete range of activities necessary to sustain them. The second and third types are very much smaller. One is normally oval, from 28 to 45 sq. m in size, and includes between 34 and 40 retouched tools. The other type is equally restricted, containing between one and three concentrations of material sometimes with a

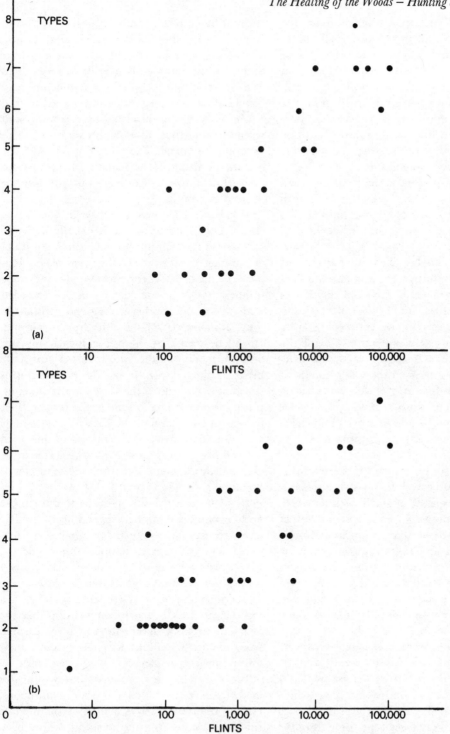

5:1 The number of flints on Mesolithic sites, (a) in Lowland Britain and (b) in Highland Britain compared with the range of functionally distinct artefacts. Sample after Mellars (1976b) with additions.

hearth. It is usually circular in overall plan and from 3 sq. m to 15 sq. m in extent. The number of retouched tools is between 6 and 37. These two types of site are harder to interpret but may, in Newall's words, be 'subordinate extraction camps'. It is interesting that the floor area of the larger sites is approximately the size of base camps in the ethnographic literature. It is also clear that the occupation group on the extraction sites was very much smaller.

Because of the quality of the excavated evidence, especially from the Netherlands, Newall was able to apply statistical analysis to these sites with a certain rigour. The British evidence does not allow this at present. Paul Mellars has, however, attempted to analyse the insular settlement pattern on more intuitive but comparable lines (1976b). He also makes a threefold division of sites. The major sites, which are much smaller than Newall's first group, are between 44 sq. m and 210 sq. m in extent and usually consist of dense, roughly circular concentrations of artefacts. The second group, on the other hand, has fewer tools and a floor area of only 10 sq. m to 15 sq. m, whilst the third is made up of more complex sites, on which a number of different nuclei can be found, at times associated with separate shelters.

Mellars sees three types of artefact assemblage which show a broad correlation with this scheme. His first group consists of small sites in which microliths are unusually prominent and other types are rare. These normally come from limited occupation floors and suggest an emphasis on hunting by a restricted human group. In northern England sites of this type occur above 300 m on the Pennines and may have been used in summer, although this last argument need not apply to less isolated sites in the south.

Mellars's second group is made up of 'balanced' assemblages: those with fewer microliths and a greater number of scrapers. In some cases there is a high proportion of burins and axes, which are generally rare in the microlith-dominated groups. Assemblages of this type come from the south east, including some sites with hollowed shelters, but also from coastal areas, especially in northern Britain. Upland sites of this group choose an intermediate location, well below the 300 m contour. A number fall within Mellars's largest size group, including the best known of all, at Star Carr. Mellars sees these as the winter camps of a larger social group. Here the analogy may be with Newall's category of 'base camp'.

Mellars's third group is more mysterious and resembles some later assemblages in its high proportion of scrapers. There are too few sites for useful analysis and Mellars suggests an occupation oriented towards skinworking in preparation for the winter months.

This threefold division is a useful one, but it should not be allowed to conceal the basically continuous relationship between the intensity of occupation on each site and the range of activities performed there. Figure 5:1a compares the range of functionally separate artefacts on well-recorded settlements in southern England with the total number of worked flints from each site. It will be seen that there is a logarithmic relationship between the two, with perhaps some break at about 5,000 items. The relationship is continuous and shows the same increase in complexity from the smallest site to the largest. This increase is not arithmetic – a site with 10,000 flints may not show twice the activities of one with 5,000 flints – but the *rate* of change seems to be constant throughout. This also applies to sites in highland areas (fig. 5:1b).

In a few cases it is also possible to discern the outlines of individual shelters, and here a similar approach can be revealing. This shows some tendency for the larger structures to be connected with a wider range of activities. Since this is a reflection of domestic floor area and not of the size of site, it may suggest a separate social grouping (fig. 5:2). It is worth commenting that the order in which different items are represented from one site to another does not represent their mutual proportions in all of the larger floors.

Clearly there is a functional cline within this evidence, even if the data is really continuous, either because work was actually structured in this way, or because the true gaps have been masked by undetected reoccupations. The actual order in which artefact types appear is relatively constant from the smaller sites to the largest, although this order must be modified by seasonal variation. The order runs: microlith – scraper – saw – burin – knife – axe – borer – fabricator – adze – punch – pick. This places the expected emphasis on extraction in the smaller sites and on the maintenance of equipment in the larger.

Apart from the functional segmentation of these camps, there are seasonal variations to consider. Local changes in climate, rainfall and plant growth are of importance (cf. Mellars, 1976b). There are already suggestions of a basic highland/lowland movement corresponding to the annual movements for red deer. On this basis, the larger social groupings would have formed in the lowland areas in winter. This basic polarity is seen in the size of living floors and shelters. Grahame Clark has linked the use of these winter camps with the working of unshed antler, and sees the high proportion of burins at Star Carr as a further aspect of this pattern (1972). Like axes, these implements are rare in upland areas. There may be some analogy with a group of smaller sites on the coastline of south-west Scotland, all with a high proportion of burins

(Coles, J., 1964). At Star Carr burins represent 27 per cent of the regular stone implements (Clark, 1972) and it is instructive to note that these can be equally common on the coast of southern England. Conversely, there is little evidence for these patterns in Ulster, where red deer was not important (Woodman, 1974a).

Clark has claimed that one group of Mesolithic structures might have a seasonal aspect (in Clark and Rankine, 1939. cf. Skenlář, 1975, 1976). By analogy with Russia and the circumpolar zone, he has suggested that Mesolithic 'living pits' might have been used in winter; and certainly, since his original discussion, fresh examples with associated post holes have come to light. There is perhaps some danger in arguments from analogy – in Somerset in the last century sunken-floored huts were used in summer, when they would not flood – but it is certainly apparent that their Mesolithic counterparts occupy only a restricted lowland segment of the full range of settled areas. They can contain hazelnuts, leading David Clarke to suggest that they were really food stores (1976a). The actual number of worked flints from these features varies from about 50 to 10,000, and

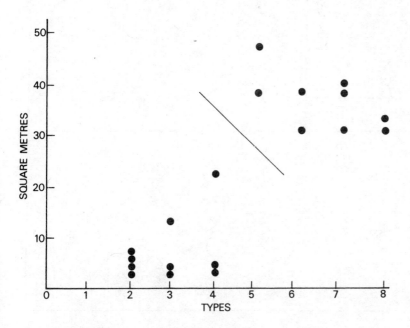

5:2   The floor area of Mesolithic shelters compared with the number of functionally distinct artefacts. Sample after Mellars (1976b) with additions.

there seems little reason to consider them all as permanent sites. In one Mesolithic pit in the Kennet valley the vertical distribution of flints suggested four occupations separated by intervals of desertion (Froom, 1972, fig. 11). In some cases there are even suggestions of group camps of this type, although the intensity of occupation and the range of activities may have varied greatly. These sites belong to Mellars's third basic plan. At Farnham, which was probably a base camp, Clark and Rankine recognised a series of about twenty pits of different sizes and functions clustered round a swallow hole (1939, and Rankine, 1936), and salvage work at Havant in Hampshire produced a minimum of ten such pits, seven of them in a compact group with an area of stained sand between them (fig. 5:3). These lay quite close to a spring and the layout of the main group of pits suggested a single coherent occupation (Bradley and Lewis, 1974).

It is not possible to tell how long this structure was maintained into the Neolithic period, and

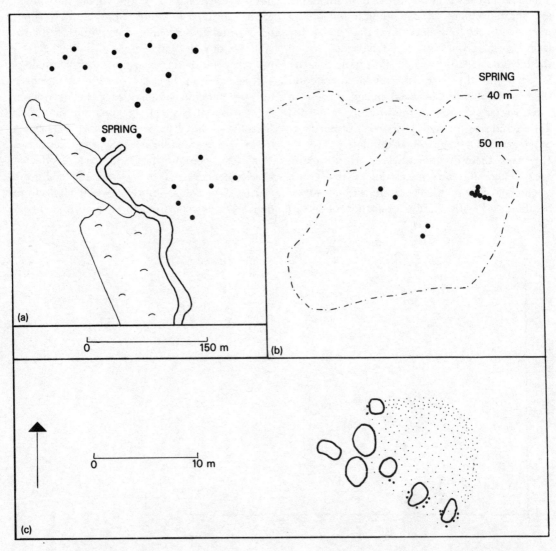

5:3   Outline plans of Mesolithic pit groups (a) at Farnham and (b) at Havant, with a detail of the main group of pits at Havant (c).

how quickly these patterns lost their original identity. On Neolithic sites there is little relationship between the numbers of game bones and of missile points, and it is not certain to what extent the latter were produced in the home. The greatest number is recorded from Carn Brae and could more closely reflect its social status than its subsistence economy (Mercer, 1975). A possible analogy is with the higher proportion of axes on causewayed enclosures (Bradley, 1972, p. 197). There is also a problem in distinguishing arrowheads made on a settlement site from those introduced with game acquired in the chase, and the discovery of missile points embedded in contemporary skeletons emphasises their alternative use as personal weapons (Pryor, 1976b). Despite these difficulties, Neolithic hunting has normally been considered in two ways: by the gross distribution of arrowheads, or through a few sites of supposedly restricted function.

The first approach raises many difficulties, not least the problem of dating simple projectile points – the leaf-shaped arrowhead is no longer considered an exclusively Neolithic form (Green, H. S., 1974, p. 106). There are also problems in examining such a chronologically insensitive artefact over a long period of time, especially in a settlement pattern where mobility is to be expected. Even so, a few preliminary observations can be made. There is now clear evidence for the improvement of browse in areas of woodland which had been affected by fire (Mellars, 1976a). Although it is by no means certain which techniques of clearance were favoured in the Neolithic, the regeneration phase of long fallow agriculture would provide an excellent context for the increased taking of game. Forest management by controlled burning has already been suggested for the Mesolithic, and it could have been the first step in the opening of the later landscape. On the North Yorkshire Moors Ian Simmons has recognised a series of Neolithic clearings which show little evidence for farming, but match the distribution of arrowheads (in Spratt and Simmons, 1976); and in the later Neolithic period in general there are signs of rather more hunting at a time when large agricultural clearings were becoming overgrown (Bradley, 1978a). The York-

shire evidence is somewhat unusual, and there is normally more integration between the distribution of arrowheads and that of other Neolithic activities. The latter could well result from a relationship between forest agriculture and hunting, and contrasts with the broader patterns which appear in the more open landscape of the Bronze Age.

There is clearer evidence on a regional scale. Two particular patterns seem to be found, each suggesting a different emphasis on hunting activities. One group of sites with a number of missile points seems to have adopted upland positions which gave the best field of vision. Examples are known in the Mesolithic on the Pennines (Jacobi, Tallis and Mellars, 1976) and in Surrey (Gabel, 1976), and they have been noted in later periods in the Sussex Weald (Tebbutt, 1974) and Herefordshire (Robinson, R., 1946, 1950). On the Pennines open conditions had been maintained by burning. Similar camps in parts of Devon preferred to follow the spring line, at times extending down into the valleys and along the streams (Greig and Rankine, 1953). The Wealden sites deliberately avoided these locations, perhaps, as Tebbutt suggests (1974, p. 36), to avoid frightening the game. By the Early Bronze Age, if not earlier, another common pattern is for arrowheads to extend uphill from the main settled areas into more marginal situations, where contemporary burial monuments were built. Examples of this pattern can be seen in the Yorkshire Dales, the Welsh borderland and perhaps on the Cotswolds (Cowling, 1946, pp. 44–60; Robinson, R., 1946, 1950; Grinsell, 1964).

In certain areas these patterns may show an increasing intensity and concentration towards the later Neolithic, and in some cases the separation of hunting and domestic activities became far more apparent. Manby has shown how in northern England this period saw an increase in the number, variety and distribution of projectile points (1974, p. 101), and in south-west Hampshire the later examples show an increasing concentration in certain areas (Calkin, 1951, maps 1–3). This is all the more striking since the later types actually cover a shorter time-span. There was also an increase in the number of arrowheads deposited. Much the same pattern can be seen on the Cotswolds, where the second millennium types are three times as common as the leaf-shaped arrowhead (Grinsell, 1964; Grinsell and Janes, 1966). It is of course known that the leaf-shaped type was not restricted to the Neolithic period, but any allowance for this revision increases the contrast still more. Even on the old chronology leaf-shaped arrowheads had a longer lifespan than other types and, making a crude conversion to calendar years, the number deposited per century would increase approximately fivefold. With a longer chronology for leaf-shaped arrowheads, even this figure may be too low. In areas where new land was being brought into use at this time the ratio of different types can be compared with that in the previously settled zones. If this is then related to the lifespan of each form, there is a comparable increase in arrowheads in the recently cleared area. In Sussex, for example, there is a slight increase in the number of Early Bronze Age arrowheads on the chalk, but a sevenfold increase in the Weald (Curwen, E., 1936). On the Wiltshire Downs the number of later types more than doubled, while in the Vale of the White Horse they increased seven times over (Bradley and Ellison, 1975, fig. 5:1). On the chalk the percentage of arrowheads at Windmill Hill rose from 7 per cent on the causewayed enclosure to 15 per cent in the late Neolithic (Smith, I. F., 1965, ch. 5). The latter figure compares well with the 19 per cent at Durrington Walls (Wainwright and Longworth, 1971, p. 164). The corresponding development of the bow has been studied by Clark (1963).

In addition to general distributional trends, there are a few instances where closer analysis is possible. One area in which detailed field survey is available is in Upper Wharfedale where there is good surface evidence from thirty sites (Cowling, 1946). These suggest a fourfold grouping of the finds, which belong mainly to the Later Neolithic or Early Bronze Age. There is every reason to believe that the varied assemblages in this area have been fully recorded. The groups considered here range from riverside locations to the Pennine uplands 200 m above.

The first group is dominated by projectile points and resembles some of Tebbutt's sites in the Weald where only arrowheads were previously collected. An excavated example of this type of site may be in the second occupation at Moêl Y Gaer, where 31 per cent of the implements were arrowheads, in contrast to a more usual figure of less than 10 per cent (Bradley, 1978b). A hearth on this site gave a radiocarbon date in the early second millennium b.c. In Wharfedale sites of this kind adopted two types of location considered earlier, the lower ground by the river and the summit areas above. At Moel Y Gaer the arrowheads were mainly associated with scrapers (43 per cent) and knives (23 per cent).

The second group consists of tools made or repaired on other sites, a phenomenon most common in areas without local materials. The majority of these items were scrapers, but some arrowheads are present. These again occurred on the higher ground. A close comparison could be with the hilltop site at the Breiddin, where over half the worked flints were finished forms (C. Musson, pers. com.). A figure of less than 5 per cent would be more usual. Apart from the evidence which they give for the transport of materials, the small quantity of waste pieces is the clearest index of mobility.

The third group consists entirely or almost entirely of by-products, a fact which suggests genuine functional segmentation, since the natural sources of the stones were no nearer to these nuclei than to any others. Two aspects of this problem may be related to hunting: the occasional discovery of cores prepared for making transverse arrowheads; and the actual discovery of arrowhead blanks. Moel Y Gaer again sheds light on this problem. A floor of the type considered here has in fact been excavated and was partly defined by a wooden windbreak. This floor gave a radiocarbon date in the earlier Neolithic. A detailed analysis of the excavated material certainly suggests that implements, arrowheads in particular, were being made and mended here. There is also oblique evidence to suggest that items were removed for use elsewhere (Bradley, 1978b). On one of the Wharfedale sites, which actually included tools, all the raw material was from older implements. Again, these sites favoured the higher ground.

The last group consists of finished forms, mainly scrapers, together with waste material. These hardly warrant separate discussion, since a specific connection with hunting cannot be shown. They may indeed relate to stock raising. In Wharfedale these sites have a wide distribution and include riverside as well as more elevated locations. In Herefordshire similar groups are clustered about waterholes (Robinson, R., 1946, p. 34).

This fourfold division is in no way rigid and lacks the complicated structure and the range of the Mesolithic evidence. As figure 5:4 makes clear, all these nuclei are found within a limited area very close to one another. Precise contemporaneity cannot be assumed. The dispersal of activities remains, suggesting in its way a finite but real mobility. What it need not imply is a full dependence on hunting. It seems equally likely that sites with arrowheads are only part of a wider variety. Not surprisingly, in the second millennium b.c. game bones are rarely found without a domestic component.

Four other classes of site have been specifically connected with this practice: kill sites, hunting stands, caves and 'burnt mounds'.

'Kill sites' have mainly been discussed in terms of Palaeolithic activity. Occasional examples of Upper Palaeolithic or Mesolithic date have been recognised in Britain, notably the elk skeleton from High Furlong, Lancashire, which was associated with two bone points (Hallam *et al.*,

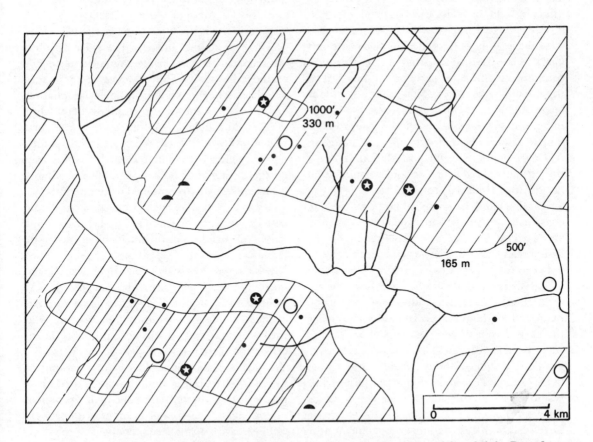

5:4   Interpretation map of Neolithic and Bronze Age flint scatters in Upper Wharfedale. Data from Cowling (1946). Stars – sites with many arrowheads; half-circles – sites dominated by scrapers; open circles – knapping or maintenance sites; small circles – other flint scatters.

1973). A less well-known example comes from Stanstead Abbots in Hertfordshire where part of a butchered pig skeleton was associated with Mesolithic artefacts and a light shelter (Gibson, 1972). The circumstances in which these animals were taken are rather obscure, although the High Furlong elk may have been driven into a lake. The same may be true of the red deer recognised in the peat below the Bronze Age settlement at Balinderry, although there is no proof of this (Hencken, 1942, p. 71). There is limited evidence for conventional traps from the British Isles. One very dubious example has been claimed beneath a Bronze Age barrow in Derbyshire (Greenfield, 1960, p. 17), and a line of shafts containing sharpened stakes close to the Glenluce Sands may represent a series of pit falls (Mann, 1903). These date to the later Neolithic. In Ireland, Wales and Scotland a number of wooden tread traps have also been recorded. These have been considered in detail by Grahame Clark who has shown that their European counterparts can be as early as the first millennium b.c. (1952, p. 51). They are most suitable for taking deer. If game animals were normally butchered at these sites, it could account for the limited range of bones found on the settlements. At Cahercommaun in the post-Roman Iron Age the leg bones of red deer were quite common but not the feet (Hencken, 1938, p. 76).

Hunting stands are artificial platforms or hides constructed to allow concealed observation or killing. This may be one explanation for the widespread construction of wooden trackways between the raised areas in regions of fenland. This evidence has already been considered and it is enough to recall that these sites occur mainly in England and in Ireland and between the early Neolithic and the end of the Bronze Age. Their construction is normally related to local fluctuations of the water table but a number of examples certainly lead to platforms which would be unsuitable for sustained occupation. One late Bronze Age site in the Somerset Levels has been considered as a possible hunting stand (Coles, J., 1972, p. 273), and it is worth noting that the peat of this area has preserved a number of bows (Clark, 1963). An analogous

structure may be the branch platform built in a similar environment at Rathjordan in Ireland. Although this has been seen as a precocious crannog, the virtual absence of settlement debris probably excludes this and the excavators suggested that its position was ideal for observing game watering in the surrounding area (O'Riordain and Lucas, 1947). The same interpretation could apply to the more famous platform at Star Carr which would again have been unsuitable for normal occupation (Clark, 1954). Perhaps the drier ground which had been stripped of trees to build this structure was in fact where the occupants lived, and the mass of artefacts were mainly secondary refuse which had been removed from this area.

Caves in inland areas have traditionally been treated as the stopping-places of hunting parties, and also as places of burial. The first view has been criticised by Green in discussing some sites in the midlands (in Kelly, J., 1976, p. 67), but the second is not in dispute. One use need not exclude the other. The evidence of these sites has already been reviewed in an earlier chapter and only a few points need emphasis here. Most of the sites belong to the second and first millennia b.c. Few of them include missile points. Of the eighteen caves reviewed by Gilks from northern England, only three included arrowheads and only two contained wild animal bones (1973, pp. 50 ff.). Indeed, Gop Cave, one of the best-known sites of this period, lies close to a scatter of missile points, but included domestic fauna (Davies, E., 1949, pp. 274–84; Boyd Dawkins, 1901). Where wild animals were taken, meat may not have been the sole motive. At Wetton Mill, Bramwell pointed out a number of smaller animals, including pine marten, wild cat, otter and fox, which were probably introduced for their fur (in Kelly, J., 1976, p. 44). There is possible evidence for leatherworking on this site. Where larger animals were hunted, their bones form a limited component of the inland assemblages. The greater number of these were red deer, with a smaller component of roe deer.

It is difficult to say a great deal about the evidence from the first millennium b.c., partly because by this period, if not earlier, flint missile points were no longer made. But to some extent the decline in 'arrowhead' production was offset by the main development of the spear. In the Late Bronze Age it is possible that hunting was sometimes carried on from horseback and the smaller number of dog bones in inland caves of the Iron Age might emphasise this contrast. If so, it is quite conceivable that hunting methods had changed. In the earlier phase the emphasis was on archery and the use of dogs; later, mounted spearmen played a part. Strabo's reference to the export of hunting dogs shows that this contrast was only partial (IV, 5, 2). The comparative rarity of red deer in upland caves, compared with finds from the seashore, could be because these sites were used in the warmer months when the animals were most dispersed. If some of the coastal sites were visited in winter, red deer would be easier to hunt, and any differences of method might also reflect these factors, with greater use of horses in the summer territory and of dogs in the winter grounds.

The 'cooking sites', 'burnt mounds' or *fulacht fiadh* have a wide chronological and geographical distribution, ranging from the Early Bronze Age to the Post-Medieval period and from the New Forest to the Shetlands. They usually consist of piles of burnt stones associated with a well-made trough (Hedges, 1975). There is clear literary evidence from Ireland and Wales that some of these were used as 'deer roasts', and their traditional name, *fulacht fiadh*, means literally the 'cooking-places of the roving hunter warrior' (O'Kelly, 1954). Experiment has shown that these sites could be used for cooking meat, but there is no direct archaeological evidence that they were specifically connected with game (cf. Hedges, 1975). In the Orkneys there is strong circumstantial evidence for normal domestic occupation. In the Northern Isles there is the added difficulty that red-hot stones were traditionally used in butter production (Fenton, 1976) and Steven Briggs has suggested that some Welsh sites were used by metalworkers (1976a, p. 278). Outside northern Scotland distributional arguments are very little help since the sites are of so many dates.

Beyond this area however there are few signs of associated settlement. One site in south-west Scotland may possibly have overlapped a palisade, but it also abutted a ring cairn (Scott-Elliott and Rae, 1965). Another Bronze Age site on the Isle of Man was close to a burial area (Cubbon, 1964), and, if its strange carbon dates are held in reserve, the cooking site at Drombeg certainly lay near a stone circle (Fahy, 1960). In no case do these sites imply a clear domestic function and these few associations are a little suggestive, if only of 'funeral feasting'. Some were conceived on an elaborate scale. Sites in Orkney, Shetland, on the Isle of Man and in Ireland all included buildings and permanent fittings (Hedges, 1975), and Drombeg even contained a well. An undated site at Ballycroghan in Ulster also included an artificial platform constructed on the edge of a stream (Hodges, 1955). There is evidence that a very similar site at Leckhampton, Gloucestershire, was in intermittent use from the Beaker period to the Late Bronze Age (C. J. Young, pers. com.).

It is unfortunate that these sites should now be found in marginal areas. They commonly occur in regions of moorland or heathland and always close to a water supply. For this reason animal bones have not survived and it is impossible to be sure that game was being cooked, despite the suggestive literary evidence. The main artefacts at Leckhampton – a site unusual in yielding finds at all – were scrapers, missile points and knives (Bradley, 1978b). There is evidence for the repeated use of these sites. As a result of O'Kelly's experiments, it is possible to work out how often they were visited; published estimates range from 30 times for the initial phase of Clay Head 1, Isle of Man, to 300 times for Drombeg. 'Autumnal debris' in the troughs excavated by O'Kelly suggested a seasonal occupation, whilst there is environmental evidence for sporadic flooding at Leckhampton. Ballyvourney 2 was probably used over four separate seasons and the mound sections certainly indicate intermittent use and cleaning (O'Kelly, 1954, pp. 112 ff.). On some sites structures were also rebuilt or refloored. No one function explains all the evidence, and meat was probably cooked by the same methods in different circumstances.

The chronology of these sites yields an interesting pattern. Most of them first appear in the second millennium b.c., when there is evidence that in some areas the distributions of arrowheads and of other items were gradually drawing apart. The ideal requirement for a proper balance between hunting and farming is an extensive tract of forest edge, and it may have been in this period that progressive clearance seriously interfered with this pattern. Despite an increase in the range, number and distribution of missile points, there is little or no increase in the proportion of game introduced into the settlements. The changes in the contemporary landscape are most important. In some regions they resulted in extensive areas of grassland, which formed the focus for barrow cemeteries; while in other areas the extension of settlement to more precarious environments eventually increased the development of moorland and heathland. By this stage parts of the landscape offered little scope for continuous settlement.

These processes may well be related. The main game animals were apparently deer and pigs. Pig, like roe deer, is naturally a woodland animal, while the red deer requires a more varied territory. In winter it favours secondary woodland, coastline, heathland and scrub clearing, and in summer a range of open heathland or moorland. Grassland areas, like those in Wessex, would have been less attractive, and the same applies to arable zones like the Cumbrian plain. At the same time such environments would be less suited to human use. The effect of these changes may have been to draw the game into areas rather remote from the lasting settlements, and as this happened hunting might well have become more of an occasional exercise, one undertaken from specialised sites at some distance from the home base. The same argument was employed by Proudfoot to reconcile the Irish literary evidence for hunting with the rarity of game bones in raths (1961, p. 113). If this suggestion is right, the game animals might have been less in competition with man, and this gave greater scope for hunting to become a social activity, one which could be undertaken at intervals for purposes essentially of prestige.

If these arguments have anything to recommend them, they could account for two parallel developments which might otherwise be hard to explain. The first is the number of archers' graves in the early second millennium b.c. The quality of items like the wrist-guard from Barnack (Kinnes, 1976) clearly shows that considerable importance was attached to these burials, and in some senses the bows, the finer arrowheads and the wrist-guards might have been 'sociotechnic' artefacts, signs of rank and status. It is easy to think of these as personal weapons, but this would hardly explain the geographical patterns seen earlier. More confusing is the virtual absence of defended sites and the rarity of skeletons with evidence of wounds (Pryor, 1976b). This might be contrasted with the information from Saxon cemeteries. The second feature which has not been discussed is the small body of metalwork known from the cooking sites (O'Kelly, 1954; Hedges, 1975). This is of particular note, in view of the virtual absence of other artefacts, but the very small number of finds does need careful emphasis. The items from Bronze Age sites listed by O'Kelly include axes, a gold ring and a gold dress ornament. To these may be added a spearhead mould from the Bronze Age site at Leckhampton (C. J. Young, pers. com.). They give one further hint that hunting conferred or accompanied status. This is consistent with the traditional evidence.

So far the argument has only considered the inland component of the Star Carr cycle and its eventual dislocation. But in other areas, for instance some of the Scottish islands, this basic cycle of movement may never have been appropriate and some of these environments could not have supported the main game animal. In fact, the shoreline and the river estuaries may sometimes have offered sufficient alternative resources. With the eventual isolation of Britain and Ireland, this coastal zone would have expanded in relation to the inland forests, which might themselves have needed human interference on a greater scale for game supplies to be maintained. There is certainly a trend in the later Mesolithic towards increasing use of the shoreline, and even in the south, where the contemporary coast has been lost, camps some way inland could have included it in their catchment areas (Jacobi, 1973, p. 249).

In some instances, the evidence from this coastal zone directly conflicts with the usual pattern. Recent work by Mellars on the Obanian shell middens has shown that the shoreline was used throughout the year (Selkirk, 1976, p. 206), and in Ulster, where red deer was unimportant, Woodman has found little evidence for major seasonal differences in the location of settlement sites (1974a). But it would be easy to take this approach too far. In a recent paper on her work at Portland, Susann Palmer has suggested that the coastal industries of southern England are so distinctive that they should constitute a 'British Coastal Culture' (1976). She considers that Portland at least could support year-round occupation and regards its inhabitants as 'gatherers rather than hunters by choice'. It is doubtful whether the elements which she feels are so distinctive of this coastal area are many or varied enough to constitute a 'culture' in normal usage, and this very concept has little application to hunter/gatherer communities. A major problem with Palmer's thesis is that one feature of the coastal sites is a rather higher proportion of burins than is found in inland areas. This might equally well indicate the pattern of deer-following envisaged by Grahame Clark, particularly since another site at Portland has produced burins (Palmer, 1968). The apparent absence of game bones should not be given undue stress. A similar problem can be seen at Morton in Scotland, where 26 per cent of the tools were burins but where the main resources recovered were fish and molluscs (Coles, J., 1971). Only two red deer were represented in an occupation spanning 31,000 man-days. At present the problem can merely be stated. Obanian sites, in contrast, do include a series of bone tools, but the burins which figure so prominently in the basic model were apparently not used to make them. These sites may actually show a progressive replacement of antler (Clark, 1956). Similarly, on the Bann, where the economy may have been directed towards aquatic resources, the 'salmon spears' and 'gorges' published by

Whelan were made of cattle bone (1952, p. 15).

The artefact evidence from later periods is hardly less diverse. It shows its first major increase early in the second millennium b.c. Here a similar dilemma is created by the rarity of arrowheads on sites with a proportion of game. For example, they were absent at Freswick Bay, where all the bones were of deer (Lacaille, 1954, p. 266). Their representation on the coastline is very erratic and varies from 1 per cent to 22 per cent of all the implements recorded. The average, 9 per cent, is similar to the figure for some inland settlements, and certainly suggests that hunting was rarely important. Some of the sites were very insubstantial and at times differ completely from the more lasting settlements in this zone. Lacaille noted the extreme thinness of many Beaker levels in Scottish dunes and referred these to an epi-Mesolithic survival (1954, pp. 288 ff.). In the same way, Cherry working in Cumbria has observed how most of the small nuclei with arrowheads only contained about fifty retouched flakes. The total weight of flint from these occupations averaged 3.6 kg (Cherry, 1963, p. 51). He also noted that there was very little evidence for the reworking of tools. Again at Dalkey Island, the unusual state of preservation of the Beaker pottery suggested that the occupation surface had not been seriously trampled. The excavator in fact envisaged 'encampments of short duration' (Liversage, 1968, p. 164).

The status of these occupations is possibly reflected in their use of raw materials. It has been noticed that some of the coastal assemblages are dominated by imported materials, even when beach flint seems to have been available. On other sites the opposite was the case. It does not seem likely that this is the result of changes in the coastline. One possibility is that imported flints were only used to any extent in the shorter occupations, or where there was regular contact with the hinterland. On the same basis the wider use of beach flint could indicate a more prolonged stay. At Dundrum, for example, two Neolithic occupations were based mainly on beach flint, but an Early Bronze Age occupation was dependent on imported material (Collins, 1952, 1959). At Port-stewart a late Larnian occupation used imported flint but local material was used in the Neo-lithic (Hewson, 1935), and on site V at Dalkey Island both raw material and finished tools were brought into the site, but were then worked to a differing extent. The percentage of waste flakes was: Larnian 75 per cent; Neolithic 94 per cent; and Beaker 64 per cent (Liversage, 1968, p. 97). It seems possible that these figures may be some index of the intensity of occupa-tion. As in the other Irish examples, the Neo-lithic occupation could have been the most extended, but this is probably the product of an inadequte sample.

The distribution of the arrowheads does not show the patterning of the inland material. Instead, it has been noticed how certain coastal dunes were favoured in one phase and not in another. For example, in Scotland it has been observed that the unusually high proportion of arrowheads on the Stevenson Sands (22 per cent) were mainly barbed and tanged, while on the Glenluce Sands, leaf-shaped arrowheads were twice as common (Callendar, 1932). On the Culbin Sands the pattern is again reversed. Similarly, in Pembrokeshire Grimes pointed out how the arrowheads on the clifftop sites were barbed and tanged, while those on the coastal sands were of the leaf-shaped variety (1932, p. 191). It is hard to see a pattern in this material but part of the answer may lie in the nature of the dunes. These volatile environments can be productive, provided vegetation cover is maintained, but with erosion or human misuse sand-blows can take place (cf. Jardine and Morrison, 1976). It was this process which sealed so many sites and these distributions may reflect very local changes. Hunting may have been only a minor adjunct to the economy.

From the later Bronze Age onwards the absence of flint missile points rules out a similar approach and game bones assume more impor-tance. This type of information creates at least as much difficulty on the coast as it does inland. Despite evidence for the limited or occasional use of many locations, there are few sites where all the bones are of game, and all these include additional resources: marine mollusca, fish, sea-birds, and, on one site, edible snails. It is cor-respondingly rare to find assemblages without any game bones at all. Jarlshof might be one example (Hamilton, 1956, pp. 212–13).

Like the inland sites, the majority of these occupations show a very limited emphasis on game. The proportion of wild animal bones on the shoreline was slightly higher in the Neo-lithic and Bronze Age periods, and higher again in the Iron Age. The limited sample suggests that red deer and pig were favoured in the later Neolithic but that by the later Bronze Age roe deer had taken second place. Since both are woodland animals, it is not necessary to envisage much change of hunting territory. There is greater evidence for the horse in the later Bronze Age, but there is no real fall in the representation of dog and no proof that either animal was specifically associated with hunting. In the Iron Age, however, hunting *was* on the increase and red deer, roe deer and pig are frequent finds. Red deer is often associated with dog. It has been suggested that hunting methods may have been adapted to the density of animals in different environments. It is also notable that there are rather few associations be-tween red deer and wild pig and again between wild pig and roe deer, despite a general pre-ference for a wooded environment. Whilst this may emphasise the diversity of the coastal land-scape, it could also point to real selectivity in the chase. The increased proportion of red deer may also reflect greater use of this environment in winter (Table 6).

One curious aspect of this predominance of red deer is its occurrence in areas outside its natural habitat and beyond at least its modern distribution. Some of these sites were on small islands, on which it could hardly have been supported. One example is the Orcadian island of North Ronaldsay; Arthur MacGregor, in dis-cussing the bones from Burrian broch, suggested that venison was brought here from elsewhere (1974, p. 105). The special importance of this animal on South Uist is emphasised by a curious find from an Iron Age house at Drimore (Fairhurst, 1971, p. 80). Here the centre of

TABLE 6: *Frequency of association between the principal domestic and game animals on Iron Age coastal sites in Scotland*

	Cattle	Sheep/goat	Pig	Dog	Horse	Red deer	Roe deer	Wild pig
Cattle	.	17	14	8	11	14	6	4
Sheep/goat	17	.	14	8	10	14	6	4
Pig	14	14	.	8	9	13	6	3
Dog	8	8	8	.	9	13	6	3
Horse	11	10	9	9	.	7	3	1
Red deer	14	14	13	13	7	.	6	3
Roe deer	6	6	6	6	3	6	.	2
Wild pig	4	4	3	1	1	3	2	.

the hut floor contained a circle of about twenty unburnt jaw bones. Another example comes from Dun Mor Vaul (McKie, 1974). Here the initial problem is that pollen analysis has shown a completely open landscape, which would not be very suitable for roe deer, despite its representation among the bones. This contrasts with the poor representation of pig. In her report Noddle argued that the phases in which young domestic animals were killed would reflect the periods in which resources came under most pressure. It is particularly interesting that the main evidence for hunting is not in these periods of strain. For this reason it would appear that hunting was more than a supplement to the basic diet. It was actually practised most while the site functioned as a broch. The faunal analysis for this site has been misused and Table 7 offers the basic evidence. This represents the minimum number of animals in each phase and not the gross number of bones. Bird bones are considered separately.

McKie has claimed that a high proportion of game bones is characteristic of sites in this region (1977, pp. 219 ff.) and if brochs *were* socially eminent forms, this could offer at least some explanation. On the shoreline, as in inland areas, hunting may have changed from an economic to a social practice.

Although there is every reason to expect that hunting would be complemented by the use of other resources, this is not easy to prove, even for the Mesolithic period. In later prehistory, when hunting was a minor supplement to farming, the evidence for other practices remains extremely slight. Plant foods will normally survive only in waterlogged or carbonised deposits and specialised techniques may be needed to recover them. Fishbones are brittle and usually poorly preserved, and the same applies to bird

TABLE 7: *Distribution of animal bones at Dun Mor Vaul*

Phase	Game animals	Domestic animals	Sheep/ Goat	Cattle	Pig	Nature of occupation	Bird bones as % of all bones
1	33%	67%	7 (4)	8 (7)	3	? open settlement	3
2	37%	63%	21 (9)	12 (7)	1	construction of broch	1
3a	43%	57%	7	7 (1)	2	use of broch	1
3b	43%	57%	8 (2)	8 (2)	2	modified use of broch	9
4	30%	70%	19 (5)	17 (4)	7	replacement by farmhouse	14
5	30%	70%	14 (4)	6	5	reduced and sporadic occupation	37

Figures in parentheses refer to newborn and juvenile animals.

bones. In each case the sample from conventional excavation will be both small and distorted. The opposite applies to shellfish, which are very well represented, although their numbers belie their low nutritional status. The following account is necessarily based on data of poor quality and until more sophisticated analysis becomes available, discussion can only be conducted in the most general terms.

This does not mean that these resources were unimportant, merely that the evidence is very badly distorted. This is so much the case that there is more evidence for gathering in Neolithic and later contexts than there is in the Mesolithic. This is partly because several waterlogged sites have been properly recorded and partly because of the durability of a few foods, hazelnuts in particular. It is probably true that until the Middle Bronze Age 'storage pits' are more likely to yield nuts than grain. In the prehistoric period hazelnuts, beechnuts, acorns, plums, cherries, raspberries, blackberries, elderberries and crab apples are the resources which most often survive.

Although the evidence for wild plant foods is normally more restricted from the Mesolithic than it is from later periods, there is every reason to resist this conclusion which runs counter to all expectations. David Clarke has argued on ecological grounds that the Mesolithic economy would have been based on gathering rather than hunting, and even suggested that the Mesolithic sites in the Weald were drawn towards one of the richest areas of nuts and roots in the whole of Europe (1976a).

There is certainly no denying the abundance of hazelnuts in Mesolithic contexts, even though this may have been only one of a far wider range of foods, and there is certainly evidence for the high representation of hazel in secondary forest. Since these nuts are so nutritious, there have been suggestions that areas of woodland were deliberately fired to increase their representation when the forest recovered (Smith, A. G., 1970). David Clarke even saw the Mesolithic economy in the Weald as a form of garden horticulture (1976a, p. 475). These arguments are very attractive, and need not be confined to the

Mesolithic, but they are almost impossible to prove. What is clear is that without some thinning of the forest, only limited areas on high ground or close to water might be suited to the smaller edible plants (Spratt and Simmons, 1976).

This point has been developed by Professor Godwin, who has shown how the wider clearance associated with farming led to the extension or the first appearance of a whole series of trees and shrubs which could, quite incidentally, be used by man (1975, p. 471). The limited forest manipulation of the Mesolithic may have had little effect on those species that were native to Britain. Four of the main plant foods represented in the surviving evidence find their origin in this situation: beechnuts, cherries, elderberries and raspberries; and at species level *prunus* and *rubus* can be added. *Prunus*, elder and beech were present in the post-Glacial period. Another four trees or shrubs associated with agricultural expansion have recorded uses as oils, drinks, medicine and cattle feed. Similarly, no fewer than twelve of the weeds and ruderals first appearing in the Neolithic or the Bronze Age have traditional uses as medicines, vegetables, fodder, pot herbs, fibres or dyes. Others were used as emergency food in peasant agriculture, notably corn spurry and dog nettle (cf. Usher, 1974).

Godwin himself saw these plants and bushes as part of the process of secondary forest growth. He argued that scrub would not be a normal component of the Mesolithic forest and that these species were part of a succession leading to regeneration. This interpretation has now been questioned by Groenman-van-Waateringe (1972, p. 297), who has pointed out how the forest edge can form an impenetrable thorny barrier, not only to browsing animals but also to the expansion of brushwood. She argues that many of the plants considered by Godwin are components of naturally grown hedges. These she views as a precocious form of land enclosure. She points out one advantage of this situation:

The *Prunetalia* bushes and the associated

outskirt vegetation are characterised by a diversity of edible fruits, like blackberries, raspberries, wild strawberries, sloe, wild apple, cherry etc. Once man had noticed that these shrubs developed spontaneously on the boundaries between field and woodland, it is quite possible that he began to help nature along.

The effects of these arguments are of some interest. It would seem that the range of plants in the archaeological record from the Neolithic onwards is a side effect of clearance for agriculture. Conversely, the *narrower* range of evidence to survive from the Mesolithic only emphasises the restricting effect of a closed woodland environment. Hazel was certainly not the only plant food in this period, but the difficulties of obtaining the wider range associated with farming in turn strengthens the case for forest manipulation.

Mellars has referred to associations between Mesolithic artefacts and hazelnuts on 'at least twenty different sites' (1976b, p. 376). In later periods the evidence is similar. Godwin's figures show a consistent representation of hazel charcoal throughout later prehistory, with perhaps a slight peak in the Bronze Age. In lowland areas hazel pollen shows an increase in zone VIII, which may correspond to a general fall in oak pollen. In Godwin's view beech increased its representation with the secondary regeneration of forest, but the charcoal evidence is limited. The record for the other resources, crab apples, nuts and berries, shows their real emergence with the Neolithic and perhaps some slight peak in the Bronze Age. However, the samples are quite inadequate for detailed comment, and very little is known of the circumstances in which these foods were collected

The evidence for inland fowling is still more limited, perhaps because appropriate techniques have rarely been used to retrieve small bones. On the other hand, this cannot be the whole explanation, since bird bones are better known in coastal regions and even more have been recovered on medieval excavations using similar techniques. It seems that fowling was mainly

TABLE 8: *Principal plant foods, Neolithic to Iron Age. Totals of macroscopic identifications*

	Neolithic	Bronze Age	Iron Age
Hazel	24	27	20
Acorns	21	45	30
Sour Cherry	1	1	1
Wild Cherry	2	–	1
Bird Cherry	–	–	1
Raspberry	1	3	–
Plum	1	1	1
Blackberry	1	4	2
Prunus sp.	3	3	4
Rubus sp.	2	1	1
Elder	3	6	6
Crab Apple	2	1	1
Beech	4	6	5

Data from Godwin (1975).

practised in two favourable areas: the sea coast, where breeding colonies could be raided, and in areas of fenland. The evidence for fowling is very limited, and no inland Mesolithic site has given material comparable in quality with that from the middens of Oban and Oronsay. Transverse arrowheads which are thought to have been used as bird bolts are known in the Mesolithic but are not frequent until the late Neolithic, when bird bones were used to decorate pottery. Otherwise the evidence is circumstantial. In East Anglia, for example, a scatter of arrowheads and other items can follow the edge of the fens (Clark, 1932), whilst the sites suggested earlier as hunting stands could have had a partial emphasis on fowling. The evidence from the Somerset Levels is especially promising here, and the largest collection of bird bones comes from Glastonbury (Bulleid and Gray, 1917, pp. 631 ff.). Unfortunately, there are not enough other groups for any discussion to be worthwhile. This contrasts with the finds from coastal areas.

Most of this evidence comes from north-west Scotland, one of the richest regions in Europe from this point of view (Fisher and Lockley, 1954). Elsewhere there were prehistoric occupations at Dunstanburgh Castle, Northumberland,

and on Lundy which correspond to modern breeding colonies (Gardner, 1972, pp. 24–5). The seabirds taken in prehistory may be divided into three groups: primary seabirds; secondary seabirds, i.e. those which originate on land or only take to the water in winter; and summer visitors (Snow, 1971; Fisher and Lockley, 1954). In Scotland the secondary seabirds are represented by only five species and the occasional visitors by only one. At least eleven of the primary seabirds breeding in the Atlantic zone were taken. Of these, up to ten include the temperate east Atlantic in their modern distribution and at least eight are recorded as breeding on islands off the Scottish coast. Such seabirds may also be classified as resident, migratory or dispersive, the latter term referring to those birds which move away from their breeding colonies to deeper water. Another distinction could be made between inshore, offshore or oceanic seabirds; the archaeological record shows at least six inshore birds, another six offshore birds and only one oceanic species. Of those that still nest off the Scottish coast, two are inshore birds, five are offshore birds and another is oceanic. On the principle of minimum effort, these birds would have been most easily taken when on the nest.

Most of them are, in fact, species commonly taken in recent centuries while they were nesting or in moult (Baldwin, 1974). Shearwater, kittiwake and petrel are present in the recent record, but rare or absent on prehistoric sites. Fulmar, too, is almost absent, despite its economic potential. Two reasons can be suggested for this. First, there is evidence that birds which lay more than one egg were normally preferred, since the occasional collection of eggs could be used to stagger births and to lengthen the period during which the breeding grounds were in use. It is significant that the tubenoses – petrel, shearwater and fulmar – lay only one egg. At the same time, the kittiwake, fulmar and petrel are oceanic by preference and can only be taken in inland waters when they are breeding. The fact that they are not found may mean that these birds were ignored in the breeding season and out of range at other times of year. However, their distributions themselves may have changed: for example, the fulmar has extended its natural range to follow the herring fleet. Since the number of oceanic birds did not increase with the fishing of deeper waters in the Iron Age, the simplest explanation may be that fowling was a land-based activity, a limitation that confines its main season to the spring and summer months (cf. Clark, 1948a) (Table 9).

There is similar evidence for coastal fishing (cf. Clark, 1948b). At least twenty-seven different

TABLE 9: *Principal bird remains on coastal sites in Atlantic Scotland by number of separate occurrences*

	Mesolithic	Neolithic	Earlier Bronze Age	Later Bronze Age	Iron Age
Fulmar	1	–	–	–	–
Herring gull	–	–	–	1	1
Great Auk	3	–	1	–	1
Razorbill	3	–	–	1	1
Guillemot	2	–	1	–	1
Puffin	–	–	–	–	4
Shag	1	–	–	1	3
Cormorant	2	1	–	1	3
Eider Duck	–	1	–	–	–
Common Tern	2	–	–	–	–
Great Northern Diver	–	–	–	–	1
Inshore	5	2	–	2	7
Offshore	8	–	2	3	13
Oceanic	1	–	–	–	–

fish are on record, in addition to crabs, seals and whales. The most widely occurring species seem to be cod, wrasse, ling, grey mullet, haddock and thornback ray. In addition to these, crabs and grey seal are quite common. The fish may be divided into two groups: those which move from one area to another, where a specific fishing season is indicated; and those which move either seasonally or at different stages of their development, from deep into shallow water (Meek, 1916). For example cod and haddock can be fished together in the West Highlands of Scotland, although cod is taken mainly in March and haddock mainly in summer, while the peak periods for fishing in the North Sea are in spring and autumn. Ling is mainly caught between March and May, and wrasse and sea bream are mainly taken in summer. The 'edible crab' moves into deeper water from autumn to February. The archaeological record also includes at least six fish which move into inshore areas for the warmer months. The pilot whale would also be caught in summer, and the grey seal and common seal, which made up the whole faunal assemblage at Porth Killier in the Scillies, would probably have been taken in spring there (Ashbee, 1974, pp. 178, 267).

In certain cases, then, analogy with recent practice indicates that fish might have been taken mainly between March – the start of fishing for ling, and November – the final fishing of hake. The main period of overlap is in the warmer months, with slightly more activity in spring than in autumn. Interestingly, this also overlaps the main breeding periods of the sea-birds which in recent centuries were mainly taken between April and August. This period also covers the time when other fish were closer inshore and probably easier to take. Outside this period, fishing for them would be more difficult and might involve navigation in more volatile conditions. This is not to say that inland waters were not used in winter, and until detailed studies of fish growth are available from British sites all these suggestions are extremely tentative.

Only a few chronological patterns appear and these may be of doubtful validity. In some ways the Obanian evidence stands out from the rest. Only two of the sites for which Lacaille has given data (1954, pp. 240 ff.) include offshore or oceanic birds, in contrast to roughly 60 per cent of the sites of later date. The commonest fish on the latter are either rare or completely absent, and most of those which *were* found could have been taken on or quite close to the shore. Some of these sites were used all year round. This compares interestingly with the Mesolithic midden at Morton on the east coast, where four of the fish were bottom-feeders and might have been caught in deeper water (Coles, J. M., 1971, pp. 351 ff.). Indeed, the high number of cod on this site may indicate a more specialised regime. The coastal climate here would have been less favourable. In later periods the situation changed radically: bottom-feeders are known in Neolithic to Iron Age contexts. Indeed, they seem to dominate the small sample from the Iron Age, a trend which is maintained into the Roman and post-Roman periods.

TABLE 10: *Principal fish remains on coastal sites in Atlantic Scotland by number of separate occurrences*

	Shallow water	Coastal	Deeper water	Unclassified
Obanian	5	6	1	1
Morton	–	–	4	2
Neolithic	1	2	2	–
Earlier Bronze Age	1	–	1	–
Later Bronze Age	–	–	2	1
Iron Age	2	4	4	2
Roman and post-Roman Iron Ages	2	–	3	–

There is little material equipment to amplify this outline. Apart from the Obanian 'harpoons', the commonest items are bored or grooved stones which may have been used as net-weights. These are not found in the Mesolithic, but occur at Skara Brae in the Neolithic (Childe, 1931, p. 112), possibly at Walney Island in the Early Bronze Age (Cross, 1949), and at Covesea in the first millennium b.c. (Benton, 1931). So-called 'netting needles' are also found at Covesea and occur from the later Bronze Age onwards. There are five bronze fish hooks from the Culbin Sands which may belong to this period (Anderson, 1886, p. 202). There is an Iron Age fish gorge from South Uist (Fairhurst, 1971, p. 100). Finds of stranded whales associated with 'blubber mattocks' have already been described by Clark (1947b).

As far as inland fishing is concerned, the evidence is slight and usually of poor quality. Such fishing was in fact of two kinds, specialised or unspecialised. Some of the waterlogged timber structures from river valleys might have been early fish weirs, but this needs more investigation. Two specific sites are of interest: at Thatcham, in an area of the Kennet valley where many fish can be taken, an elongated pit on the edge of the reed swamp was interpreted as a possible fish trap (Wymer, 1962, fig. 5); and at Branthwaite in Cumbria Ward has examined a Middle Bronze Age platform built in another area of marsh. There was no sign of normal domestic settlement, and the platform itself was associated with a dugout canoe. One interesting feature of this site was a carefully built wooden 'box' which had been recessed into the platform (Ward, 1974). This was interpreted as a 'fish store', and its very damp position might support such a view. The few bones from inland sites are mainly pike and salmon. Ehrenberg has suggested that barbed spearheads from the Thames could have been for taking sturgeon (1977); and there is a bone fish gorge from the Manifold Valley (Kelly, J., 1976, p. 74).

Two types of specialised fishing can also be envisaged. Eel fishing is still a matter for informed speculation, although Pryor has suggested that some of the transverse arrowheads at Fengate were connected with this practice

(1974b). They may have been parts of eel spears, but might equally have been used in hunting or fowling. Neolithic missile points have also been connected with fishing in the estuary of the Bann (May and Batty, 1948). The evidence for salmon fishing is more extensive, but still geographically confined, since almost all the evidence is from northern Ireland.

This evidence is quite complex. Much of the dated material is Mesolithic and is only being understood through the sensitive work of Peter Woodman (1974a and b, and 1976). He has shown that most Larnian sites were on rivers or the coast, with very few in upland areas. The relative importance of hunting is reflected in the late Mesolithic tool kit; at Newferry on the Bann burins and scrapers were rare, whilst 60 per cent of the implements were one type of knife. This brings to mind the laurel leaves of the Neolithic, which also cluster towards the northern Irish coast. In the Mesolithic period it seems clear that seasonal changes of settlement locations were not particularly abrupt. At Newferry there was occupation of an intermittently flooded area in summer and autumn, whilst the earlier winter site of Mountsandal was on higher ground in the same general area. The distribution of these sites may emphasise the seasonal salmon runs, and Movius's excavation at Newferry disclosed hearths and spreads of ash interstratified with layers deposited in damper conditions (1936). He interpreted the main activity on this site as 'fish drying', and Woodman's more recent excavation has produced bones. Such a specialised site could have been used for preserving fish taken in the seasonal run, and it should be contrasted with the winter site at Mountsandal, which contained a series of pits and circular huts. While Movius's excavation produced hazelnuts and raspberries at Newferry, Mountsandal also included pits, bird and animal bones. But it is not yet clear how far the economy could have changed between the occupations of such differently dated sites.

Other evidence for seasonal fishing comes from finds dredged out of Irish rivers close to the exits of lakes. Whelan published a series of bone points from one such area, including two which he felt were used for hunting land mammals (1952). However, their date is not really clear. The same reservation applies, but with more force, to a series of 'clubs' and other stone implements from similar locations published by Mahr (1937, p. 283). These might have been suitable for clubbing salmon in their seasonal migration, perhaps at artificially constructed weirs, but their chronology remains uncertain. Mahr used this material to create a 'Riverford Civilisation', the pantomime horse of Irish archaeology. He identified this imaginary group with the original Picts.

On the coast another resource was provided by shellfish (cf. Bailey, 1975). These fall into two basic groups: those which favour soft sandy or muddy shorelines, such as cockle, oyster, razorshell and mussel; and those which prefer a rocky coastline, such as limpets and periwinkles. Although these are all available throughout the year, they provide more meat in the warmer months. Not all are of equal nutritional status; limpets, for example, provide four times as much meat as mussels. Some may have been gathered as bait (Clarke, D. V., 1976). In general, the rocky shores are less productive, and here post-Mesolithic middens include a broader range of supplementary resources, including wild and domestic animals, birds, fish and plants. Other shellfish can be found offshore, such as dogwhelks, and these are less common. The hard coastal areas tended to be used more in the Iron Age, perhaps reflecting a preference for defensible positions.

Certain middens seem to have been restricted to particular species. One undated example at Polmonthill, Falkirk, included an estimated six to seven million oysters (Stevenson, 1945), while on the Culbin Sands in the Middle Bronze Age two phases of use on the same site showed a quite different molluscan component (Coles, J. and Taylor, 1970). This was attributed to changes in local coastal conditions. Neighbouring middens sometimes differ from one another entirely. At Walney Island, on the other hand, a single Beaker pot contained five varieties of shellfish (Cross, 1939, p. 274).

Size variations can be important, and reductions in the number and size of a particular species may be related to periods of over-exploitation, during which other varieties would be used. Collection was not always systematic. J. G. Evans has given an elegant demonstration of this point by considering the changing relationship between the coastal environment and the supply of shellfish on the Neolithic and later settlement at Northton (1971a, pp. 52–62). He has shown that the composition of shell mounds may indicate the catchment area from which they were formed. For example, at Dalkey Island shellfish were being collected from the rocky shores of the island and not from the richer sands of Dublin Bay (Liversage, 1968).

There is no doubt that some large middens were accumulated over a very long period. One site at Inveravon in West Lothian produced radiocarbon dates spanning two millennia (McKie, 1972b). But studies by Bailey have shown that the nutritional value of shell meat is very low, with the result that the size and volume of these sites is extremely misleading (1975). The main reason for their formation was the large quantity of shellfish needed for a satisfactory meal. This made it difficult to transport enough of them inland, so that they were often consumed where they were collected. Even before Bailey's study, Professor Atkinson had made this same point about the Mesolithic midden at Stannergate (1962, p. 6). The total food resources at Morton, including plants, meat and fish, would only allow an occupation of 31,000 man-days (Coles, J., 1971, p. 361). This compares with Atkinson's more subjective estimate of about 25,000 man-days for Stannergate. A further reason for accumulating shells may have been to spread them on arable fields. This has been suggested by Paul Ashbee for sites in the Scilly Isles (1974, p. 265), and scattered seashells were found on the Bronze Age fields at Gwithian (Megaw, Thomas and Wailes, 1961). Presumably shell sand and seaweed might also have been added.

The associated artefacts are few and very confusing. The 'limpet scoops' and 'limpet hammers' of the Atlantic coast have probably been correctly identified, a view supported in experiments by Lacaille (1954, p. 224). Pointed flint flakes at Killellan Farm, Islay, and at Walney Island could have been used for extracting meat, and on Islay several examples were found inside winkle shells (Burgess, 1976b). A similar function could have been served by the rod microliths at Portland (Palmer, 1968). Another type with a coastal emphasis is Susann Palmer's 'Portland Pick', but this she associates with plant foods.

Because of the poor quality of most primary data, it is not easy to see wider themes in this material, but a few points are still worth making.

First of all, there is a contrast between the full settlements on the shoreline, and the majority of recorded finds, which probably come from sites of more limited status. In some cases these coastal nuclei are essentially adjuncts to a pattern with its centre of gravity elsewhere, either in a more favourable coastal position or lying further inland. Two sites on the island of Lewis illustrate this point. Both were of Iron Age date and may have been contemporary with one another. One site was an 'earth house' and seems to have formed part of a permanent settlement, whilst the other, not far along the shore, was an isolated midden. Both were analysed and published together, and it was found that the settlement included domestic animal bones and a few sea shells, but only the midden contained fish and birds (Baden-Powell and Elton, 1937). This dispersal of activities is perhaps significant, and it may be that food was being dried on the shore.

Different forms of coastal exploitation can share similar seasonal constraints, and for this reason early fishing, fowling and strandlooping are all compatible with one another. But certain difficulties arise once their relationship to hunting and farming is considered. If the Star Carr model of deer-following is accepted, for example in south-west Scotland, it would imply a winter occupation of the lowlands and a summer occupation of higher ground. This pattern would then conflict with the tenuous evidence that these other activities were often undertaken in the warmer months. Where Clark considered that

the occupants of Star Carr hunted on the hills in summer, Butzer suggested that they fished (1972, p. 540). Again salmon, trout and pike could all be taken inland between May and September, the optimum period for activity on the shoreline. These problems could have been offset by rather more varied movements by smaller groups – the interpretation in fact favoured at Morton – but the problem is not resolved, especially if coastal resources were favoured to an increasing extent as the inland landscape was invaded by trees. Another answer, which seems more appropriate where game sources were rare, would be to remain on the rivers and shoreline, perhaps using different segments in rotation. This was the Larnian solution, and it is one which may have become increasingly feasible after Britain became an island. By remaining in one basic zone different resources might be exploited in turn.

There is little evidence for earlier Neolithic activity in this coastal zone, despite theoretical arguments which might suggest it (Evans, J. G., 1971b, p. 13), and in remote areas earlier patterns may have been maintained for some time. Only towards the end of this period is there evidence for specialised activities on the shoreline and in upland areas, and neither is easy to interpret. It is not difficult to suggest some relationship between the hunting of red deer and the summer pasturing of livestock, but it is far less satisfactory to look for a similar relationship on the coast. Here the evidence of fish and bird bones suggests visits in summer, but the remains of red deer do not. One solution envisages the winter pasturing of younger animals in this area, while another interpretation sees the increase in red deer as a reflection of more permanent settlement in this zone. Where this solution does not apply, and the shore was visited from other areas, there is a further problem in reconciling the evidence for inland hunting with the evidence for fowling and fishing. Both *could* have been fitted into the slack period of the farming cycle, but to some extent it must have been necessary to choose between them. The prestige which attached to hunters could have been a decisive factor.

These problems become serious in the Iron Age, when there is more evidence for hunting on the coast than there is inland. Since red deer was still the main animal hunted, it seems likely that this reflects a greater use of the coastal zone in winter. Such a solution is perfectly feasible, since there is a clear increase in the settlement evidence from this area. Although part of the shoreline had been cultivated since the Neolithic, there is more evidence for *farming* in the Iron Age than there is from earlier periods. Some of the newer sites were impressive stone-built structures which must have a social aspect. The brochs are the most important of these.

Case (1969) and Renfrew (1976) have both stressed the role of sea fishing in the spread of Neolithic culture, but in some respects the evidence for this practice is disappointing. But in the Iron Age there is at least evidence of a socially complex coastal culture. This chapter has stressed the importance of hunting to these communities. It is now clear that fishing was also important, and the catchment areas of individual brochs certainly bear this out. Euan McKie has put forward an interesting case for the development of these structures in the Western Isles and their eventual adoption in Orkney and Shetland (1965). Surely it was with this exploitation of marine resources that such contacts could be formed and maintained. If this were so, these coastal economies may also have attained a social dimension.

The Magnitude of Antique Fragments
Possibilities and Suggestions

We do not like to look out of the same window, and see quite a different landscape.
We do not like to climb a stair, and find that it takes us down.
We do not like to walk out of a door, and find ourselves back in the same room.
     T. S. Eliot, The Family Reunion

What business, added the corporal triumphantly, has a soldier, 'an please your honour, to know anything at all of geography?
Thou would'st have said chronology, *Trim, said my Uncle Toby.*
     Laurence Sterne, Tristram Shandy

The fragments have been assembled. Do they fit together? Each chapter has explored one aspect of the settlement pattern. Little of the evidence is satisfactory and it has always been easier to suggest areas for future work than to draw together what is available. And yet each separate study *has* revealed a divergence from the cultural chronology which forms the normal framework for prehistoric studies. This evidence must be allowed to have its head. What follows is hardly a synthesis, since any definitive study must await more subtle techniques of social archaeology. The most that can be claimed is that the tendencies described in the separate chapters are real and are connected. It is not easy to find a structure to information scattered so prodigally through space and time. The chapter heading is taken from a drawing by Fuseli, 'The Artist in Despair over the Magnitude of Antique Fragments'. It offers its own comment.

This final discussion really falls into seven continuous sections. To avoid difficulties of terminology and chronology, the periods considered can be defined as follows: late Mesolithic and pioneer Neolithic (up to *c.* 3300 b.c.); mature Neolithic (*c.* 3300–2700 b.c.); later Neolithic (*c.* 2700–2000 b.c.); Beaker and earlier Bronze Age (*c.* 2000–1300 b.c.); later Bronze Age (1300–700 b.c.); earlier Iron Age (*c.* 700–200 b.c.); and later Iron Age (*c.* 200 b.c. to the Roman Conquest). Finer distinctions will only be made where the *settlement* evidence demands this.

The first of these phases spans the earlier fourth millennium b.c. – perhaps starting even sooner – and ends towards the Elm Decline. It was a period of change and experiment which saw the most elusive process in all prehistory: the meeting of hunter gatherers and farmers and their eventual integration.

It may be helpful to distinguish the situation of each group before the first contacts were made. Three aspects of the Mesolithic are crucially important. First of all, a massive increase in the number of occupation sites clearly shows that the population was growing in this period, with a corresponding extension in the areas settled. Jacobi has shown that there is no evidence for contacts with the mainland after the formation of the English Channel (1976), and any increase in population probably resulted from internal expansion. Second, the separation of the British Isles increased the range of coastal habitats suitable for settlement and widened the possible scope of the Mesolithic economy. And, just as this last process was a result of the warmer climate, so too was the development of the vegetation. Areas which were tundra in the late Glacial were all but closed forest by the late Mesolithic.

In view of this background, it would be surprising if the archaeological evidence did not show signs of strain. The most direct archaeological evidence is of course provided by artefacts. Here, two developments are important: the wider dissemination of the axe, particularly the development of a polished axe in Ireland, and a greater diversity of microliths. It is not certain that all of these were used in the chase, and Mellars has pointed out that later Mesolithic sites also show a greater variety of other tools (1976b, p. 395). There may have been some economic specialisation. The closed forest would change the migratory cycles of the game and plant foods would only be found where the light could penetrate.

One response to these pressures was greater use of the shoreline, or of other resources which would reduce the need for mobility. On the Irish salmon rivers it is likely that fishing communities were semi-sedentary, and the same may apply to the occupants of the Kennet valley, where fish might have been almost as plentiful (Froom, 1972). On the coast, there is evidence from western Scotland for year-round occupation associated with fishing and shell-gathering. Both activities were made possible by the warmer climate, and it would have been in these situations, where the forest cover was broken, that plant and animal resources were most accessible.

But it is clear that this change of emphasis away from plants and game was not sufficient to offset a crisis. There is now a substantial body of evidence to suggest that Mesolithic man was using fire to resist the pressures of environment and population and was bringing about improvements in his own food supply. This evidence is not found in Denmark, or in Ireland, which will be considered separately. Burning of the woodland has two principal effects: it can alter the plant composition of an area and so increase the supply of natural foods, and it can lead to an increase in browse. This in turn will increase the supply of game animals and can lead to improvements in their meat yield and fertility (Mellars, 1976a). There is also evidence for careful culling of these animals and, perhaps, for the provision of fodder in winter (Jarman, 1972; Dimbleby and Simmons, 1974). In each case Mesolithic man was reacting positively to the crisis brought on by afforestation. It seems likely that burning was of two types: limited clearance around the edges of the forested area to improve the food supply, and more extended activity to *maintain* open conditions in the face of climatic change. As Simmons has noted, the first type of clearance would be most frequent close to water, where the cover was broken, or at the tree-line on higher ground (in Spratt and Simmons, 1976, p. 197). In each case, one immediate effect would have been to produce more hazelnuts from the forest edge. Burning often took place close to the springheads which had always been favoured for hunting. In other areas, however, there are signs of recurrent firing, perhaps on a larger scale or following a more regular cycle. This was the case in the Pennines, where there was extensive settlement on high ground below the tree-line. It now appears that burning was sufficiently regular and intensive to stunt the growth of trees and to maintain large open areas which were eventually consumed by peat (Jacobi, Tallis and Mellars, 1976). These areas were probably used for the hunting of large mammals in summer.

In Ireland the situation was probably rather different, and microliths do not occur in the late Mesolithic. It is evident that there was a smaller range of potential game and that a different economy was followed. The Larnian is in fact remarkable for its isolation. It is even possible that the bow had to be reintroduced in the Neolithic. There are however 'some indications for late Mesolithic communities acquiring a new range of equipment' (Woodman, 1976, p. 300), rather as in England there is a greater typological diversity (Mellars, 1976b, p. 395). But there is no evidence for precocious clearance by fire, and the coastal distribution of Mesolithic artefacts suggests that the population had little experience of inland soils. Instead there was a concentration of effort on the coast and rivers, where fish and molluscs in particular offered enough resources to support a large, possibly sedentary, population. The status of the pig in this economy is a little ambiguous and it is conceivable that it was domesticated in the Mesolithic. It should be noted that Jewell has suggested that domestic cattle could be descended from the native aurochs (1963).

The contrast, then, is very striking. In Ireland a particularly specialised economy was practised in an environment which was probably empty in the late Glacial. This economy was evidently successful, although it relied to an unusual extent on fish, and perhaps plants, and very little upon livestock. For this reason these communities may be considered as relatively stable. In other areas of Britain, notably on the west Scottish coast, a similar pattern may have emerged with year-round use of the shoreline, this time accompanied by the taking of land mammals. The same *might* be true of the most productive rivers. But even with this allowance, the contrast is a real one. Over much of Britain an economy which had placed some emphasis on game and plant foods was under growing pressure from two sources: its own internal growth and the gradual increase of the forest. Although it is fashionable to think of hunter-gatherer populations as deftly adjusting to their environments, this may not have been the case here, and by the late Mesolithic natural changes in the British landscape may have upset the kind of equilibrium enjoyed by their counterparts in Ireland. It is this disturbance which may account for the range of economic practices which have been interpreted as 'incipient agriculture'.

Farming communities in this phase were little better placed. Here again there is evidence for internal population growth promoted by improvements in nutrition and in overall fertility, but tempered to some extent by the recurrent exhaustion of the soil. It was for this reason that agriculture spread so rapidly through northern Europe: not because of its immediate adoption by an indigenous population, but because pioneer agriculture might so easily lead to crop failure and renewed migration. Two difficulties resulted: first, the frequent wasting of environments which needed careful nurture if they were to sustain the impact of population growth and, subsequently, the pressures which built up in more marginal lands, especially around the rim of north-west Europe. Renfrew may be correct in seeing the Atlantic wall as a stimulus to the social organisation which was to lead to megalith building (1976). But, as Case has pointed out (1969), the expansion of these communities into Britain involved a new range of difficulties. It was necessary for a population which may have been essentially land-based to undertake the colonisation of these islands by sea, together with the introduction of staple resources, both plants and animals, which could not be found in the wild. For this reason the difficulties of pioneer agriculture discussed in the first chapter may have been exacerbated and the cohesion of the immigrant groups lost. It is not surprising that the mature Neolithic, as it emerges from this period of strain, should prove such an eclectic mixture of continental ideas.

It is worth recalling some of the basic characteristics of pioneer agriculture, especially in an environment where closed forest was already causing problems for a technically ill-equipped population. The important point is that food is produced only gradually in this situation. John Coles has stressed the slow rate of clearance and the crucial importance of hunting and gathering as an initial means of survival (1976). He illustrates this by pointing out how the Somerset Levels were initially selected not for their agricultural potential but for their mammals, plants and fish. To this extent, the first Neolithic activity was not particularly different from Mesolithic practice, especially since pioneer *agriculture* may have been on too small a scale to register clearly in the pollen record. By the period of contact Mesolithic demographic and environmental stresses had led to a period of experimentation, involving a more concerted effort to control plants and animals, and sometimes more use of resources which could permit a less nomadic existence. In the European Neolithic at this time an analogous crisis had occurred, in which outward migration had been checked at the Channel coast, while population may have continued to outstrip the capacity of the soil to support it. The colonisation of Britain probably involved a far greater dislocation than previous shifts of settlement. And if Jacobi is correct in suggesting the total isolation of Britain from the sixth millennium b.c., this would have been a difficult undertaking. Both communities were in fact engaged in a period of change.

This may explain why there are so few ways of distinguishing between the environmental impact of the two groups, save perhaps by the increased number of pollen episodes leading up to the Elm Decline. The point was made by Simmons in discussing a number of these episodes on the North Yorkshire Moors:

> The similarity of clearance phases between the Mesolithic period and the middle of the Neolithic suggests a continuity of a hunting and gathering economy on the upland plateaux and the evidence is of gradual rather than sudden changes in both culture and environment (in Spratt and Simmons, 1976, p. 207).

This of course refers to a rather isolated area, but it was seen in Chapter 2 that pollen analysts have experienced similar difficulty in separating the impact of the two communities in other regions. As Woodman has pointed out, the main evidence for the first Neolithic in Ireland is still from unassociated pollen cores (1976, p. 300). The important point is not a chronological one – the practical arguments for a long period of pioneer farming must be accepted – but that the impact of the two populations on the landscape should have been so similar for so long.

Before any specific hypothesis is proposed, it is necessary to isolate those areas in which the two economies could have come into contact. Pollen analysis cannot be the arbiter here. The first difficulty concerns hunting. Jarman has suggested that Mesolithic hunting of pig and red deer shows a carefully calculated structure, designed to maintain a breeding population and ensure a continuing game supply (1972). But hunting by pioneer farmers may have been undertaken for a short-term result, so that this pattern was distorted and the composition of the herd was upset. Indiscriminate killing by early farmers could also have affected the migratory cycle of the animals relied upon by Mesolithic hunters, although it is possible that a similar age and sex structure could have resulted fortuitously from killing those which were harming the crops. Because both groups were killing migratory animals, it is not enough to show that the distributions of Mesolithic and Neolithic *sites* do not overlap. Mesolithic sites in the Weald, for example, would have included the South Downs in their catchment areas, and game taken at one time of year on the sands could at another time have been killed on the chalk. In any case, the catchment areas exploited by the two populations might have been very different. Fleming suggests that a community of four hundred people practising shifting cultivation may have required a clearing of between 1·8 and 3·6 km radius (1972a); Jochim suggests a radius of 15 km for the land used from a hunter-gatherer base camp (1975). A second problem is that it would have been no less logical for pioneer farmers to begin clearing the forest from its edges than it was for Mesolithic man. Just as Mesolithic burning may have been undertaken close to rivers and the coast, Neolithic man could have begun clearance in these same areas, thus adding to the existing ambiguity. It seems that the first clearings in the Lake District were mainly near the sea, and in Ireland the discovery of domestic animal bones in raised beach deposits represents some of the earliest evidence for farming. Powell has also argued that Neolithic settlers may have preferred lowlying lakeside or waterside situations, like those in Europe (in Powell, Oldfield and Corcoran, 1971). The evidence from upland areas close to the tree-line is less clear-cut, but on the North Yorkshire Moors, and possibly on Dartmoor, there may be evidence that Neolithic clearings were being made in the course of hunting, just as they were in the Mesolithic settlement pattern (Spratt and Simmons, 1976;

Simmons, 1969). In Ireland there is even evidence that cereals were growing at a high altitude.

How far could these conflicts be reconciled? Here it is important to review the chronological evidence for contacts between both communities. In most areas there is no demonstrable overlap: although artefacts in both styles can sometimes be found in the same areas, and even on the same sites, the radiocarbon dates for Mesolithic and Neolithic occupations are usually mutually exclusive. To some extent this is an argument for a prolonged phase of pioneer agriculture, insubstantial in physical terms, but of critical economic significance. But it also seems to imply fairly rapid acculturation. There are significant exceptions. In other areas overlapping carbon dates can allow a longer Mesolithic occupation, although the actual question of its social contacts remains unsolved. Two major areas seem to be the Bann and Kennet valleys, both regions within the basic distribution of earlier Neolithic activity. By contrast the third millennium b.c. carbon dates from western Scotland refer to Mesolithic settlement on the limits of Neolithic activity, although this should not be given too much weight. The third situation is more elusive. This is where physical associations between material of both groups is either certain, or at any rate possible. The two best-known instances are at High Rocks in the Weald and Torbryan Cave in Devon (Money, 1960; Rosenfeld, 1964). High Rocks has given two radiocarbon dates of 3710 ± 150 b.c. (BM 40) and 3780 ± 150 b.c. (BM 91), which seem to be too early for the associated Ebbsfleet Ware, whilst there is a radiocarbon date of 2500 ± 200 b.c. (1.549) from Torbryan Cave. The common feature of these occupations is that they are not found with full Neolithic settlements, but with what may be hunting sites. High Rocks site F included three arrowheads and a scraper, whilst Torbryan Cave contained a 'point' and an arrowhead. This is reminiscent of the situation on Dartmoor, where Neolithic arrowheads again occur with Mesolithic items in surface scatters. This overlap, however it is explained, does not occur on the

lower ground. Pollen evidence shows only slight clearings in this general period and does not demonstrate that the Neolithic activity was connected with farming (Simmons, 1969). Exactly the same pattern is seen on the North Yorkshire Moors, where Simmons has argued for 'continuity of a hunting and gathering economy' into the third millennium b.c. (in Spratt and Simmons, 1976, p. 207).

If these rather isolated observations are representative, they seem to suggest a fairly complex pattern. It has already been seen that both populations were undergoing a period of experiment and stress. This may account for a certain similarity between the environmental impacts of the two groups. In this unusual setting the introduction of additional staples by immigrant farmers could have offered a valuable supplement to resources which were already hard pressed. Agriculture may have been particularly acceptable, in spite of its greater demands. But in those zones where a new equilibrium had been attained, in Ireland and perhaps more widely, there was no reason to accept these economic changes and the original patterns retained their cohesion rather longer. These were possibly areas in which semi-sedentary occupation may have been possible already. In Ireland it certainly appears that Mesolithic and Neolithic artefacts have a partly complementary distribution, although it does seem likely that the native inhabitants had made little use of inland soils (Woodman, 1974b and 1976). Where any overlap can be seen, Neolithic items were introduced into indigenous sites, rather than the reverse. As Woodman has pointed out: 'Many of the innovations found in the Irish Neolithic . . . are filling gaps in the equipment range of the Late Mesolithic' (1976, p. 301). There must have seemed little reason to alter the economy in areas which were already rich in resources, and it may only have been with the availability of a new range of large animals that there was any incentive or need for change. Otherwise, what probably happened was the gradual encroachment of farming communities upon these resources, as agriculture eventually allowed new economic growth. The remaining hunter-gatherers may now have moved into rather poorer zones, and it is no coincidence that the areas where their equipment is associated with Neolithic artefacts were marginal land used by the farmers not for agriculture but for hunting.

In the literature it has been usual to treat the Neolithic period as one of continuous growth, without accounting for the fate of the native population or for the reasons which led to expansion. Both questions have been evaded because they are so intractable. Although economic growth is certainly characteristic of Neolithic groups both in Britain and Europe, their overall effect on the landscape is not easy to explain.

One point is of basic importance. If the Elm Decline itself is not treated as an anthropogenic feature, however frequently it coincided with episodes of clearance, basic contrasts are seen at once in the scale of early activity. Rarely can these clearings be precisely located by pollen analysis, and the limits of this method may mean that what seems one massive episode was really the cumulative effect of a sequence of smaller onslaughts. If this is true, the real contrast may not be between different economic practices, but between relatively mobile and sedentary occupations. This contrast is apparent in Cumbria, where numerous clearings of this period are documented. Fleming has suggested three routes towards the creation of large open areas: permanent degradation of the soil, which prevented the regeneration of trees; increasingly intensive and demanding clearance, of the type which Boserup connects with population growth; and deliberate use of a single core area with a steady evolution of agricultural techniques (1972a). There is little evidence for the first suggestion, since Neolithic settlers were clearly concerned to avoid those areas in which permanent damage could be done. But it is difficult to discriminate between the remaining alternatives, although they do possess the common factor that prolonged clearing might only be feasible where the soil could withstand continued use. In practice, such areas have been recognised mainly in Ulster, Cumbria, Wessex, Somerset and East Anglia, although

further environmental work will undoubtedly extend this list. There may be a regular relationship between the last two approaches. If the land proved unproductive, it could hardly permit the growth of population; and if in turn population became a problem, it might be simplest to provide food from land of proven capacity. If this is true, the contrasting scale of clearance would have had its social aspect. Only on the most productive land could lasting settlements be established and only here would population grow to a point at which social manifestations left a permanent trace. This is what Case means by a phase of 'stable adjustment', and this very term implies other episodes which were cut short. If the Elm Decline was partly a climatic feature, it may have quickened the pace, not only of land clearance, but also of the contacts between these different groups (cf. Sims, 1973).

One basic stimulus to these developments may have been the dispersed settlement pattern which now appeared in Britain. It is uncertain how far this was a reflection of a traditional model, and how far it arose from the difficulties of colonisation. But there is little question that outside a few areas, where village communities do seem to have existed, settlements normally consisted of a very few houses, each of which was capable of sheltering a small family and no more. Instead of social growth resulting from the gradual nucleation of these into larger communities, as may have happened in the first millennium, it is more likely that a 'clan' structure evolved, in which small communities maintained kinship ties across a dispersed pattern of settlement. Fleming has compared the structure of such a community to the segmentary layout of chambered tombs, in which different families were possibly buried in separate compartments beneath the same monument (1972b). If this is true, it could imply a typological sequence in which tombs might show an increase in the number of chambers. In the same way Morris suggests that double court cairns were built later than single cairns 'as the original social groups expanded and segmented' (1974).

A related argument has been put forward by

Jack Scott in a study of chambered cairns on Arran, but he does not consider the social implications of his data (1970). He works from the reasonable assumption that on an island with a limited area of productive land near the coast there should be some correlation between the height of each monument above sea level and its own structural complexity: the sequence of colonisation should match a typological sequence. He has shown that this does apply on Arran, and has extended the same approach to include Bute and Kintyre (1969, table 5). It may be possible to extend this over an even wider area, and it is clear that the mean number of compartments in all well-preserved Clyde cairns does increase with elevation (data from Scott, 1969).

Here, then, is one integration of social practice with the progress of settlement. In another sense, the capacity to build the more elaborate monuments will have depended on economic success. For this reason it is striking that the annual work of land clearance around Hockham Mere should have been equivalent to building a long barrow. Both might need organisation, and the small number of individuals eventually placed in these mounds does more to establish social distinctions. The contrast between extended and less-lasting clearings has its own social implications since its immediate effect was to create an economic imbalance between these two areas. Although there was a general sequence from smaller to more extended clearings, this was not an inevitable progression but the result of careful calculation and prospecting. It cannot be assumed that the appearance of large open areas, let alone the building of monuments within them, was an inevitable triumph of Neolithic technology. That is to fall back on crude evolutionary judgments. The manpower needed to build

these would often have come from areas of greater population, but it does not follow that the monuments themselves were built on the most productive land, and it may be wrong to see each site as the *centre* of a social territory (cf. Renfrew, 1973a). Morris even suggests a change to the usual sequence of events: 'Before a territory is inhabited, it must be sacralised' (1974). It is clear that barrows and enclosures in Wessex were being built in areas of grassland, but it is not known if that grassland was *deliberately* created, especially if the area had already experienced soil loss. In fact there seems to be a general tendency to place public monuments not at the centres of their territories but at the edges, and in southern England causewayed enclosures are not found amidst the areas of barrows but alongside them. Some are set on the interface between the chalk and other soils, and this suggests that one of their functions was to integrate the economies of these different regions (cf. Bradley and Ellison, 1975, p. 208). These would include the extended and the more ephemeral clearings.

The extent to which an increasingly open landscape lent itself to this type of integration appears from a well-known example. Renfrew has used a simple geographical model to suggest that Windmill Hill was the centre of a social unit covering some 300 sq. km and containing twenty-one long barrows (1973a). But in making this calculation he has ignored the environments beyond the chalk, some of which may have been less suited to Neolithic settlement. Some of these areas were in contact with Windmill Hill and figure 6:1 maps the region from which exotic items were introduced to the chalk. This area has several flint axes imported from the down. As might be expected, this diagram shows the enclosure lying towards the edge of the downland, but at the centre of a zone of great economic variety (data

TABLE 11: *The mean number of compartments in Clyde cairns in relation to their height above sea level*

	Height above sea level		
	0–49 m	50–99 m	over 100 m
Mean number of separate compartments	2	3	3

Based on data from Scott, J. (1969)

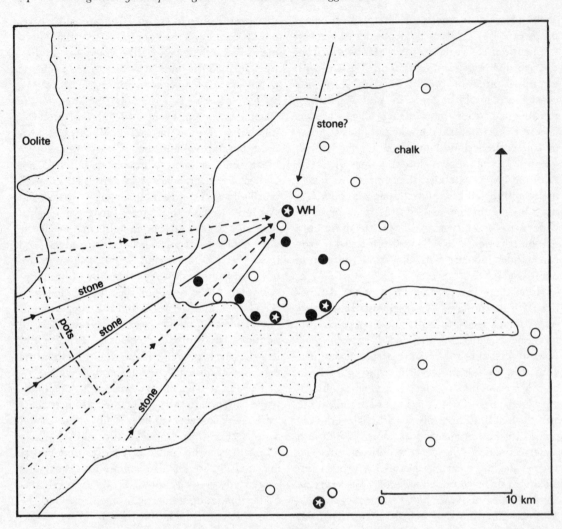

6:1   The siting and external contacts of Windmill Hill. Stars – causewayed enclosures; filled circles – long barrows with imported Oolite; open circles – other long barrows. The arrows indicate the direction of the sources represented by imported items at Windmill Hill.

from Piggott, S., 1962, fig. 1; and Smith I. F., 1965). The mastering of this diversity was the principal achievement of the first farmers.

These developments followed a period of general uncertainty and may be summed up by drawing a series of contrasts with the earlier patterns. The greatest difference would perhaps have been a completely different arrangement of resources, whether or not this involved seasonal movement between highland and lowland areas. In the earlier period the winter migration of red deer led Mesolithic man to congregate in the shelter of lower ground. But by this stage of the Neolithic it seems likely that the main period in which different communities came together would have been summer, perhaps in the slack period of the agricultural cycle between sowing and the harvest. This transformation could only have happened in a fairly stable landscape, since in pioneering agriculture these months are taken up with clearance. Only in those few areas where a grassland landscape had formed, fortuitously or by design, can the possibility of transhumance be entertained. It is quite possible that the Wessex downs were one such area and Windmill Hill in particular includes a high proportion of bones of dogs and cattle. The same interpretation is suggested by the siting of some of the enclosures in the river valleys and of the long barrows on higher ground.

This increased appreciation of the diversity of the newly cleared areas has other aspects. Dennell has pointed to the variety of arable practices within the area in contact with Windmill Hill (1976, pp. 14–16), and it is possible that similar contrasts will be found with more work on the animals. The landscape was also prospected for building materials, and Wessex is not the only area into which large quantities of specific stones were introduced from some distance. Their transport would have presented major problems and attention was obviously paid to the colour, texture and structural properties of these rocks (Powell, 1969). In no sense are the stone monuments of this phase mere side-effects of clearance. There is less evidence for the transport of timbers, but it is partly compensated for by indications of careful forest management, and by the evidence for skilled woodworking from the late fourth millennium (Rackham, 1977). Another aspect of this general movement of resources is the wide distribution of specialist-made pots, perhaps through the ceremonial centres in which such a variety of styles is found (Peacock, 1969). The same applies to the interchange of axes, which may have met an intensive but quite regional demand. These may well have been made seasonally, again between sowing and the harvest, and the location of some production sites in highland Britain surely demands this. Interestingly, there is little continuity in the use of stone sources in Ireland, where Mesolithic acculturation was delayed, and more evidence for this from southern England (Woodman, 1976; V. Care, pers. com.).

Despite the movement necessary to form these distribution patterns, there are increasing indications of lasting settlement. The burial monuments may have been attached to specific communities and could even have served as territorial marks, whilst the provision of storage pits, which are probably absent in the Mesolithic, also implies a reduced mobility. The same point is made by Groenman-van-Waateringe's evidence for the development of hedges. The rectangular houses of this phase are more complex structures than the circular shelters used by hunter gatherers (cf. Skenlář, 1975 and 1976).

By the end of the fourth millennium b.c. there was in fact a renewed equilibrium after a prolonged phase of experimentation shared by natives and immigrants alike. The areas over which particular ceramic or axe groups were distributed are generally equivalent and there may already be some regularities in the spacing of public monuments across the landscape. Even though the details of these constructions vary greatly, there remains a further equivalence in the work invested in them and in the number of burials which the sepulchral sites contain. This balance was no more than provisional, but it could only occur in a landscape in which some of the major physical and cultural barriers had fallen.

This new accommodation was not to last. Although it is customary to see the Neolithic as a period of continuous growth, there is little reason for doing so. Atkinson assumes an exponential rise in population throughout this period (1968, fig. 15), but there is no support for this view. There is no demonstrable increase in the number of monuments to the dead; there is little continuity of economy; and the physical evidence for Neolithic settlements actually diminishes sharply.

Two phenomena occurring towards the middle of the third millennium b.c. might help to explain this difficulty. The first, which is well known, is the disuse or more restricted use of the types of public monument associated with Neolithic expansion. There are fewer burial sites, except perhaps in Ireland, where the chronology of passage graves remains a problem, and there is no proof that causewayed enclosures were being built late enough to influence the development of henges. This disturbance is broadly contemporary with another phenomenon, which has been described both by Whittle (1977) and by the author (Bradley, 1977). Only in recent years have pollen analysts in Ulster questioned the conventional picture of Neolithic Britain as a patchwork of temporary clearings. In a number of areas it is now seen that the soil withstood a far longer cycle of land use, beginning with a phase of cultivation and only reverting to woodland after further use as pasture. In many cases this process took several centuries. Similar evidence is now recognised in Wessex, Cumbria, Somerset and East Anglia. Not all clearings did in fact regenerate, but the point of interest here is that so many should have done so within a fairly restricted period towards the middle of the third millennium. The fact that so many areas reverted to woodland at this time cannot support a model of continuous growth, particularly when there are few new clearings dated to the same period. Not only were appreciable areas going out of use; fewer new areas were being settled (fig. 6:2; cf. Bradley, 1977).

This recession corresponds in time to the lapse in the building of monuments. It is not likely to have a single explanation. Although it could represent any check on the population growth seen earlier, other significant factors could be famine, disease, crop failure and soil erosion. There is no specific evidence which would allow us to arbitrate between these, although just this cycle of growth and decline has been suggested by

Brothwell (1971). It is not a pattern which is confined to Britain, and similar disturbances occurred in areas of Europe once the loess came under pressure. It seems likely that Neolithic expansion had temporarily outstripped the capacity of the system to support it. Recovery when it did come was slow and rather distinctive.

Certain areas, however, were affected less seriously than others. In Wessex, for example, John Evans sees a period of more relaxed land use, perhaps as scrub grazing, instead of full regeneration (1972), and other clearings in East Anglia, Cumbria and Ireland remained altogether open. These were among the areas in which Neolithic expansion had been most successful, and they seem to show a greater continuity than other parts of the country. In Wessex and perhaps East Anglia, there may be some continuity in the areas in which causewayed enclosures and henges are found, whilst axe production continued unchecked at Grimes Graves and at Langdale. In Ireland, burial monuments were probably built throughout the third millennium, despite some change in the main settled area (Herity and Eogan, 1976, p. 70).

The scale of this disturbance is still unknown, but its consequences were profound. It can be

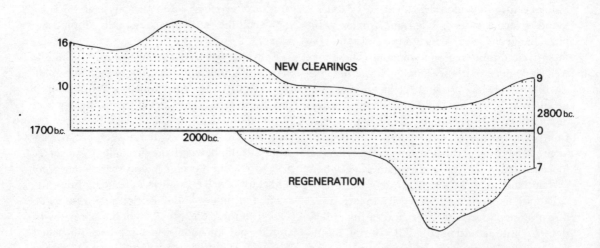

6:2   The chronological distribution of new and abandoned clearings 2800–1700 b.c. Based on radiocarbon dates plotted at two standard deviations. Data from Bradley (1977).

argued that nearly all the distinctive economic patterns of the next few centuries have their roots in this situation. There was, first of all, a profound disturbance in the structure of the landscape. Only locally can a continuous escalation be seen in the scale of ceremonial monuments, and where there is some continuity in their location, their scale may alter radically. Late Neolithic cemeteries are much smaller than the long barrows of the earlier phase, even when the number of deposits was the same. Long barrows were widely displaced by round barrows or by open cremation cemeteries of the type first seen at Dorchester on Thames. The common feature is a smaller investment of organisation and work. This point is best illustrated by comparing the scale of the first henge monuments with that of causewayed enclosures. The henges themselves follow a general typological sequence, in which the earlier sites are normally the smallest, and in this respect they seem to symbolise both the crisis and the period of recovery. The evidence of radiocarbon suggests that the number of clearings only picked up towards the end of the third millennium, at the time of the first large enclosures but before the general dissemination of Beakers (Bradley, 1977).

It is possible to say something about the areas into which this recovery was directed. There are signs of fresh onslaughts on the forest, but not all of these were in the same areas and some of the sites which had been cleared before were left undisturbed. Instead there was an increasing emphasis on environments which had not been intensively used. The building of the great henges in Wessex and beyond may have been part of this process, and at Durrington Walls enormous tree trunks were clearly being introduced from areas of greensand or alluvium. It also seems likely that other sites reflect a period of exploration and land use in areas which were still forested. There is less evidence from the river gravels, although some were apparently coming into widespread use for the first time. The problem should not be over-simplified; some areas had already been occupied by causewayed enclosures but only occasionally by burial monuments, which tended to occur on higher ground.

In the later third millennium b.c. a more balanced pattern was achieved, and there are certainly more finds of what seems to be settlement material. Cremation cemeteries become a particular feature of this zone and a number of ring ditches have been recognised which could allow of both ritual and domestic interpretations (cf. Kinnes in Jackson, 1976, pp. 42–6).

Another zone where settlement became more extensive was the shoreline. There is a distinct peak of finds of this period, principally, though not exclusively, on the large tracts of coastal sands. This cannot be attributed to changes of sea level, and the rarity of earlier material does seem to be genuine. There is comparable evidence for settlement on sand hills in areas of fenland, and slighter traces of the occupation of small islands, both on the coast and inland.

Finally, there is rather ambiguous evidence for greater exploitation of the uplands, including areas which must certainly have been of little interest to earlier colonists. The clearest demonstration of this extension to the settlement pattern is from sites of very limited status, particularly caves. Undoubtedly many of these were principally of burial, but in some cases domestic settlement is also likely. It would be difficult to explain the use of such areas for burial if they were otherwise unexplored. A common feature of all these new environments is the frequency with which sites used in the Mesolithic were chosen. This is a difficult issue since it may again raise the question of Mesolithic survival. However, two other explanations are possible: these locations may have had particular geographical advantages, and the surface cover perhaps showed lasting modification by the earlier inhabitants.

As might be expected, the later Neolithic economy was more broadly based. There was perhaps an increase in stock raising, possibly accompanied by transhumance. This surely accounts for small nuclei with a domestic fauna in all the newly settled zones. One characteristic of these sites was the unusually high proportion of scrapers. It can be argued that these were associated with cattle. Pastoralism on a more systematic basis is harder to prove, although it has often been assumed. There is far too little evidence for any dogmatic statement, but by 2000 b.c. there was a strong emphasis on pastoral weeds in the clearance horizons. Unfortunately there is too little evidence from the preceding centuries. The absence of grain imprints in pottery may not be relevant. There may, however, have been fewer sites with querns. Morris has commented that the use of cremation in the Irish passage graves is consistent with ethnographic evidence from pastoral nomads (1974).

On the coast, the new occupants made full use of the available resources, and in some cases they may have planted crops, although it is not known how widely. These areas were almost certainly used for grazing and, like the uplands, often yield a high proportion of scrapers. Most of these sites seem to have been short-lived and probably seasonal. They indicate an eclectic economy which also featured fish, molluscs and seabirds. A possible innovation during this phase is net weights. Finds of shellfish, and on other occasions the use of imported materials, indicate the inland contacts of these people. In Ireland this may be reflected by the introduction of shells into passage graves; Herity particularly emphasises this feature, since shells are not found in the earlier court cairns (1974, pp. 172–4). But here again greater chronological precision is needed before this view becomes dogma.

In all these new environments there was an apparent increase in hunting. The stylistic range of missile points certainly broadened, and there is also some widening of the distribution pattern. Occasional sites of this date could be interpreted as hunting stands, and a group of pit traps is known in Scotland. This increase in hunting possibly explains the greater use of dogs.

Few of these observations are new, but they have in the past been interpreted differently. Attention has been focused upon a certain formal similarity to the economy of the late Mesolithic. There is a similar diversity, and to some extent similar resources were used. The structural resemblance perhaps goes further, since the very diversity of the late Mesolithic economy was really a response to a series of pressures, created by the increase in population and by drastic changes

in the environment. This resemblance to the practices just described did at one time suggest a quite specific continuity. The result was that this period was referred to as the 'Secondary Neolithic', on the explicit assumption that this pattern resulted from the acculturation of the natives (Piggott, S., 1954, pp. 276 ff.). This view is now more difficult to accept, partly because there is little or no typological evidence for physical continuity between the artefacts of the respective groups, and partly because the longer Neolithic chronology now in vogue would imply a preliminary period of perhaps 1500 years during which the two populations avoided contact. It is more likely that the eclectic economy of this particular phase was the response to further difficulties: it represents a movement away from a period of intensive land use to one which was more extensive and involved far fewer risks. This change of emphasis may reflect a check in population growth and perhaps a temporary breakdown of the social framework which had made expansion possible. Later, as the pollen evidence shows, there was a genuine recovery, with a series of newer clearings and a resumption of co-operative labour (Bradley, 1977). But, except in a very few areas, continuity of social organisation cannot be proved. The wide range of habitats now being used may indicate that individual communities were ranging more widely over the landscape; but it could equally well mean that some social units had disintegrated. Either way, it is clear that for a time the demands upon individual groups were perhaps rather less. Hunting, for example, would have been an ideal adaptation to an extension of secondary forest, and could also have relieved any difficulties in maintaining the protein supply. An extension of transhumance, or even nomadism, would have eased the pressure on individual areas of land.

One region which demonstrates this well is the area around Lough Gur, where a number of distinct sites have now been examined. It is reasonable to assume that they were basically complementary, even if specific sites were not all used at the same time. Their characteristics can be set out as follows:

Knockadoon – scattered houses with evidence of stock raising and arable plots (O'Riordain, 1954).

Rathjordan – a hunting stand constructed on the edge of an area of marshland and probably used in autumn (O'Riordain and Lucas, 1947).

Rockbarton – hearths incorporating imported materials, built in an area of fenland and including wild plant foods collected in summer (Mitchell and O'Riordain, 1942).

Geroid Island – a small wooded island probably used as seasonal grazing for pigs and cattle (Liversage, 1958).

In another area the economy might have shown a coastal element.

There are other signs of mobility in the settlement pattern, some of which reveal the breakdown of the earlier system. Any unity in house or settlement types disappears and in many instances structures have been completely elusive, even on well-excavated sites (McInnes, 1971). Those which are known show a greater variety of form than the buildings of the preceding phase, and in a few cases are as insubstantial as the shelters of the Mesolithic. This diversity of form is matched by a greater range of sizes and by a fall in the mean floor area. Earlier Neolithic houses have floor areas of between 30 and 65 sq. m, with a mean of 50 sq. m. In the later phase the largest structures are no more than 50 sq. m in area, and the mean falls to 30 sq. m. There is less evidence for the storage of food in pits and more evidence that flat-based pots were used for this purpose. One reason might have been that sites were occupied for a shorter period. This increase in mobility is also indicated by the breakdown of the regional ceramic styles of the earlier phase and the emergence of a more confused pattern. In Ireland there is little evidence of regional ceramic groups, and Dr Isobel Smith has argued that in the rest of Britain potting was no longer the prerogative of local specialist groups (1974, p. 113). A similar tendency is evident in the distribution of axes. It appears that the products of a few workshops were now being distributed over a much wider area. Hodder has applied regression analysis to some of these distributions and argues that this pattern indicates

the greater value of these items (1974).

In a few cases, however, signs of recovery can be seen. With more extensive excavation, later Neolithic enclosures, fields, paddocks or droveways are at last being found, and all of them suggest some organisation of the landscape. The evidence is slender, but it seems possible that a number of innovations including granaries, paddocks, palisaded enclosures, droveways and wells could predate the first appearance of metallurgy (cf. Bradley and Ellison, 1975, pp. 160 ff.). And in Ireland, where recovery was more rapid, there is already evidence for the development of regular walled fields. There is insufficient evidence to deal with these questions at the moment, but suffice it to say that the renewed attention paid to public monuments did not stand in isolation.

Although it is customary to consider the appearance of Beakers as a radical step in British pre-history, as perhaps one of the few periods of immigration with an adequate backing, the actual reflection of this phase in settlement evidence is remarkably hard to define. So much depends on one's historical interpretation of the phenomenon. Was there really a 'Beaker culture', and how much evidence is there that what is discussed is a new population, rather than a social phenomenon associated with the spread of metals? Although the cultural explanation of Beakers has been an unshaken dogma for a century, once it is criticised, as it has been lately, it is hard to return to the orthodox view (cf. Burgess and Shennan, 1976; Case, 1977).

Certainly the evidence of settlement archaeology cannot justify a division at this point. The recovery from the middle Neolithic hiatus was almost certainly under way before the introduction of copper or bronze and there was already a resurgence in the ritual activity which produced the great public monuments. In addition to henges, which have already been discussed, the cursus probably belong to this phase, although a satisfactory chronology has yet to be established. In Wessex the large ceremonial centres had already adopted a spacing that resembles Renfrew's Early State Module (1975, pp. 12 ff.), and the same basic pattern had emerged in Ireland in the location of most important Passage

Grave cemeteries which show a mean spacing of *c.* 40 km (Herity, 1974, fig. 137).

The comparison between Wessex and Ireland may not be fanciful. In both areas a particular style of pottery already occurred with some frequency in 'ritual' deposits, even if it was not confined to specialised sites. Just as the great henges were associated with Grooved Ware, the Passage Graves are linked with Carrowkeel Ware. There may even be features in common: stylistic traits in the pottery; the association of bone pins with both groups and even the duplication of motifs from Passage Grave art in the Grooved Ware ceramic repertoire. There may be henges in the Boyne valley, and Silbury Hill may be related not to the round barrows of Wessex but to the great Irish tombs. Indeed Passage Graves probably show the earliest combination of astronomical observation and formal design. Morris has suggested that the Boyne tombs belong to a 'chiefdom-type socio-political framework' (1974). This resembles Renfrew's interpretation of the southern English henges (1973a). All this is naturally speculation, but the interesting point is that here are two instances of an association between a type of ritual monument and a specific style of pottery, both of which predate the Beaker experience. It is especially interesting to see that among the main items associated with Grooved Ware are a variety of arrowheads (Wainwright and Longworth, 1971, pp. 254 ff.). Archery is also an integral part of the Beaker phenomenon.

When the Beaker settlement evidence is assembled, a further problem arises: there is no structural feature which is actually new to Britain. Even the rare enclosures or houses are of types which have been recognised in native contexts. As Derek Simpson has pointed out, this is a pattern which is also found in Europe (1971); the 'Beaker folk' evidently had no minds of their own. The most that can be said is that there are settlements in Britain with different proportions of Beakers among the pottery (Clarke, D. L., 1976b, p. 472), and even this observation may be misleading if some of these vessels were made on living sites. The distinctive nature of this phenomenon becomes even clearer when it is realised that in Britain Beakers are the first vessels which are consistently found in graves. If they had a specialised role, perhaps in the serving of drink, their social importance may have equalled that of the fine vessels which entered Britain in the middle of the first millennium b.c. (cf. Barrett in Bradley and Ellison, 1975, pp. 112 ff.). Like them, beakers are associated with ornaments and weapons, but in each case the evidence for a major movement of population is unsatisfactory.

It is worth returning to the public monuments. Whether these show continuity with earlier sites or had developed in freshly opened areas, they do again belong in regions of ecological diversity. Such a variety could only be enhanced by the range of economic practices of the late Neolithic. There are two conspicuous features of these sites: first, that both the supposedly precocious finds of metalwork, those from Mount Pleasant and Castell Bryn-Gwyn, occur on sites of special status (Wainwright, 1970 and 1962); and second, that on each of the main henges at least Beakers only appear *after* the sites were established in the social landscape. This seems to be true even though Beakers were already current when these sites were being built.

This digression is necessary if settlement history is to be disentangled from the traditional ethnology. But it would be wrong to replace one dogma by another (cf. Case, 1977). The evidence for a British Beaker 'culture' may be unsatisfactory but it is still true that the late Neolithic recovery accelerated rapidly at about this time. It is not possible to decide how far this evidence shows the impact of immigrants and how far the social reverberations associated with metalworking found their ultimate reflection in the landscape. At any rate, the experimental data rules out the most naive hypothesis: that the forest fell before a wave of flat axes.

Although much of this intensification had its social aspect, it would be wisest to begin with a simple account of where the impact was felt. It is once more necessary to stress that these are not new patterns but merely an elaboration of old ones. The greatest impact was through continued colonisation, often ranging well beyond the better soils into regions which are now moorland and heath. This process is represented by a continued fall in the proportion of arboreal pollen and in some areas it may also be connected with the 'Lime Decline'. Judith Turner links this with the collection of fodder and bast (1962). There may also have been a change in the actual techniques of felling. The adoption of the beetle and wedge perhaps enabled the pioneer farmers to attack more substantial trees than had previously been possible without fire setting. There is corresponding evidence for the use of tree trunks for making coffins and dug-out canoes. In this phase stone artefacts were again produced and distributed on a *regional* scale, as they had been in the earlier Neolithic period of expansion The newly settled area took in a range of less resilient soils and Helbaek may well be right in seeing this as one reason for increased barley growing (1952, p. 200). In lowland Britain one difficulty to be faced was the clearance of areas which had already been invaded by grassland. Although this provided an opportunity for increased stock raising, a number of sites have shown plough marks from this early period (Fowler and Eváns, 1967). Cultivation of this kind would normally follow hand-stripping of the turf. It is interesting to note that there are several contemporary sites where spade furrows have been found.

In highland areas there is even more evidence for an attack on the landscape, the later · of which are evidently marked by the first real peak of stone clearance. It may be no coincidence that only in this period, after a lapse of many centuries, was stone employed once more as a building material, and the relevant phases of most henge monuments are known to be linked with the appearance of Beakers (Case, 1977). As this implies, the long-distance transport of stone was also resumed in this period. This onslaught on highland areas may have accompanied the discovery of metal sources. In each of these new areas, however, there was a danger of falling fertility and an all but inevitable progression from cultivation to grazing and hunting. This is nowhere clearer than in the arable/pastoral curve.

Corresponding pressure was exerted on the shoreline, and here, too, barley was grown. There continued to be an eclectic economy, at least part of it practised seasonally. The use of dune pasture possibly increased, but fishing, fowling, hunting and strandlooping still retained their importance. Almost certainly, greater areas of shell-sand came under cultivation, and the number of substantial structures in these areas may have increased. Some of these were undoubtedly used all year round. A last development was completely new, the use of the coastal zone for the production of artefacts. There is clear evidence for potting, and reason to suspect both metalworking and the production of faience.

Hunting continued to be of importance, as it had been in the late third millennium b.c. There was an increase in the number, variety and distribution of missile points, and in some areas it is possible to isolate a number of minor nuclei, lookouts, maintenance camps and stands which were probably associated with hunting. Hunting and farming proved to be increasingly incompatible, and as the landscape underwent further changes hunting became less practical from the home base. At the same time the rapid degradation of soils some distance from the main settled areas created ideal hunting grounds which could be served by specialised camps, usually temporary shelters equipped with hearths and cooking troughs. These specialised sites are one new development of the second millennium b.c. and closely follow the first attack on the landscape. Alongside this increase in hunting there may have been some emphasis on gathering but the data is very sparse and it is hard to decide whether this is anything more than a continuation of the broadly based patterns of the Neolithic.

An emphasis on animal husbandry remained. This may be related to earlier practice, but the late Neolithic evidence is very limited. Pastoral weeds feature prominently in the clearings and the artefact evidence shows an emphasis on leatherworking, with a distinctive tool kit which has been recognised from burials and settlements alike. The areas in which these items are found are those in which late Neolithic activity has been suggested and in some cases these environments also produce flint groups dominated by scrapers.

They include the coastline, the chalk plateau, upland caves and areas of fenland. Such indications gain further weight from the evidence for leather clothing. As far as this evidence goes, it is consistent with cattle farming which may have been quite important in the early second millennium b.c. But there could be indications that the wider availability of grassland allowed more emphasis on sheep, and before the end of the Early Bronze Age there might have been an increase in the use of woven cloth. At the same time leatherworking tools disappear from the record.

The general picture which emerges is of a diverse but quite intensive economy in which new areas were constantly being brought into use. There are certainly signs of pressure. There was a constant process of soil degradation, this time concentrated in the more marginal areas, and there was probably competition for land. This is largely a social question but it can be documented from the location of burials. These were increasingly placed either on abandoned agricultural land or at the very edges of the cleared area. In some regions they lie on the edge of the floodplain, in others in remote positions high above the settled land. Frequently they were placed in grassland, where they would be no obstacle to cultivation.

But to say this is of course to shirk the issue in favour of a crude functionalism. The reason why the earlier second millennium b.c. is so distinctive is not because of its economic patterns, which may have been a continuation of existing practice, but because of the social nuances which now went with them. Some part of this social patterning must go back into the third millennium b.c. but the problem here is one of archaeological visibility. As a working hypothesis it can be argued that the main impetus came with the spread of metals (cf. Renfrew, 1973b and 1974).

It is clear from Beaker burials that at least four groups were accorded special status (cf. Case, 1977, p. 81). The best known are of course the 'warriors' with their daggers and the archers with their arrowheads and wrist-guards. Stephen Green has now added a distinctive class of leather-worker's graves (in Kelly, J., 1976), and at least two burials in Wessex include 'metalworkers' hammers'. All this naturally permits speculation on the precise status of sites with similar equipment. The finds of leatherworking tools, already mentioned, may suggest that such sites were of some importance, whether they were used continuously or not. The limited evidence for bronze and faience production could have the same significance, and the great increase in hunting now seems more clearly a social phenomenon. The discovery of metalwork of various dates on the 'burnt mounds' or 'cooking sites' seems to support this conclusion, which gains added weight from the fact that these sites are occasionally found with burial and ceremonial monuments. It is harder to establish the status of some of the other sites, although one problem experienced in Chapter 4 is worth recalling. Here a number of limited occupations were tentatively connected with stock farming and it was argued that many of these would be used on a discontinuous basis. The main groups were on the shore and in upland caves. But in each case the associated burials gave no indication that these sites were being used by a restricted segment of a farming community, as might have been usual with transhumance. Instead it was necessary to suggest a group specifically of pastoralists. Nowhere is this clearer than in the Early Bronze Age graves of the Wessex downland, which may have been built in the summer pasture of one such group. It seems conceivable that the lower ground towards the rivers was under cultivation. Andrew Fleming has argued that with the emergence of large areas of grassland pastoral communities might well have developed and that this resource could have become the subject of competition (1971b and 1972a). He even suggests that the stock raisers might have driven other farmers on to the marginal soils. This model, however speculative, at least portrays the two groups, pastoralists and arable farmers, not only as economic partners but also as ranks in society. Fleming aptly comments that it is characteristic of pastoral communities to accumulate wealth in the form of personal adornments. In a sense the investment of labour on earlier sites was replaced by an investment of wealth.

But, as long as this discussion remains so close to economic practice, it continues to skirt the main problem. The major monuments throughout this period were ritual and not explicitly domestic. Not only had large workforces to be mustered, organised and fed, but also large areas, of evidently productive land, were sacrificed to non-functional ends (cf. Renfrew, 1973a). Public works such as cursus, stone alignments, great cemeteries or formal enclosures represent a disproportionate investment of time and effort for a farming community. There is also convincing evidence for mathematical and astronomical expertise (Thom, 1967). This evidence has been sorely abused (e.g. McKie, 1977), but there can be little doubt that a fifth class must now be envisaged: a priesthood, or its equivalent, whose role cannot be rationalised in terms of subsistence agriculture. It makes little difference whether the social structure which supported this development

was strictly a chiefdom, or whether the necessary surplus was administered through the particular agency of redistribution; what is quite clear is that a surplus had been attained and that it was carefully controlled, through a hierarchy which formed part of an exchange network that extended into Europe as well as Ireland (cf. Briggs, 1976b). Its effect was to place on the landscape an overlay of abstract design, incorporating astronomical alignments, geometric forms and an array of visual effects. The elaborate patterns of intervisibility in the Dorset Ridgeway cemetery are just one example (RCHM, 1970, pp. 425–9); there are regularities in the spacing of henges, stone circles and barrow groups (Renfrew, 1973a; Burl, 1976, p. 69; Fleming, 1971b, fig. 14; Green, H. S., 1974). The creation of these effects shows a total command of resources, skills and materials which emphasises more than anything else the success of this particular economy.

But such success is often vulnerable. The increased number of clearings in the second

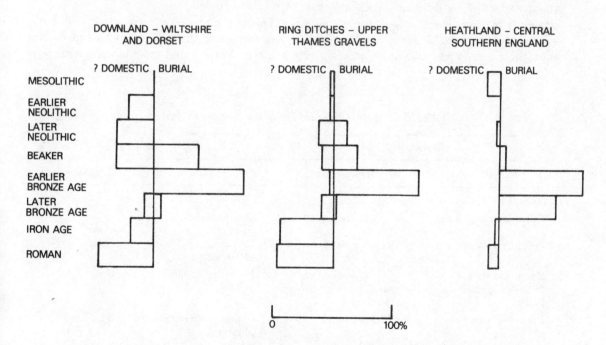

6:3   Continuity or discontinuity of land use as reflected by finds from well published barrows in southern England. Earlier finds usually come from the buried soils and later finds from the barrow ditches. Data from Bradley (1977).

millennium b.c. was not simply a result of outward growth and expansion. Although such growth could have spectacular effects in regions of lasting productivity, these regions were increasingly surrounded by areas which could not support such pressures. Even on the Wessex downland it cannot be proved that the appearance of grassland was actually intended; whilst it might have supported a flamboyant class of pastoralists it could in fact have fed more people as arable. The less resilient soils must now be considered. In some mountainous areas peat was already invading agricultural land by the beginning of the second millennium b.c., although this is no argument for overall climatic change. And in other upland areas deforestation followed by farming rapidly truncated the soils, with the result that stone clearance soon became a necessity. On some sites this followed one or more phases of burning, but in other areas Fleming has suggested an overall wastage rate of no more than three years (1971a). In this environment there was an ever-present danger of erosion or acidification, and even on the chalk itself soil loss certainly took place. There is also some evidence for wind erosion of arable land. Similar effects could follow over-grazing. In other areas forest clearance raised the threat of podsolisation. Many of the round barrows were being constructed on land which was already unusable.

This can be illustrated in two ways. Figure 6:3 charts the history of three environments in southern England where the continuity or discontinuity of settlement can be assessed from dated barrows (cf. Bradley, 1977). On the downland it seems that most well-published examples were built in areas which had already been cleared and which retained sufficient potential for use at a later date. Much the same pattern is seen on the river gravels. But when the heathland barrows are considered it is noticeable how few were built in areas which had been occupied before, and how completely these areas were abandoned for permanent settlement after the barrows had been built. One example from a comparable environment shows how erratic land use could be. Table 12 is an interpretation of land-use history at Swarkestone in the Trent valley, based on the pollen evidence from two neighbouring barrows (data from Posnansky, 1955 and 1956 and from Greenfield, 1960).

This interpretation is merely tentative, but it does emphasise the risks which attended these habitats. As more and more of such areas were

TABLE 12: *Bronze Age land use at Swarkestone, Derbyshire*

	Barrow 2		Barrow 4	
	Data	Interpretation	Data	Interpretation
1	Pollen from buried soil	Cultivation	—	—
2	Pollen from buried soil	Podsolisation	Occupation site, many scrapers,	Beaker
3	Pollen from buried soil	Regeneration	no querns (all under barrow)	occupation?
4	Open land surface with furrows and querns. Pollen	Cultivation – open woodland with grassy clearings	Pollen in primary turf stack	Grassland
5	Barrow structure	Turf grassland	Building of barrow phase 1	
6	*Building of barrow*		Pollen in secondary turf stack	? cultivation and then grassland
7	—	—	*Building of barrow*	

attacked, so the cultural growth of the richer 'core areas' was threatened. It seems hardly necessary to turn to climatic deterioration to account for the collapse of this system.

But the rapidity of this change should not be exaggerated. The beginning of the later Bronze Age marks one of the fundamental transformations in British prehistory, but there has been a temptation to compress events too closely. At first it was thought that this period was one of immigration (cf. Gerloff, 1975, p. 242), but such a view has little to commend it. There has also been a tendency to set too precise a date to the climatic deterioration which other authorities consider to be the main agent of change. It seemed that the Deverel Rimbury culture of southern England must have emerged quite abruptly to have filled the space between the last Wessex graves and finds of the Late Bronze Age.

This reading of the evidence was over-simplified, so much so that it became easy to explain events in catastrophist terms. But a recent review of the status of the Deverel Rimbury culture suggests that it may represent only one section of the community who were producing their distinctive pots whilst the last dagger graves were in use (Barrett, 1976). Although there is a genuine chronological succession, such an overlap would conform to a model which allows a period of reorganisation and retrenchment. There is an overlap of at least two centuries between the carbon dates for the late Wessex Culture and those for Deverel Rimbury pottery, and it now seems that the associated metalwork may itself need backdating if it is to conform to the European chronology (Burgess, 1976d; B. O'Connor, pers. com.). It also appears that several of the regional concentrations of Middle Bronze Age metalwork had precursors in the Arreton phase (Burgess and Cowen, 1972; B. O'Connor, pers. com.). This was not the case in Dorset, where a concentration of Arreton material had no successor. It is interesting that this group is known around Mount Pleasant, for which the latest carbon date is 1324 ± 51 b.c. (BM 669) (Wainwright, 1975).

This is not to deny that climatic change was important. It has simply been given too much weight. Not so long ago, when this phenomenon was set rather later in time, it was used to explain some of the developments at the beginning of the Iron Age (cf. Piggott, S., 1972b); what has happened now is that the same explanation has been transferred to a different set of events (e.g. Burgess, 1974, pp. 195 ff.). Over much of Britain the *real* decline was in the earlier Bronze Age and was the result of settling areas of unsuitable soil. Many of the changes which forced those areas out of cultivation did involve climatic agencies, but these changes could have been reduced or avoided had the ground never been stripped of trees. The dates for barrows on heathland and moorland demonstrate that there was no single phase which shows this type of decline. In some cases monuments were certainly covered by peat, but possibly some time after their desertion. Perhaps the real effect of climatic change was to prevent such extensive use of the uplands again. What matters, then, is not those sites which were deserted as a direct effect of these changes, but those in which land use would henceforth be restricted. Peter Fowler has pointed out that only from the middle of the Bronze Age do Fox's Highland and Lowland Zones show a consistent contrast (Fowler, 1975).

The direct effects of climatic change on lowland Britain have also been over-stressed. For example, Burgess sees a 'water cult' as one response to natural change (1974, p. 196). What is really apparent is a reorganisation of the best farming land and a concerted attack on new areas which could sustain a long period of use. There was a drastic increase in the number of clearings from about this time, both in Britain and in Ireland, and more evidence of weeds of cultivation. There was a range of innovations connected with both arable and pastoral farming, and pollen evidence that new areas were being cleared of trees. Part of this process has been monitored from artefact distributions. In Lincolnshire Davey has demonstrated a concentration of resources on the lower ground towards the rivers (1971) and the same pattern has been observed in Berkshire by Justin Ball (pers. com.). The work of Calkin on the Hampshire/Dorset border suggests a similar landscape (1962), and site catchment analysis of settlements on the Sussex downland has revealed a preference for the richer but more demanding lowland soils (Ellison and Harriss, 1972). In some instances the distribution of chance finds coincides with Earlier Bronze Age metalwork, in particular domestic items. Emphasis upon these productive zones was aided by the development of a more extensive tool kit. There is some evidence for the renewed coppicing of woodland, and the amount of timber which was eventually incorporated into domestic and defensive structures suggests that pollarding might also have been practised.

The most radical change of all was in the physical appearance of the landscape. It has never been easy to establish the extent of cultivation in the second millennium b.c., although it has probably been underestimated. One difficulty is that the development of organised field systems may have removed the evidence, so that earlier arable land can only be recognised where it is preserved under later monuments, or where land use has been curtailed by changes in the natural environment. Despite this, it seems likely that the situation described above brought about the 'Celtic' field system. There is evidence for a massive reorganisation of the landscape in a number of different areas. In Wessex very large field systems were laid out on the downland, sometimes incorporating barrows in the existing landscape, a number of which date to the Early Bronze Age. The main characteristics of these systems were their considerable size and their complex internal structure. They were evidently imposed on the landscape in a single operation, and for the most part they conform to clearly defined baselines, which can run across country for several kilometres, ignoring the subtleties of local topography (Bowen, H. C., 1975). The parallel axes of one such system in Dorset ran straight across a stream. The earlier barrows often formed sighting points for these axial blocks, and were sometimes incorporated into the edges or corners of fields. It is not clear whether any of them served as a boundary in the earlier landscape, but burial mounds are recorded as fulfilling this role in the early Irish laws (Charles-Edwards, 1976). The mean size of the individual fields was about 2,500 sq. m (Bradley, 1978a).

Similar arrangements can be seen in two other areas. At the fen edge at Peterborough recent excavation has disclosed a highly organised landscape which also took shape in this phase. Here the dating is securely based on artefacts and radiocarbon. The basic structure of this system was composed of parallel droveways running inland at right angles to the fen edge and defining a series of linear land blocks which were broken up into fields and paddocks. This time there is evidence that the arrangement was for pastoral rather than arable land use. Excavation at Fengate is still in progress at the time of writing, but it already appears that similar layouts can be recognised as crop marks in the Welland valley, in parts of Essex including the Thames estuary and, possibly, in the Great Ouse valley (Pryor, 1976a; P. Woodward, pers. com.). In each case the basic alignments respect earlier ring ditches, much as the Wessex fields respected the barrows.

Finally, fieldwork currently under way on Dartmoor is revealing a radically organised landscape based on an extensive series of land boundaries which show a similar respect for earlier cairns. These are perhaps associated with settlements of this phase and are sometimes covered by peat which formed in the first millennium b.c. In some instances these boundaries or 'reaves' run parallel to one another and form the basis for whole field systems (Fleming, 1976). There are hints of similar arrangements in Northumberland (Hogg, A. and N., 1956, fig. 1; Hogg, A., 1975, fig. 83), although this has not been clearly confirmed on the ground, and rather similar boundaries at Achnacree Moss also date to this period (Barrett, Hill and Stevenson, 1976). The unitary structure of these large areas of the landscape is remarkably clear, and the field systems are on a scale hardly equalled before the Roman period. They may be thought of as 'cohesive' systems, as distinct from 'aggregate' systems which form by piecemeal addition. This terminology suggests analogies with the planning of settlements and their internal buildings (cf. Bradley, 1978a). The first evidence for a planned settlement may be from Rams Hill and could itself date to the eleventh century b.c. (Bradley and Ellison, 1975).

Although it has been suggested that some of the population of highland Britain moved south as the climatic deterioration took effect, it is far simpler to relate these changes to quite local changes. There is other evidence for the pressures which were now being felt, and it seems that by this phase land boundaries were also being built. Occasional instances occur of linear earthworks overlain by round barrows, but normally these were constructed either at the same time as the large field systems or not long afterwards.

These early boundaries have already been discussed. Three main possibilities have emerged. The first is that their construction does reflect a change in the balance of the later Bronze Age economy, from a revival of cereal farming to a greater emphasis on livestock. Some modifications could have taken place and there is a fluctuation in the arable/pastoral curve which could reflect this. It is possible that over-energetic arable farming was already damaging the more resilient soils and that local changes of balance were needed to provide enough food. This could also account for their building if the change were intended to secure a better integration of arable and pasture. Appelbaum postulates an infield/outfield system, the chief characteristic of which would be the emphasis placed upon intensive and controlled manuring (1954). This system would offer an alternative to the use of byres in the long houses of north-west Europe (cf. Bradley, 1978a). But neither of these suggestions need exclude a third possibility. This places greater emphasis on the fact that these are among the first extended land boundaries to have left a trace in Britain. The size and shape of some of the larger land blocks suggests that they should be considered as whole 'territories', and not simply as the internal land divisions of particular farms. It is tempting to compare these land units with Saxon estates, or even parishes. It is possible that enclosure was

connected with competition, and even with raiding. Some of the upland enclosures, which could have defined grazing areas, may have been shared by several communities, and Cunliffe has suggested that his 'plateau enclosures' may be an important precursor of hill forts (1976a and c). It is certainly true that some of these boundaries were reconstructed on an increasingly impressive scale and that in their developed form they can be integrated with defended sites.

In all this, one element is really new. Because of the accident of survival, a complex landscape can be recovered in a number of upland regions, in particular the chalk downland and Dartmoor. The higher parts of the Wessex downland were long used mainly for sheep, and it is this feature which accounts for the large areas of fields that can be traced today. At the same time, there may be evidence that this area was used as summer grazing in the earlier Bronze Age; and that by the Roman period settlements were already being located on lower ground. The use of this zone as arable resulted from a period of crisis, when pasture was converted in order to provide more food. How was this change effected?

Several important innovations appear to provide the answer. In this period ponds were first being built, and wells may also have been sunk. They would have overcome some of the difficulties of permanent settlement on the high unwatered downland. The form of the numerous square fields indicates the widespread practice of cross-ploughing, and some at least of the linear earthworks could have made efficient manuring rather easier. Although cattle provided most meat, sheep were also becoming important. They need far less water and their manure is particularly crucial in sustaining arable production. Hulled barley was also favoured, and the use of this variety may have cut down losses in the harvest.

The effect of these changes in lowland Britain was to produce a landscape with fixed boundaries and the potential for great continuity. Once lasting fields and enclosures had been established, they proved very difficult to supersede. A range of domestic compounds also came into being, although it is not known how far their different forms reflect variations of status, population or economy. Inside at least some of these earthworks robust houses were being constructed which were significantly larger than those of the preceding phase. Storage pits were also adopted, and these confirm that the sites were conceived on a more long-term basis. All in all, settlement on the downland had an energy and permanence unmatched since the early third millennium.

The major problem, however, is that this was in fact a relatively marginal area, and .it was probably in Taylor's 'Zone of Destruction' that the most important developments took place. In spite of evidence which suggests a greater density of settlement on more lowland soils, there are two genuine difficulties. In areas of relatively unbroken topography lynchets cannot be expected to survive, with the result that the great field systems of the downland have few counterparts on the richest land; these have already been listed. Considerable difficulty has also been experienced in locating lowlying settlements. This perhaps results partly from the loss of earthworks and partly because surface finds of this date are notoriously friable. There are two further reasons: the difficulties of identifying Late Bronze Age pottery when it is found, and a tendency to treat metal finds separately from settlement material. It is true that with fewer burials in the first millennium b.c. finds of metalwork become more common both in rivers and in hoards; but this is no argument for viewing them entirely in a ritual context. Davey and Ball have both shown that the distribution of metal finds shows a changing centre of gravity, and Burgess's 'wet places' cult cannot account for all the evidence, even if it does explain the high proportion of weaponry recovered intact from the rivers (Davey, 1971; J. Ball, pers. com.). A number of workers have suggested that some of these metal finds could have come from very rich settlements in use throughout the later Bronze Age (Ehrenberg, 1977, p. 18). In the Thames valley there are several sites in which metalwork has been directly associated with pottery and structural features,

and it can now be argued that this was one zone where wealth and power were concentrated (e.g. Longley, 1976).

At present it is not known whether the economic complexion of these areas was different from that of the chalk. The evidence from Fengate is no basis for any general hypothesis, since it lies in such an unusual environment, but it is clear from finds of querns and grain in the Thames valley that theories of an exclusive dependence on livestock must be discounted. What is difficult to establish is the relationship between the economic potential of this zone and the social status of the sites. One interpretation suggests that these might have been supported by the work of a peasantry and that a class society, not unlike the Wessex culture, may have maintained itself while the economy altered (cf. Coombs, 1975, p. 76). According to another view, a social elite may have appropriated the most fertile land and forced part of the population into more marginal areas. There is no way of deciding between these theories. The social status of the few rich settlements is better compared with crannogs than with hill forts.

Before the vexed question of defended sites is considered, more must be said about developments in highland Britain. These have perhaps been misunderstood, since it was here that the greatest effects of climatic change were felt. The suggestion has already been made that the rapid wastage of upland soils was initially more important than climatic change as such. Many of the most damaging changes to the soil had already occurred before the beginning of zone VIII. It might be expected that changes were being made similar to those seen in the south. There was apparently more emphasis on lower or newly cleared ground, and there are comparable signs of rich and important centres closer to the rivers. The complex of finds associated with the Holderness region may be an example (Smith, R., 1911). In the north-west this is matched by the waterlogged structure at Branthwaite (Ward, 1974), and in Ireland one of the main settlements was Balinderry (Hencken, 1942).

On the higher ground some reorganisation was perhaps achieved. One area which demonstrates this is Dartmoor, which lies at the extreme edge of the highland zone. Here an extensive and highly organised landscape did in fact develop *before* large areas became unsuitable for settlement. This is an important point, since the sequence is similar to that in lowland areas. There seems to have been time for complicated systems of fields and boundaries to have developed out of the earlier landscape before the natural balance was overturned (Fleming, 1976; Simmons, 1969). It is not clear whether this pattern is seen anywhere else, but the excavators' interpretation of the linear banks at Achnacree Moss is especially relevant at this point. It appears that here early land use had resulted in podsolisation. The excavators suggest that the building of these boundaries, in particular the digging of ditches, was meant to restore the land for agricultural use (Barrett, Hill and Stevenson, 1976). Only when this had failed did the area become overgrown by peat. Bearing this in mind, one might suggest that the large highland field systems recognised by Feachem (1973) may at times have undergone a similar process. Not all of them need reflect the earlier Bronze Age expansion; some at least could proceed from a later attempt to arrest the decline. This can only be tested by excavation.

Whatever the merits of this view, it is clear that by the first millennium b.c. a genuine distinction was developing between the highland and lowland zones. As Fowler has pointed out, few artefact distributions cut across this boundary any longer, and the Middle Bronze Age metal industry apparently shows a time-lag in northern England (cf. Burgess, 1968). There were other changes: more evidence is known for mobile pastoralism in the north, both from finds in upland caves and from others in areas of peat. In some cases finds of metalwork have seemed to suggest that pastoralism remained a prestigious activity. The same may be true of horsemanship. There is evidence for continued hunting, with greater use of the spear and less dependence on dogs. On the coast there is similar evidence, although it may be true that rather fewer marginal locations were used. The later Bronze Age has been described as a settlement vacuum in the north, and sites are certainly elusive. Possibly the areas which need more attention are in the 'zone of destruction' on the lower ground.

The exceptions to this pattern are the defended sites. These have only been recognised during the last few years, with the development of a radiocarbon chronology. For a while, it seemed as if the backdating of the earlier hill forts might fill the so-called 'settlement vacuum' between the Deverel Rimbury and the Iron Age. But this was in fact based on a false premise, since the defended sites are clustered in areas of relatively low agricultural potential, and are far less common in those regions from which most fine metalwork is known. For some time the growing production of weaponry throughout the later Bronze Age has been equated with the emergence of a distinct class of defended hilltop enclosure. The difficulty is that such weaponry rarely comes from those particular sites, which produce mainly personal utensils. Almost as many caves have produced bronzes. The weapon hoards of this period have a quite different distribution and are more common in eastern England than in those areas where the defended sites occur (Coombs, 1975). This even applies to areas like the Wessex downland, and it seems to suggest that 'hill forts' are a rather peripheral phenomenon (cf. Avery, 1976, figs 1 and 2). Wealth and possibly power were concentrated in lowlying but more fertile regions, many of which have been levelled by centuries of cultivation. These are the areas in which the rich riverside occupations are known.

It is not easy to account for this development. The few hilltop enclosures of the Middle Bronze Age are of uncertain character. They were not sited in particularly effective positions for defence, and their status in the landscape is not clearly understood. Up to six large enclosures of this date may be identified: Rams Hill, Norton Fitzwarren, Martin Down and Highdown are quite well known (Bradley and Ellison, 1975; Pitt-Rivers, 1898, pp. 185–215;

Wilson, A., 1940 and 1950); possible additions may be Drumcoltran in southern Scotland, which included a hoard of rapiers in its ditch, and Hook in the Hampshire Basin, which was notable for the massive post holes in its entrance (Coles, F., 1893, pp. 105–6; Ashbee, 1955). The first two sites may have originated in an earlier phase. Rams Hill, Norton Fitzwarren and Highdown all occupy rather insignificant hill tops. Hook is on level ground, and Martin Down is in a shallow valley at the edge of the Wessex linear ditch system. As a group these sites lack cohesion. They show little continuity with 'hill

forts' proper, and may have played a social role similar to that of henges. Rams Hill is very near one of the main barrow cemeteries in Wessex; Priddy Circle 1 shares this distinctive siting, and, like Rams Hill, has a timbered rampart (Tratman, 1967). Rams Hill, Martin Down, Hook and Highdown all lie on the interface of several ceramic style zones (A. Ellison, pers. com.) and all of the sites except Drumcoltran lie close to the centre of major areas of metalworking (fig. 6:4). This recalls Rowlands's comment that: 'the direct or indirect linkage of political control to the elaboration

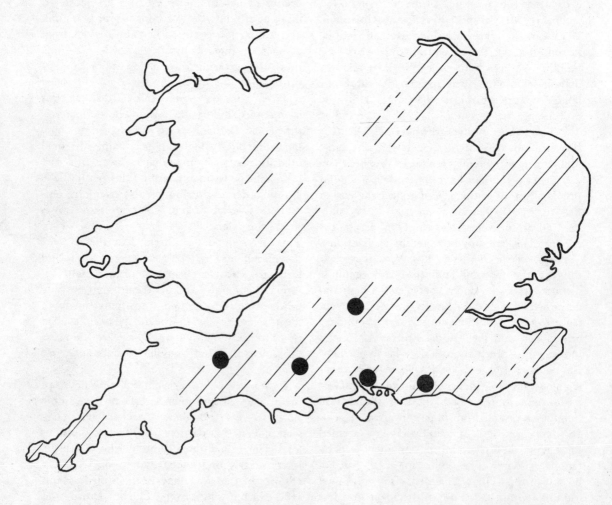

6:4   The main concentrations of Middle Bronze Age metalwork in southern England (data from Rowlands, 1976) in relation to major enclosures of the period.

of craft production could well lie behind the changes in the organisation of metalwork production detected for the late Middle Bronze Age' (1976, p. 167). There are hoards from the defences of Norton Fitzwarren and Drumcoltran. It is reasonable to suspect that these sites played some part in the pottery and metal distributions.

But the later 'hill forts' represent a more complex development, which postdates the organisation of the landscape and at times may have grown out of it. Some sites are an embellishment of areas of enclosed upland grazing, whilst others span earlier boundaries. One aspect of these hill forts is particularly important. In the Middle Bronze Age the defended enclosures occurred in areas with their own schools of metalworking. By the end of the Bronze Age the areas with defended sites and those which produced most of the metalwork no longer coincided. Rowlands has made an important study of how metalworking was organised and has suggested a contrast between the Middle and Late Bronze Ages (1976). The prevalent model in the earlier period was for smiths to operate from fixed workshops for a limited part of the year, and to distribute their products over a small area, of perhaps 10-to-15-km radius. North of the Thames, production was more probably organised to meet immediate rather than anticipated demand. In the later period, however, output was greatly increased and more attention had to be paid to collecting and transporting large quantities of scrap. It is possible that these changes took place under political control. If so, this only emphasises the contrast. The division is not between the highland and lowland zones; there is more contrast between the north and west on the one hand and the Thames valley and the east on the other.

A number of defended sites were clearly in areas where land use might have been restricted by the effects of climatic change. Even areas where reorganisation had begun may have proved vulnerable, and the chalk itself remained under pressure. The areas dominated by hill forts were probably those in which the greatest pressures had been felt, and sometimes where

least could be achieved. The growth of defensive sites was possibly an aggressive posture accompanying competition for land, and perhaps raiding. However, the relative material poverty of these sites does seem to imply that they were not an equivalent of the rich lowland settlements and certainly that they did not control bronze production. This is particularly so where the origins of individual sites were basic economic practices like summer grazing. Cunliffe has observed that the main characteristic of the early hill forts is the number of ancillary buildings, rather than houses (1976c). The rows of four-post structures on some of these sites may well have been for storage, and their overall planning recalls the organisation of the surrounding landscape. One interesting possibility is that these sites were fortified food stores, central places in which an economic surplus could be collected and administered. The close fusion of such sites with the landscape, in southern England at least, suggests that they might be the culmination of the economic changes that define this phase.

If this theory has any merit, it would imply that the entire structure of the landscape underwent an unprecedented transformation between about 1300 and 700 b.c., and that the so-called 'Late Bronze Age vacuum' was in fact a major period of change. A few relevant contrasts should be stressed. The landscape of the Early Bronze Age conceals its own organisation, and represents the visible outcome of a huge investment of organised manpower. As such, it was the culmination of trends which began in the later Neolithic. But the entire emphasis of this landscape, and of the society that formed it, was towards ritual and ceremonial presentation. Large areas of land were made over to great public monuments or to elaborate formal designs. Any structural link these may have had with the agricultural cycle can only be guessed at. The best example of 'ritual landscape' is even earlier in date. In a recent paper Patrick has shown that the Passage Grave at New Grange was orientated to allow the sun to light the central chamber at the midwinter sunrise (1974). He has also demonstrated that the passages of some of the major tombs within 60 km were orientated on New Grange itself (Patrick, 1975). An equally structured landscape may have existed around Stonehenge in the Early Bronze Age. But, outside Ireland, by the first millennium b.c. manpower seems to have been wholly re-directed to subsistence activities. Even the major enclosed sites apparently possessed an economic, even aggressive, role; burial monuments were few and in the Iron Age some of the earlier ceremonial centres were being re-used as settle-ments. Before this stage was reached, cultivation was impinging on the old burial areas. An appetite for flamboyant display was never lost and was perhaps directed more into actual con-flict. The appearance of the sword, together with the evidence for horse riding, suggests an aris-tocracy who retained rather similar tastes, but depended on an economy which had changed completely.

The very configuration of Britain had also changed. Not only did Fox's two zones represent a real division for the first time, but also the entire emphasis of settlement had shifted from upland into lowlying areas. There is little similarity between Burl's regional groups of henges (1969) and Forde-Johnston's different styles of hill fort (1976, pp. 262 ff.), and there is scarcely any continuity between the areas with rich metalwork in the Early Bronze Age and those with the greatest wealth a few centuries later. But a substantial resemblance exists be-tween regions which had fine metalwork in the Middle Bronze Age and those which continued to do so throughout prehistory. Burgess has suggested that some of these regional styles pre-figure tribal groupings known in the late Iron Age (1974, pp. 221–2), and Eogan has also argued that Ireland developed some of its historical structure in the Bronze Age (1974). These theories will be difficult to prove, but they must be made a priority for research.

These tendencies have been discussed at some length, since they are a source for ensuing developments in prehistory. This is ironic, since it is the Iron Age which has been most discussed in terms of settlement archaeology. This is a fair reflection of the abundance of published and unpublished material, but it is becoming harder to treat the Iron Age in isolation. Since so much work has already been done to synthesise the settlement evidence, it would be wrong to offer a summary with pretensions to complete-ness, and this account will therefore be largely thematic. In fact it seems as if the Bronze Age/ Iron Age transition is not very significant in terms of a process which was only really dis-turbed by the impact of the Roman world. So great was this impact when it came that the final phase of the Iron Age must be considered an entirely separate topic.

In the conventional terminology, the Iron Age succeeds the Late Bronze Age. In reality, it was its consequence. The best argument for substan-tial immigration has been an increase in the number of sites, following an apparent vacuum in the Late Bronze Age. It now seems far more likely that the chronology of settlement finds has been misunderstood. A variety of ceramics have been conflated into an Early Iron Age horizon, with the result that many sites which belonged to the earlier period have been dated too late. Professor Harding, for example, has assembled a number of unrelated features to make up a period of change, which naturally coincides with a peak of wrongly dated sites (1974). This procedure has concealed a real but less dramatic growth. A phase of immigra-tion can still be envisaged, but there is no break in the material culture to locate this. It seems more reasonable to suggest that the larger number of sites was principally the result of internal developments, based on the reorganised economy of the preceding centuries. Population increase has been inferred in Iron Age studies because of the changes which it seems to have caused; the difficulty has always been to account for this increase in the first place.

In any event a better division in the material culture would be made at the end of La Tène I, even if this takes no account of the appearance of iron. At this later date the interchange of weaponry was finally curtailed, after an unbroken sequence of invention since the Middle Bronze Age. Also at this time the first phase of hill fort building ended and only now did elements of the so-called 'Woodbury Economy' assume any real prominence. There may be something in Avery's paradox that the building of so many fortified centres had stabilised British society (1974, p. 60).

One basic change could have been a consequence of these earlier developments: the intensification of cereal farming, most prominent in the Lowland Zone. Economic differences may now have been resolved more by increased production than by administration of a surplus through the defended centres. The provision of deep storage pits on just these sites suggests such an arrangement. Reynolds has shown that these pits are most suitable for keeping seed corn (1972); and the corollary might be that sites with many four-post buildings were storing a higher proportion of *food*. It is still not known how common these structures were on unenclosed sites.

The intensification of arable farming is widely documented. There is a high proportion of cereal weeds in clearings, and a series of important innovations, in particular an increase in the capacity of storage pits and the adoption of spelt as a staple crop. The changes in the pits are a little ambiguous, but could be linked with greater cereal growing. Spelt can be autumn sown and by planting other crops in spring it would be possible to spread the work load over a longer period. The effect would be to increase arable production and to divide the harvest into two periods of intensive activity. There is literary evidence for this practice in Britain around 500 BC (Diodorus Siculus, *Bibliotheca historica*, ii, 47). Once again, these changes are unlikely to have been made unless population pressures had demanded a greater investment of labour. Such changes would have been made easier by the availability of iron tools; and the evidence from Gussage All Saints also suggests the adoption of the rotary quern.

Some changes were perhaps effected by ploughing up areas of pasture. The opening of more productive soils, so prominent a feature of the later Bronze Age, still continued unabated, and there is renewed pollen evidence for a high rate of clearance. This is in contrast with the position in Ireland, where the early Iron Age has been extraordinarily elusive. It has been estimated that in south-eastern England 22 per cent of the early or middle Iron Age sites known to the Ordnance Survey in 1962 were situated on heavy soils, and that 61 per cent of all sites were at the junction of two or more natural zones. Despite the long-standing equation between early Iron Age agriculture and the chalk, 44 per cent of the sites were on gravel-based soils and only 34 per cent on chalk itself. Of the sites which they assign to their earlier phase 45 per cent were occupied to the close of this period (information from G. Moreland-Smith). A significant proportion of downland sites eventually went out of use. One other practice is relevant: marling, for which there is literary support (Pliny, *Natural History*, xvii, 5–8). With marling cultivation could possibly have been extended to otherwise unfavourable soils and productivity could have been maintained for longer.

A noticeable proportion of the new sites were in areas which would be used as pasture, and it is possible that some of the enclosures of this period had a specialised function. The linear ditch systems continued to develop, and with the opening of wider areas of the landscape, sites dominated by sheep became common for the first time. The animal bones from this phase reveal a remarkable diversity, and in specific cases it has been possible to infer relationships between the economies of separate sites. The contrasting assemblages from different terraces of the Thames are just one example.

This intensification was a continuing process, and it brought its own problems in its wake. Not all areas could sustain the demands being made upon them. In the Weald, for example, there is evidence for podsolisation of arable land (Money, 1968; Piercy-Fox, 1969 and 1970), and on the chalk some of the sites used in the earlier Iron Age had been abandoned by the end of this period. Over large areas of southern England it was in this phase that ploughwash began to accumulate in downland valleys, whilst the flood plains of some major rivers contain deposits of alluvium laid down under similar conditions. These pressures also affected the choice of building materials. A characteristic of the earlier hill forts was the vast quantity of timber used in their ramparts. It is noticeable that later defensive structures made more sparing use of wood, and the adoption of dump ramparts in different areas could perhaps betray the difficulty of maintaining supplies. This may also account for a fall in the size of round houses, after a phase in which some very elaborate structures had been built. Equally significant could be the change from timber to stone houses in the north.

As part of this expansion, new systems of linear ditches were being built, notably in Yorkshire, where their full extent and chronology is still uncertain (cf. Challis, 1975, pp. 160 ff.). Whatever their precise economic role, these ditches may indicate competition for resources. The same may be true of the shorter earthworks which accompany defended sites in the southwest. Under the pressures of expansion areas which had hitherto been respected were now occupied once more. In a few instances, notably on the river gravels, earlier ring ditches were levelled by cultivation, and where barrows were still respected, as they were on the chalk, they might be incorporated in the edges of fields. Some earlier cemeteries were certainly ploughed, notably the Beaker graves at Overton Down, which were disturbed in this phase (Fowler, 1967, p. 18). This tendency is exemplified by the treatment of ceremonial enclosures. Generally speaking, these sites were abandoned throughout the later Bronze Age. There are two aspects to this question: the re-use of ceremonial centres for domestic activity, and the renewed fortification of some of these sites. The first tendency is represented by casual Iron Age occupation inside Durrington Walls and Mount Pleasant (Wainwright and Longworth, 1971, p. 24; Wainwright, 1970). Part of the Dorset cursus was also re-used by a settlement (RCHM, 1972, p. 24), whilst in North Wales the henge at Llandegai was converted for domestic use (Houlder, 1968). The second tendency is demonstrated by all those sites where hill forts overlie ceremonial enclosures. The earliest of the hill forts, at the end of the Bronze Age, may be Crickley Hill (Dixon, 1976); the latest of the enclosures might be Castell Bryn-Gwyn, in the early second millennium b.c. (Wainwright, 1962). This convergence has often been noted, and it has led to speculations about ritual continuity. Another way to interpret the evidence is to suggest that the earlier use of these hill tops had 'neutralised' these locations for further settlement until this period. If so, this phenomenon might exemplify, not a continuing respect, but the very opposite.

There are two final aspects to this outward growth. First, there is some evidence that settlements were expanding towards their limits. Atkinson and Hogg have both suggested a regular relationship between the size of Iron Age defended sites and the number of houses which they contain (Atkinson, 1972, p. 64; Hogg, 1971, pp. 114 ff.). Atkinson has also shown that the pressure were greatest on the smaller sites, where the density of houses was twice that of the major hill forts. The same pattern can perhaps be seen in Jobey's crucial work on settlements in northeast England. Evidence also exists for the extension of some of the defended sites and for local increases in the size of open settlements. In parts of Wales there may have been regular local limits to this expansion. Given such evidence, it is not surprising that only towards the middle and later years of the Iron Age do regular distributions of sites exemplify the principles of spatial competition postulated in Central Place Theory.

It is less clear how far such an expansion occurred throughout highland Britain, partly because of an uncertain chronology, and partly because so much of the information comes from a few small areas. However, there are some indications of comparable changes, even if the economic composition of entire areas remains elusive. Pollen evidence suggests a continued, perhaps an increased, onslaught on the landscape, and there are signs of local differences of emphasis between arable and pastoral farming. To some extent this recalls earlier developments in the south and exemplifies the 'time-lag' which first emerges in the Middle Bronze Age. The important fact is simply that Iron Age sites *can* be found, whereas earlier settlements are far rarer. The artefact evidence is similar to that from southern England, with increases in agricultural tools, weaving equipment and querns. However, there may have been a higher proportion of spindle whorls and leatherworking tools, and there is no doubt that sheep were more common than in the south. These again suggest an open landscape.

In the extreme north-west more provision was made for livestock and their products. Byres were not built until the Iron Age, and most of the earlier souterrains also belong to this period. It is not clear how all of these were used, but some of them may be equivalent to the storage pits of the south, whilst most were probably intended to house dairy produce. There is increased evidence for transhumance in Highland Britain, and Alcock has associated this with the development of some of the larger hill forts (1965). There is less evidence of nomadism proper, and a more intensive use of upland caves, which show greater evidence for the processing of animal products. The large-scale movement of livestock may have been controlled from horseback, and cheek pieces are a regular feature of these sites. The increased use of these upland habitats, perhaps as a result of greater pressures on the lower ground, can be combined with limited evidence for the longer use of such sites. Certain caves on the Mendips were undoubtedly in use throughout the year. These particular sites may have produced Glastonbury Ware, and seem to include bone 'potting tools' and potter's clay. A further tendency was for more of these shelters to be found near settlements, perhaps fulfilling a specialised role, such as shelters for animals, workshops or stores. One explanation could be that more sites were being used all year round, and that the expansion of permanent settlement followed an earlier transhumance cycle. This has recently been suggested by Atherden from environmental evidence (1976).

A similar intensification appears on the coast. There was a greater emphasis on fishing, especially in deeper waters, and more dependence on sea birds. Settlements on the shoreline now possessed substantial stone buildings, and a higher proportion must have been used all year round. There is more evidence for cereal growing on the shoreline, and also signs of industrial activity, notably the smelting of iron. Hunting became

more important, and almost certainly extended into winter. There was perhaps a greater selectivity in the animals taken. It is rarely possible to prove the expansion of individual sites, but this is certainly evident in those regions for which adequate surveys are available.

Possibly a third zone needs to be considered. It has already been shown that the lowlying soils of eastern England had achieved an identity of their own before the end of the Bronze Age. The greatest wealth was concentrated in this area, rather than in the uplands with their defended enclosures. It is difficult to trace a continuous development through the Iron Age, partly because of the destructive effect of later agriculture, but also because there was a general decline in the production of portable wealth towards the middle of the period. Champion has suggested that this area had more in common with parts of Europe than with the highland zone (1975), and Cunliffe has supported him by arguing that the rarity of defensive structures may follow an essentially continental pattern (1976a, p. 142). Clearly, the rarity of surviving sites is no proof that the landscape was sparsely settled, and where adequate fieldwork has been done, notably in Essex, the traditional view is rapidly changing. Of particular importance is the excavation of a large nucleated settlement at Little Waltham (Drury, 1973). Pits and weaving combs, the traditional emblems of the period, are quite common in this area, which also contains a variety of fine decorated pottery as well as small bronze objects. What is still uncertain is whether the *relative* distribution of wealth remained the same. The answer to this depends on still unresolved problems of chronology.

Despite the difficulties posed by the evidence from all three areas, certain general propositions appear well founded. Throughout large areas of Britain there was a greater continuity of settlement, with a far more sustained period of use at particular locations. This is best demonstrated by the increased domestic use of defended sites. There is more evidence for the physical expansion of settlements, not only from the open sites, where changes in the occupied area can present problems, but also from those that were enclosed.

There is greater evidence for a steady evolution of settlement types and for an increasing investment of manpower in ostentatious defensive works.

The consequences of these developments varied greatly between, and within, the three zones. In southern England the results are particularly clear. The expansion of settlement throughout the first millennium b.c. had shown three significant tendencies: an increase in the number of sites located at the interface of two or more natural zones; a widening typological range of different enclosures, some of which could have played a specialised social or economic role; and greater emphasis on clusters of discrete settlements in areas of complementary economic potential.

These tendencies may have had a profound impact on the final development of the prehistoric landscape. Quite clearly in the Iron Age there seems to have been a period of strain, which caused a reorganisation of farming. This might have been effected under centralised direction. The symptoms included the addition of defences to a number of arable farms. However, the eventual proliferation of enclosed sites does not suggest the growth of large political units, but rather a period of aggressive competition. This expansion of settlement nevertheless produced a greater economic specialisation from site to site, with the result that balance could only be achieved through forms of regular exchange.

This may have been the reason why certain hill forts eventually emerged at the expense of others. Only at the climax of this growth did defended centres really begin to conform to a regular territorial pattern (Cunliffe, 1974, pp. 260 ff.). In some cases their spacing may even be consistent with Central Place Theory. In Wiltshire, for example, it appears that the larger multivallate hill forts were spaced across the landscape at intervals of about 15 km (Hodder and Orton, 1976, pp. 45–6; Cunliffe, 1974, pp. 261–2). Brian Perry has classified the other enclosures in Hampshire (1969), and, using his data, it is interesting to note that the *range* of different enclosure types is greatest within 5 km of the large hill forts. If economic expansion had generated a system of centralised exchange, this would provide a natural stimulus towards the standardisation of artefact types. This pattern may represent the effective limit of expansion within this zone, particularly in Wessex. Although there is clear evidence for cross-channel trade, mainly through Hengistbury Head, the basic structure of the downland landscape remained the same and the imported items may have been distributed through existing networks connecting the coast and inland areas (cf. Bradley, 1975b).

In the highland zone there was less cohesion. The major trend was towards defence and ostentation without the corresponding development of a settlement hierarchy. Such a variety of sites cannot be examined in detail, but there do seem to be two widespread trends: an orthodox evolution towards defensive arrangements on sites only capable of housing fairly small units; and a tendency for these sites to adopt a fairly regular spacing, often without the emergence of a network of more massive centres. Instead, individual sites developed flamboyant architectural modes of their own, especially in Atlantic Scotland. There are many exceptions to this pattern but the crucial contrast is nowhere clearer than in Ireland. Here it seems that the relatively few hill forts which had begun to develop in the Late Bronze Age had by the post-Roman Age largely given way to a dense distribution of small earthwork homesteads and open sites (cf. Raftery, 1976).

All these developments reached their fullest extent in eastern and south-eastern England. Here, discussion has been bedevilled by the phenomenon of the 'Belgae', an immigrant group of unknown size and importance who are specifically mentioned by Caesar (*Bello Gallico V*, 12; ii, 4). Numerous attempts to give the Belgae archaeological substance have been made by both British scholars and their European colleagues, but these have so far failed (Evans, A., 1890; Hawkes and Dunning, 1931; Allen, 1961; Hawkes, 1968; Harding, D., 1974; Hachmann, 1976; Rodwell, 1976). The close contacts between the Continent and south-eastern England provide a general background. Discussion of the Belgae is based on six major developments, all of which must be carefully kept distinct: the evidence for a cross-channel trade in luxury goods;

the emergence of coinage in Britain; the distinctive burials of the Aylesford-Swarling group; the spread of Fécamp style defences; the appearance of so-called *oppida*, defined by massive linear earthworks; and the settlement of heavier soils.

Some of these features necessarily involve cross-channel contacts, but their relevance to the Belgae is too often assumed without argument. Any 'Belgic' *horizon* seems to be illusory. Stead, following an earlier paper by Birchall (1965), has shown that the Aylesford burials, which do have European counterparts, are post-Caesarian in date (1976). This is sufficient to detach them from the earliest imported coinage, even though its own chronology needs reassessment (cf. Mackensen, 1974). And in southern England the first major port of trade was at Hengistbury Head, which lies outside the 'primary Belgic area' altogether. On the Continent the problem is no easier. It has not been possible to give the Belgae archaeological substance, even though their tribal area can be recognised from Caesar's account (Hachmann, 1976), but on any basis Fécamp defences occur too widely in France to have any relevance to the argument (Ralston and Büchsenschütz, 1975). From Caesar's account it does not appear that the continental Belgae took much interest in commerce, or imported luxuries from the Roman province of Gaul.

There is evidence for fitful trade with Europe throughout the Iron Age. Haselgrove has pointed out that there were at least three areas of cross-channel contact: south-west England, central southern England and the Thames estuary (1976). These contacts may have been made at a time when important economic changes were already affecting the native communities. These insular changes include the specialist production of pottery and weapons, and the interchange of standard units of salt and iron (cf. Bradley, 1975b). It has already been suggested that a regular network of defended settlements had come into being, which perhaps regulated the economies of settlements in the surrounding areas. These regions were the first to feel the impact of cross-channel trade. The early contacts may have been through Hengistbury Head, perhaps following the same networks as earlier salt cakes made on the shoreline. It is perfectly possible that the movement of high-value coinage was only one aspect of social and economic relationships which had already been formed. If so, it may not shed light on the merits of the invasion hypothesis (Collis, 1971b). The basic point has been well made by Avery:

> It is on this infrastructure that British aristocrats and kings of the first century BC built their wealth and were, for the first time for centuries, rich enough materially to emphasise their social superiority by conspicuous consumption. . . . This insular reawakening led to shattering economic and social changes and it seems [unnecessary] . . . to ascribe its causes to Belgic invasions, particularly when . . . the economic organisation on which these developments could be based were already in existence (1974, pp. 61–2).

According to this argument, continental activity was first directed into the increasingly centralised landscape of southern England, a region where rapid changes were creating an elite of rich consumers. The same may be true of eastern England, which eventually became the other major focus of contact. This argument is not easy to elaborate, but it was certainly this region which had shown the closest contacts with the European mainland, and where the richest late Iron Age metalwork has been found. Current work by Dr Mansel Spratling is beginning to suggest a close relationship between the gold coins of this area and other forms of wealth (pers. com.). A recent analysis by Hodder suggests that a number of major sites, including Camulodunum, were regulating cross-channel and regional trade, whilst the hinterland contained a number of minor markets. It is in the *external* relations of these major sites that the main contrast with Wessex is felt; the one exception to this was Hengistbury Head (Hodder, 1977). In eastern England, however, much less is known of earlier settlement. Here two further arguments have been employed to give the Belgae an identity: the movement of settlement onto heavier soils, first claimed by Cyril Fox (1932) and later amplified by Woolridge and Linton (1933), and the development of linear dyke systems. The first point has often been questioned but without compelling justification. Several writers have pointed out that even defended sites could change their preferred location from hilltop to valley-side positions (e.g. Cunliffe, 1976a). In fact most 'hill forts' proper went out of use. The analysis of 250 Iron Age sites in south-east England has confirmed this preference for riverine locations and for heavier and deeper soils (G. Moreland-Smith, pers. com.). The change was of the order of 15 per cent. This need not be related to a major change of population. The progressive expansion of settlement onto more productive soils was a process which had begun in the Middle Bronze Age, and this evidence for further settlement must be judged against a proportion of earlier Iron Age sites on the chalk, which had gone out of use. Although it is not clear whether this marks a phase of over-exploitation, changes of this order are not without precedent.

The great dyke systems, like some smaller but outstandingly rich settlements, have been described as *oppida* (e.g. Rodwell, 1976, pp. 288 ff.). The precise connotations of this term to the classical mind remain a matter of dispute, but in common usage it has usually been taken to denote the presence of two features: a large, possibly proto-urban, community with a political sphere of influence; and a market. In this sense it can only apply to *some* of the great dyke systems, since not all of them included a large settlement. In some cases these earthworks may be simply a device for enclosing large tracts of lowlying ground. The sites discussed in this context have been somewhat arbitrarily chosen. The Chiltern Grims Ditches, which have no obvious political role, have rarely been mentioned, and linear dykes connected with late Iron Age 'multiple settlements', like those in Arundel Park, have also been neglected, even when they lay close to supposed tribal borders (cf. Bradley, 1969; Curwen, E. C., 1929, pp. 126, 136 ff.).

This hesitation is understandable, since the great dyke systems can be only partially correlated with the conventional evidence for 'Belgic'

activity. Furthermore, they have no close counter-parts on the Continent. Linear earthworks, some of them progressively increasing in scale, are a characteristic of the British landscape from the Middle Bronze Age onwards and appear relatively often in areas and periods of stress. Not all the larger examples need be associated with the so-called 'Belgic' settlement. Dyer has argued that the earlier Iron Age Dray's Ditches define a series of regularly spaced territories along the Icknield Way, each dominated by a major hill fort (1961). The Chiltern Grims Ditch equally respected the hill forts of the area, and may even be integrated with one such site, which shows structural similarities to Wheathampstead (Bradley, 1969). A possible outlier of this group was associated with saucepan pots (Hinchcliffe, 1975).

There may be wider precedents for such an arrangement. In Wessex the linear ditches often show a clear increase in scale, and may at times be connected directly with the major hill forts. One well-known example is the linear dyke attached to the entrance of Sidbury. Yarnbury is surrounded by similar earthworks. The second area with large tracts of enclosed land is in Yorkshire, but here again the chronology is imprecise. It is even possible that the earliest dykes at Silchester were connected with an orthodox hill fort (Boon, 1969, pp. 22 ff.).

If these theories are correct, the late Iron Age landscape of south-eastern England can be seen as the natural successor, if not the direct consequence, of preceding developments. A 'Belgic' settlement as such has yet to be proven. But although the elements of the landscape were not radically new, the society which produced them had been transformed. Attracted by the economic wealth of this region, Roman traders exercised a form of economic imperialism over the native inhabitants. As Collis has pointed out, the appearance of bronze and potin coinage suggests a genuine market economy (1971b). The areas which had the greatest economic potential and perhaps the greatest material prosperity were particularly susceptible to Roman innovations, and the inhabitants imitated classical institutions just as they accepted classical imports. Under this stimulus there can be little doubt that the region's centre of gravity was permanently altered, as some of the newly settled areas rose to a dominant position as centres of economic and political power. In Wessex this had been achieved by the modification of an existing pattern, but in those areas of the south-east which had never been dominated by hill forts the structure could be built from the start. The social and economic changes of the century before the Claudian invasion belong to Roman history, but it was in this period that the structure of the modern landscape seems to have been marked out. In highland Britain and in parts of the south, the expansion of Iron Age settlement had perhaps reached its effective limits, but in a landscape where earlier activity had left fewer constraints, a different pattern could appear: a complex network of markets, ports and intermediate settlements. This partially conforms to Central Place Theory but is equally closely related to the urban structure of Roman Britain (Hodder, 1977). With these developments the prehistoric period comes to an end. But the major problem remains: could these changes have taken place without the decisive influence of the classical world?

There is no solution. At the confluence of history and prehistory let us end with a hypothetical question.

Abbreviations

Agric. Hist. Rev.   Agricultural History Review
Amer. Antiq.   American Antiquity
Antiq. Journ.   Antiquaries Journal
Archaeol. Aeliana   Archaeologia Aeliana
Archaeol. Cambrensis   Archaeologia Cambrensis
Archaeol. Cantiana   Archaeologia Cantiana
Archaeol. Journ.   Archaeological Journal
Beds. Archaeol. Journ.   Bedfordshire Archaeological Journal
Berks. Archaeol. Journ.   Berkshire Archaeological Journal
Bull. Inst. Archaeol. Univ. London   Bulletin of the London
    University Institute of Archaeology
CBA   Council for British Archaeology
Cornish Archaeol.   Cornish Archaeology
Current Archaeol.   Current Archaeology
Derbs. Archaeol. Journ.   Derbyshire Archaeological Journal
Glasgow Archaeol. Journ.   Glasgow Archaeological Journal
HMSO   Her/His Majesty's Stationary Office
Herts. Archaeol. Rev.   Hertfordshire Archaeological Review
Int. Journ. Nautical Archaeol.   International Journal of Nautical
    Archaeology
Irish Archaeol. Research Forum   Irish Archaeological Research
    Forum
Journ. Archaeol. Science   Journal of Archaeological Science
Journ. Cork Hist. Archaeol. Soc.   Journal of the Cork
    Historical and Archaeological Society
Journ. Ecol.   Journal of Ecology
Journ. Roy. Inst. Cornwall   Journal of the Royal Institute of
    Cornwall
Journ. Roy. Soc. Antiq. Ireland   Journal of the Royal
    Society of Antiquaries of Ireland
Medieval Archaeol.   Medieval Archaeology
N. Munster Antiq. Journ.   North Munster Antiquarian
    Journal
Northants. Archaeol.   Northamptonshire Archaeology
Phil. Trans. Roy. Soc.   Philosophical Transactions of the Royal
    Society
Proc. Andover Archaeol. Soc.   Proceedings of the Andover
    Archaeological Society
Proc. Cambridge Antiq. Soc.   Proceedings of the Cambridge
    Antiquarian Society
Proc. Devon Archaeol. Exploration Soc.   Proceedings of the
    Devonshire Archaeological Exploration Society
Proc. Dorset Natur. Hist. Archaeol. Soc.   Proceedings of the
    Dorset Natural History and Archaeological Society
Proc. Hants. Field Club   Proceedings of the Hampshire Field
    Club

Proc. Isle of Man Natur. Hist. Antiq. Soc.   Proceedings of
    the Isle of Man Natural History and Antiquarian Society
Proc. Prehist. Soc.   Proceedings of the Prehistoric Society
Proc. Prehist. Soc. E. Anglia   Proceedings of the Prehistoric
    Society of East Anglia
Proc. Roy. Irish Acad.   Proceedings of the Royal Irish Academy
Proc. Roy. Meteorological Soc.   Proceedings of the Royal
    Meteorological Society
Proc. Roy. Soc.   Proceedings of the Royal Society
Proc. Soc. Antiq.   Proceedings of the Society of Antiquaries
Proc. Soc. Antiq. Scotland   Proceedings of the Society of
    Antiquaries of Scotland
Proc. Suffolk Inst. Archaeol.   Proceedings of the Suffolk
    Institute of Archaeology
Proc. Univ. Bristol Spelaeological Soc.   Proceedings of the Bristol
    University Spelaeological Society
Proc. W. Cornwall Field Club   Proceedings of the West
    Cornwall Field Club
RCAM   Royal Commission on Ancient Monuments
RCAHM   Royal Commission on Ancient and Historical
    Monuments
RCHM   Royal Commission on Historical Monuments
Rep. Trans. Devon Ass.   Report and Transactions of the
    Devonshire Association
Scottish Archaeol. Forum   Scottish Archaeological Forum
Surrey Archaeol. Collect.   Surrey Archaeological Collections
Sussex Archaeol. Collect.   Sussex Archaeological Collections
Trans. Bristol and Gloucs. Archaeol. Soc.   Transactions of the
    Bristol and Gloucestershire Archaeological Society
Trans. Cumberland and Westmorland Antiq. Archaeol. Soc.
    Transactions of the Cumberland and Westmorland Antiquarian
    and Archaeological Society
Trans. Dumfriesshire and Galloway Antiq. Soc.   Transactions
    of the Dumfriesshire and Galloway Antiquarian Society
Trans. E. Riding Archaeol. Soc.   Transactions of the East
    Riding Archaeological Society
Trans. Hunter Archaeol. Soc.   Transactions of the Hunter
    Archaeological Society
Trans. Inst. British Geographers   Transactions of the Institute
    of British Geographers
Trans. Woolhope Club   Transactions of the Woolhope Club
UP   University Press
Ulster Journ. Archaeol.   Ulster Journal of Archaeology
Wilts. Archaeol. Mag.   Wiltshire Archaeological Magazine
World Archaeol.   World Archaeology
Yorks. Archaeol. Journ.   Yorkshire Archaeological Journal

Bibliography

Aalen, F. H. A., 1964. Clochans as transhumance dwellings in the Dingle peninsula, Co. Kerry. *Journ. Roy. Soc. Antiq. Ireland,* 94, 39–44.

Addyman, P. V., 1972. The Anglo-Saxon house: a new review. *Anglo-Saxon England* 1, 273–307.

Alcock, L., 1965. Hill forts in Wales and the Marches. *Antiquity* 39, 184–95.

Allen, D. F., 1961. The origins of coinage in Britain: a reappraisal. In Frere, S. S. (ed.) *Problems of the Iron Age in Southern Britain,* 97–308. London: Council for British Archaeology.

Ammerman, A. J. and Cavalli-Sforza, L. L., 1971. Measuring the rate of spread of early farming in Europe. *Man,* new series 6, 674–88.

Anderson, J., 1885. Notice of a bronze cauldron found with several kegs of butter near Kyleakin in Skye. *Proc. Soc. Antiq. Scotland* 19, 309–15.

Anderson, J., 1886. *Scotland in Pagan Times.* Edinburgh: David Douglas.

Apling, H., 1931. Bronze Age settlements in Norfolk. *Proc. Prehist. Soc. E. Anglia* 6, 365–70.

Appelbaum, S., 1954. The agriculture of the British Early Iron Age as exemplified at Figheldean Down, Wiltshire. *Proc. Prehist. Soc.* 20, 103–14.

ApSimon, A. M., 1976. Ballynagilly and the beginning and end of the Irish Neolithic. In De Laet, S. J. (ed.) *Acculturation and Continuity in Atlantic Europe,* 15–30. Bruges: De Tempel.

ApSimon, A. M. and Greenfield, E., 1972. Excavation of the Bronze Age and Iron Age settlement at Trevisker Round, St Eval, Cornwall. *Proc. Prehist. Soc.* 38, 302–81.

Ashbee, P., 1955. Excavations at Hook in Hampshire 1954. *Proc. Hants. Field Club* 19, 70–2.

Ashbee, P., 1960. *The Bronze Age Round Barrow in Britain.* London: Phoenix House.

Ashbee, P., 1963. The Wilsford Shaft. *Antiquity* 37, 116–20.

Ashbee, P., 1974. *Ancient Scilly.* Newton Abbot: David & Charles.

Atherden, M. A., 1976. The impact of late prehistoric cultures on the vegetation of the North York Moors. *Trans. Inst. British Geographers,* new series, 1, 284–300.

Atkinson, R. J. C., 1942. Archaeological sites on Port Meadow, Oxford. *Oxoniensia* 7, 24–35.

Atkinson, R. J. C., 1962. Fishermen and farmers. In Piggott, S. (ed.) *The Prehistoric Peoples of Scotland,* 1–38. London: Routledge & Kegan Paul.

Atkinson, R. J. C., 1965. Wayland's Smithy. *Antiquity* 39, 126–33.

Atkinson, R. J. C., 1968. Old mortality: some aspects of burial and population in Neolithic England. In Coles, J. M. and Simpson, D. D. A. (eds) *Studies in Ancient Europe,* 83–93. Leicester: Leicester UP.

Atkinson, R. J. C., 1972. Demographic Implications. In Fowler, E. (ed.) *Field Survey in British Archaeology,* 60–5. London: Council for British Archaeology.

Avery, M., 1974. Review of Cunliffe 1973. *Irish Archaeol. Research Forum* 1.1, 59–64.

Avery, M., 1976. Hillforts of the British Isles: a student's introduction. In Harding, D. W. (ed.) *Hillforts: Later Prehistoric Earthworks in Britain and Ireland,* 1–58. London: Academic Press.

Baden-Powell, D. and Elton, C., 1937. On the relationship between a raised beach and an Iron Age midden on the island of Lewis, Outer Hebrides. *Proc. Soc. Antiq. Scotland* 71, 347–65.

Bailey, G. N., 1975. The role of molluscs in coastal economies: the results of midden analysis in Australia. *Journ. Archaeol. Science* 2, 45–62.

Balch, H. E., 1914. *Wookey Hole – its Caves and Cave Dwellers.* Oxford: Oxford UP.

Baldwin, J. B., 1974. Seabird fowling in Scotland and Faroe. *Folk Life* 12, 60–103.

Barrett, J., 1976. Deverel-Rimbury: problems of chronology and interpretation. In Burgess, C. and Miket, R. (eds). *Settlement and Economy in the Third and Second Millennia BC,* 289–307. Oxford: British Archaeological Reports.

Barrett, J., Hill, P. and Stevenson, J., 1976. Second millennium BC banks in the Black Moss of Achnacree: some problems of prehistoric land use. In Burgess, C. and Miket, R. (eds) *Settlement and Economy in the Third and Second Millennia BC,* 283–7. Oxford: British Archaeological Reports.

Benton, S., 1931. The excavation of the Sculptor's Cave, Covesea, Morayshire. *Proc. Soc. Antiq. Scotland* 65, 177–216.

Beresford, G., 1974. The medieval manor of Penhallam, Jacobstow, Cornwall. *Medieval Archaeol.* 18, 90–145.

Beresford, M. and Hurst, J. G. (eds), 1971. *Deserted Medieval Villages.* London: Lutterworth Press.

Bersu, G., 1940. Excavations at Little Woodbury, Wiltshire, part 1: the settlement as revealed by excavation. *Proc. Prehist. Soc.* 6, 30–111.

Birchall, A., 1965. The Aylesford-Swarling Culture – the problem of the Belgae reconsidered. *Proc. Prehist. Soc.* 31, 241–367.

Birks, H., 1965. Pollen analytical investigations at Holcroft Moss, Lancashire, and Lindow Moss, Cheshire. *Journ. Ecology* 53, 299–314.

Birks, H. J. B., Deacon, J. and Peglar, S., 1975. Pollen maps for the British Isles 5000 years ago. *Proc. Roy. Soc.* B. 189, 87–106.

Boon, G., 1969. Belgic and Roman Silchester: the excavations of 1954–8, with an excursus on the early history of Calleva. *Archaeologia* 102, 1–82.

Boserup, E., 1965. *The Conditions of Agricultural Growth.* London: Allen & Unwin.

Bowen, E. G. and Gresham, C., 1967. *History of Merioneth, volume 1.* Dolgelly: Merioneth Historical and Record Society.

Bowen, H. C., 1969. The Celtic background. In Rivet, A. L. F. (ed.) *The Roman Villa in Britain,* 1–48. London: Routledge & Kegan Paul.

Bowen, H. C., 1972. Air photography: some implications in the south of England. In Fowler, E. (ed.) *Field Survey in British Archaeology,* 38–49. London: Council for British Archaeology.

Bowen, H. C., 1975. Pattern and interpretation: a view of the Wessex landscape. In Fowler, P. J. (ed.) *Recent Work in Rural Archaeology,* 44–55. Bradford on Avon: Moonraker.

Bowen, H. C. and Fowler, P., 1961. The archaeology of Fyfield and Overton Downs, Wilts. (interim report). *Wilts. Archaeol. Mag.* 58, 98–115.

Boyd Dawkins, W., 1901. On the cairn and sepulchral cave at Gop near Prestatyn. *Archaeol. Journ.* 53, 322–41.

Bradley, R., 1967. Excavations on Portsdown Hill, 1963–5. *Proc. Hants. Field Club* 24, 42–58.

Bradley, R., 1969. The South Oxfordshire Grims Ditch and its significance. *Oxoniensia* 33, 1–13.

Bradley, R., 1970. The excavation of a Beaker settlement at Belle Tout, East Sussex, England. *Proc. Prehist. Soc.* 36, 312–79.

Bradley, R., 1971. Economic change in the growth of early hill forts. In Hill, D. and Jesson, M. (eds) *The Iron Age and its Hill Forts,* 71–83. Southampton: Southampton University Archaeological Society.

Bradley, R., 1972. Prehistorians and pastoralists in Neolithic and Bronze Age England. *World Archaeol.* 4, 192–204.

Bradley, R., 1975a. Maumbury Rings, Dorchester: the excavations of 1908–13. *Archaeologia* 105, 1–97.

Bradley, R., 1975b. Salt and settlement in the Hampshire Sussex borderland. In de Brisay, K. and Evans, K. (eds) *Salt – the Study of an Ancient Industry,* 20–25. Colchester: Colchester Archaeological Group.

Bradley, R., 1977. Colonisation and land use in the late Neolithic and early Bronze Age. In Evans, J. G., Limbrey, S. and Cleere, H. (eds) *The Effect of Man on the Landscape: The Lowland Zone,* 95–103. London: Council for British Archaeology.

Bradley, R., 1978a. Prehistoric field systems in Britain and north west Europe: a review of some recent work. *World Archaeol.* 9, 265–80.

Bradley, R., 1978b. A reconsideration of the Late Neolithic site at Playden, East Sussex. In Pryor, F. *Excavations at Fengate: Second Report.* Toronto: Royal Ontario Museum.

Bradley, R. and Ellison, A., 1975. *Rams Hill – a Bronze Age Defended Enclosure and its Landscape.* Oxford: British Archaeological Reports.

Bradley, R. and Hooper, B., 1974. Recent discoveries from Portsmouth and Langstone Harbours: Mesolithic to Iron Age. *Proc. Hants. Field Club* 30, 17–27.

Bradley, R. and Keith-Lucas, M., 1975. Excavation and pollen analysis on a bell barrow at Ascot, Berkshire. *Journ. Archaeol. Science* 2, 95–108.

Bradley, R. and Lewis, E., 1974. A Mesolithic site at Wakefords Copse, Havant. *Rescue Archaeology in Hampshire* 2, 5–18.

Bradley, R., Over, L., Startin, D. W. A. and Weng, R., 1978. Excavation of a Neolithic site at Cannon Hill, Maidenhead. *Berks. Archaeol. Journ.* 68, 5–19.

Brandon, P., 1974. *The Sussex Landscape.* London: Hodder & Stoughton.

Breeze, D., 1975. Plough marks at Carrawburgh on Hadrian's Wall. *Tools and Tillage* 2, 188–90.

Brewis, P. and Buckley, F., 1928. Notes on prehistoric pottery and a bronze pin from Ross Links, Northumberland. *Archaeol. Aeliana* 4th series, 5, 13–25.

Briggs, C. S., 1976a. Notes on the distribution of some raw materials in later prehistoric Britain. In Burgess, C. and Miket, R. (eds) *Settlement and Economy in the Third and Second Millennia BC,* 267–82. Oxford: British Archaeological Reports.

Briggs, C. S., 1976b. The indigenous minerals and metallurgy of the earliest Irish Bronze Age. *Irish Archaeol. Research Forum* 3.1, 9–13.

Brongers, J. A., 1976. *Air Photography and Celtic Field Research in the Netherlands.* Amersfoort: Nederlandse Oudheiden 6.

Brongers, J. A. and Woltering, P. J., 1973. Prehistory in the Netherlands: an economic-technological approach. *Berichten van de Rijksdienst voor het Oudheidkundig Bodermonderzoek* 23, 7–47.

Brothwell, D. R., 1971. Diet, economy and biosocial change in late prehistoric Europe. In Simpson, D. D. A. (ed.) *Economy and Settlement in Neolithic and Early Bronze Age Britain and Europe,* 75–88. Leicester: Leicester UP.

Brunsting, H., 1962. De sikkels van Heiloo. *Oudheidkundige Mededelingen* 43, 107–115.

Buchanan, R. H., 1973. Field systems of Ireland. In Baker, A. and Butler, R. (eds) *Studies of Field Systems in the British Isles,* 580–618. Cambridge: Cambridge UP.

Buckland, P., 1976. The use of insect remains in the interpretation of archaeological environments. In Davidson, D. and Shackley, M. (eds) *Geoarchaeology,* 369–96. London: Duckworth.

Bulleid, A. and Gray, H. St G., 1917. *The Glastonbury Lake Village,* vol. 2. Glastonbury: Glastonbury Antiquarian Society.

Burgess, C., 1968. *Bronze Age Metalwork in Northern England.* Newcastle-upon-Tyne: Oriel Academic Publications.

Burgess, C., 1974. The Bronze Age. In Renfrew, C. (ed.) *British Prehistory – A New Outline,* 165–232. London: Duckworth.

Burgess, C., 1976a. Britain and Ireland in the third and second millennia BC: a preface. In Burgess, C. and Miket, R. (eds) *Settlement and Economy in the*

Third and Second Millennia BC, i–iii. Oxford:
British Archaeological Reports.

Burgess, C., 1976b. An Early Bronze Age settlement at
Killellan Farm, Islay. In Burgess, C. and Miket, R. (eds),
Settlement and Economy in the Third and Second Millennia BC,
181–207. Oxford: British Archaeological Reports.

Burgess, C., 1976c. Burials with metalwork in the later
Bronze Age in Wales and beyond. In Boon, G. and
Lewis, J. (eds) *Welsh Antiquity,* 81–104. Cardiff:
National Museum of Wales.

Burgess, C., 1976d. The Gwithian mould and the
forerunners of the South Welsh axes. In Burgess, C.
and Miket, R. (eds) *Settlement and Economy in the Third
and Second Millennia BC,* 69–79. Oxford: British
Archaeological Reports.

Burgess, C. and Cowen, J., 1972. The Ebnal Hoard and
Early Bronze Age metalworking traditions. In Burgess, C.
and Lynch, F. (eds) *Early Man in Wales and the West,*
167–181. Bath: Adams & Dart.

Burgess, C. and Shennan, S., 1976. The Beaker
phenomenon: some suggestions. In Burgess, C. and
Miket, R. (eds) *Settlement and Economy in the Third and
Second Millennia BC,* 309–31. Oxford: British
Archaeological Reports.

Burl, A., 1969. Henges: internal features and regional
groups. *Archaeol. Journ.* 126, 1–28.

Burl, A., 1976. *The Stone Circles of the British Isles.* New
Haven: Yale UP.

Burstow, G. P. and Holleyman, G. A., 1957. Late Bronze
Age settlement on Itford Hill, Sussex. *Proc.
Prehist. Soc.* 23, 167–212.

Butzer, K. W., 1972. *Environment and Archaeology* 2nd edn.
London: Methuen.

Calkin, J. B., 1951. The Bournemouth area in Neolithic
and Early Bronze Age times. *Proc. Dorset Natur.
Hist. Archaeol. Soc.* 73, 32–70.

Calkin, J. B., 1962. The Bournemouth area in the Middle
and Late Bronze Age with the 'Deverel-Rimbury'
problem reconsidered. *Archaeol. Journ.* 119, 1–65.

Callendar, J. G., 1932. A collection of prehistoric relics
from the Stevenson Sands, Ayrshire. *Proc. Soc.
Antiq. Scotland* 67, 26–36.

Campbell-Smith, W., 1963. Jade axes from sites in the
British Isles. *Proc. Prehist. Soc.* 29, 133–72.

Carrier, E. H., 1932. *The Pastoral Heritage of Britain.*
London: Christophers.

Case, H. J., 1963. Notes on the finds (from Stanton
Harcourt) and on ring ditches in the Oxford region.
Oxoniensia 28, 19–52.

Case, H. J., 1969. Neolithic explanations. *Antiquity* 43,
176–86.

Case, H. J., 1976. Acculturation and the earlier Neolithic
in Western Europe. In De Laet, S. J. (ed.) *Acculturation
and Continuity in Atlantic Europe,* 45–58. Bruges.
De Tempel.

Case, H. J., 1977. The Beaker Culture in Britain
and Ireland. In Mercer, R. (ed.) *Beakers in
Britain and Europe: Four Studies,* 71–101.
Oxford: British Archaeological Reports.

Case, H. J. *et al.,* 1964. Excavations at City Farm,
Hanborough, Oxon. *Oxoniensia* 29/30, 1–98.

Caulfield, S., 1974. Belderberg prehistoric settlement
and field system. In Delaney, T. (ed.) *Excavations 1974.*
Belfast.

Challis, A. J., 1975. *Later Prehistory from the Trent to
the Tyne.* Oxford: British Archaeological Reports.

Champion, T., 1975. Britain in the European Iron Age.
Archaeologia Atlantica 1(2), 127–45.

Charles-Edwards, T., 1976. Boundaries in Irish law.
In Sawyer, P. (ed.) *Medieval Settlement,* 83–7.
London: Arnold.

Cherry, J., 1963. Eskmeals sand-dunes occupation sites.
Trans. Cumberland and Westmorland Antiq. Archaeol. Soc.
63, 31–52.

Childe, V. G., 1931. *Skara Brae: A Pictish Village in Orkney.*
London: Kegan Paul, Trench & Trubner.

Chisholm, M., 1968. *Rural Settlement and Land Use.* London:
Hutchinson.

Clack, P., 1973. The effect of the Roman Conquest on the
native population of the Tyne-Forth province. *CBA
Regional Group 3 Archaeological News Bulletin* 5, 10–11.

Clark, J. D. G., 1932. A Stone Age site on Swaffham
Prior Farm. *Proc. Cambridge Antiq. Soc.* 32, 17–23.

Clark, J. D. G., 1936. Report on a late Bronze Age site
in Mildenhall Fen, West Suffolk. *Antiq. Journ.* 16,
28–50.

Clark, J. D. G., 1947a. Sheep and swine in the husbandry
of prehistoric Europe. *Antiquity* 21, 122–36.

Clark, J. D. G., 1947b. Whales as an economic factor
in prehistoric Europe. *Antiquity* 21, 84–104.

Clark, J. D. G., 1948a. Fowling in prehistoric Europe.
Antiquity 22, 116–30.

Clark, J. D. G., 1948b. The development of fishing in
prehistoric Europe. *Antiq. Journ.* 28, 45–85.

Clark, J. D. G., 1952. *Prehistoric Europe – The Economic
Basis.* London: Methuen.

Clark, J. D. G., 1954. *Star Carr.* Cambridge: Cambridge
UP.

Clark, J. D. G., 1956. Notes on the Obanian.
Proc. Soc. Antiq. Scotland 89, 91–106.

Clark, J. D. G., 1960. Excavations at the Neolithic site
at Hurst Fen, Mildenhall, Suffolk, 1954, 1957 and
1958. *Proc. Prehist. Soc.* 26, 202–45.

Clark, J. D. G., 1963. Neolithic bows from Somerset,
England, and the prehistory of archery in north-
western Europe. *Proc. Prehist. Soc.* 29, 50–98.

Clark, J. D. G., 1972. *Star Carr – a case study in bioarchaeology.*
Reading, Massachusetts: Addison-Wesley.

Clark, J. D. G. and Godwin, H., 1940. A Late Bronze
Age find near Stuntney, Isle of Ely. *Antiq. Journ.*
20, 52–71.

Clark, J. D. G. and Rankine, W. F., 1939. Excavations at
Farnham, Surrey (1937–38): the Horsham Culture
and the question of Mesolithic dwellings. *Proc.
Prehist. Soc.* 5, 61–118.

Clarke, D. L., 1968. *Analytical Archaeology.* London:
Methuen.

Clarke, D. L., 1969. *The Beaker Pottery of Great Britain
and Ireland.* Cambridge: Cambridge UP.

Clarke, D. L., 1972. A provisional model of an Iron Age
society and its settlement system. In *id.* (ed.)
Models in Archaeology, 801–69. London: Methuen.

Clarke, D. L., 1976a. Mesolithic Europe: the economic
basis. In Sievking, G., Longworth, I., and Wilson,
K. (eds) *Problems in Economic and Social Archaeology,*
449–82. London: Duckworth.

Clarke, D. L., 1976b. The Beaker Network – social
and economic models. In Lanting, J. N. and Van der

Waals, J. D. (eds) *Glockenbecher Symposion*, 459–76. Harlem: Fibula-van-Dishoek.

Clarke, D. V., 1976. Excavations at Skara Brae: a summary account. In Burgess, C. and Miket, R. (eds) *Settlement and Economy in the Third and Second Millennia BC*, 233–50. Oxford: British Archaeological Reports.

Coles, F. R., 1893. The motes, forts and doons in the east and west divisions of the Stewartry of Kirkcudbright. *Proc. Soc. Antiq. Scotland* 27, 92–182.

Coles, J. M., 1964. New aspects of the Mesolithic settlement of south-west Scotland. *Trans. Dumfriesshire and Galloway Antiq. Soc.* 41, 67–98.

Coles, J. M., 1971. The early settlement of Scotland: excavations at Morton, Fife. *Proc. Prehist. Soc.* 37.2, 284–366.

Coles, J. M., 1972. Late Bronze Age activity in the Somerset Levels. *Antiq. Journ.* 52, 269–75.

Coles, J. M., 1973. *Archaeology By Experiment*. London: Hutchinson.

Coles, J. M., 1976. Forest farmers: some archaeological, historical and experimental evidence relating to the prehistory of Europe. In De Laet, S. J. (ed.) *Acculturation and Continuity in Atlantic Europe*, 59–66. Bruges: De Tempel.

Coles, J. M. and Hibbert, A., 1975. The Somerset Levels. In Fowler, P. J. (ed.) *Recent Work in Rural Archaeology*, 12–26. Bradford on Avon: Moonraker Press.

Coles, J. M., Hibbert, F. A. and Orme, B. J., 1973. Prehistoric roads and tracks in Somerset: 3. The Sweet Track. *Proc. Prehist. Soc.* 39, 256–93.

Coles, J. M. and Orme, B., 1976. A Neolithic hurdle from the Somerset Levels. *Antiquity* 50, 57–60.

Coles, J. M. and Taylor, J. J., 1970. The excavation of a midden in the Culbin Sands, Morayshire. *Proc. Soc. Antiq. Scotland* 102, 87–100.

Collier, S. and White, J. P., 1976. Get them young: age and sex inferences on animal domestication in archaeology. *Amer. Antiq.* 41, 96–102.

Collins, A. E. P., 1952. Excavations in the sandhills at Dundrum, Co. Down, 1950–51. *Ulster Journ. Archaeol.* 15, 2–25.

Collins, A. E. P., 1959. Further investigations in the Dundrum sandhills. *Ulster Journ. Archaeol.* 22, 5–20.

Collis, J., 1971a. Excavations at Owslebury, Hants.: a second interim report. *Antiq. Journ.* 50, 246–61.

Collis, J., 1971b. Functional and theoretical interpretations of British coinage. *World Archaeol.* 3, 71–84.

Conklin, H., 1957. *Hanunóo Agriculture*. Rome: Food and Agriculture Organisation of the United Nations.

Coombs, D., 1975. Bronze Age weapon hoards in Britain. *Archaeologia Atlantica* 1.1, 49–81.

Coppock, J. T., 1964. *An Agricultural Atlas of England and Wales*. London: Faber.

Cowling, E. T., 1946. *Rombalds Way*. Otley: William Walker.

Crampton, C. B., 1966. Hafotai platforms on the north front of the Brecon Beacons. *Archaeol. Cambrensis* 115, 99–107.

Crampton, C. B., 1968. Hafotai platforms on the north front of Carmarthen Fen. *Archaeol. Cambrensis* 117, 121–6.

Crawford, O. G. S., 1936. The work of giants. *Antiquity* 10, 162–74.

Cross, M., 1938. A prehistoric settlement on Walney Island. *Trans. Cumberland and Westmorland Antiq. Archaeol. Soc.* 38, 160–3.

Cross, M., 1939. A prehistoric settlement on Walney Island, Part II. *Trans. Cumberland and Westmorland Antiq. Archaeol. Soc.* 39, 262–82.

Cross, M., 1946. A prehistoric settlement on Walney Island, Part IV. *Trans. Cumberland and Westmorland Antiq. Archaeol. Soc.* 46, 67–76.

Cross, M., 1949. A prehistoric settlement on Walney Island, Part VI. *Trans. Cumberland and Westmorland Antiq. Archaeol. Soc.* 49, 1–9.

Cubbon, A. M., 1964. Clay Head cooking place sites. *Proc. Isle of Man Natur. Hist. Antiq. Soc.* 6, 566–96.

Cunliffe, B. W., 1973. Chalton, Hants.: the evolution of a landscape. *Antiq. Journ.* 53, 173–90.

Cunliffe, B. W., 1974. *Iron Age Communities in Britain*. London: Routledge & Kegan Paul.

Cunliffe, B. W., 1976a. The origins of urbanisation in Britain. In Cunliffe, B. W. and Rowley, R. T. (eds) *Oppida in Barbarian Europe*, 135–61. Oxford: British Archaeological Reports.

Cunliffe, B. W., 1976b. *Iron Age Sites in Central Southern England*. London: Council for British Archaeology.

Cunliffe, B. W., 1976c. Hill forts and oppida in Britain. In Sievking, G., Longworth, I. and Wilson, K. (eds) *Problems in Economic and Social Archaeology*, 343–58. London: Duckworth.

Cunliffe, B. and Phillipson, D. W., 1968. Excavations at Eldon's Seat, Encombe, Dorset. *Proc. Prehist. Soc.* 34, 191–237.

Cunnington, M. E., 1929. *Woodhenge*. Devizes: Simpson.

Cunnington, M. E. and B. H., 1913. Casterley Camp excavations. *Wilts. Archaeol. Mag.* 38, 53–105.

Curle, A., 1948. The 'wag' at Forse, Caithness: excavations of 1947–8. *Proc. Soc. Antiq. Scotland* 82, 275–83.

Curwen, E., 1936. On Sussex flint arrow-heads. *Sussex Archaeol. Collect.* 77, 15–26.

Curwen, E., 1939. Blunted axe-like implements. *Proc. Prehist. Soc.* 5, 196–201.

Curwen, E. C., 1929. *Prehistoric Sussex*. London: The Homeland Association.

Curwen, E. C., 1954. *The Archaeology of Sussex*. 2nd ed. London: Methuen.

Dacre, M., 1970. Kimpton excavations. *Proc. Andover Archaeol. Soc.* 4, 13–18.

Davey, P., 1971. The distribution of later Bronze Age metalwork in Lincolnshire. *Proc. Prehist. Soc.* 37(1), 96–111.

David, N., 1971. The Fulani compound and the archaeologist. *World Archaeol.* 3, 111–31.

Davies, E., 1949. *The Prehistoric and Roman Remains of Flintshire*. Cardiff: William Lewis.

Davies, O., 1950. *Excavations at Island MacHugh*. Belfast: Belfast Natural History and Philosophical Society.

Dennell, R., 1972. The interpretation of plant remains: Bulgaria. In Higgs, E. S. (ed.) *Papers in Economic Prehistory*, 149–60. Cambridge: Cambridge UP.

Dennell, R., 1976. Prehistoric crop cultivation in southern England: a reconsideration. *Antiq. Journ.* 56, 11–23.

Dieck, A., 1961. Die Moorleiche vom Gunzer See bei Straslund vom Sommer 1879 und das Problem der Moorbutter. *Greifswald-Straslunder Jahrbuch* 1, 26–39.

Dimbleby, G. W., 1954. Pollen analysis as an aid to the dating of prehistoric monuments. *Proc. Prehist. Soc.* 20, 231–6.

Dimbleby, G. W. and Bradley, R. J., 1975. Evidence of pedogenesis from a Neolithic site at Rackham, Sussex. *Journ. Archaeol. Science* 2, 179–86.

Dimbleby, G. W. and Evans, J. F., 1974. Pollen and land snail analysis of calcareous soils. *Journ. Archaeol. Science* 1, 117–33.

Dimbleby, G. W. and Simmons, I. G., 1974. The possible role of Ivy *(Hedera Helix L)* in the Mesolithic economy of Western Europe. *Journ. Archaeol. Science* 1, 291–6.

Dixon, P., 1976. Crickley Hill, 1969–72. In Harding, D. W. (ed.) *Hillforts – Later Prehistoric Earthworks in the British Isles,* 162–75. London: Academic Press.

Drewett, P. L., 1970. The excavation of two round barrows and associated fieldwork on Ashley Down, Isle of Wight, 1969. *Proc. Hants. Field Club* 27, 33–56.

Drury, P., 1973. Little Waltham. *Current Archaeol.* 36, 10–13.

Dunn, C. J., 1975. Ring ditches in the Derwent Valley. *Annual Report of the Yorkshire Philosophical Society* (1975), 60–5.

Dyer, J., 1961. Dray's Ditches, Bedfordshire, and Early Iron Age territorial boundaries in the eastern Chilterns. *Antiq. Journ.* 42, 44–62.

Ehrenberg, M., 1977. *Bronze Age Spearheads from Berkshire, Buckinghamshire and Oxfordshire.* Oxford: British Archaeological Reports.

Ellison, A. and Drewett, P., 1971. Pits and post holes in the British Early Iron Age: some alternative explanations. *Proc. Prehist. Soc.* 37 (i), 183–94.

Ellison, A. and Harriss, J., 1972. Settlement and land use in the prehistory and early history of southern England: a study based on locational models. In Clarke, D. L. (ed.) *Models in Archaeology,* 911–62. London: Methuen.

Eogan, G., 1974. Regionale Gruppierungen in der Spätbronzezeit Irlands. *Archäologisches Korrespondenzblatt* 4, 319–27.

Evans, A. J., 1890. On a Late Celtic Urnfield at Aylesford, Kent. *Archaeologia* 52, 369–74.

Evans, E. E., 1975. Highland landscapes: habitat and heritage. In Evans, J. G., Limbrey, S. and Cleere, H. (eds) *The Effect of Man on the Landscape: The Highland Zone,* 1–5. London: Council for British Archaeology.

Evans, J. G., 1969. The Exploitation of molluscs. In Ucko, P. and Dimbleby, G. W. (eds) *The Domestication of Plants and Animals,* 479–84. London: Duckworth.

Evans, J. G., 1971a. Habitat change in the calcareous soils of Britain: the impact of Neolithic man. In Simpson, D. D. A. (ed.) *Economy and Settlement in Neolithic and Early Bronze Age Britain and Europe,* 27–74. Leicester: Leicester UP.

Evans, J. G., 1971b. Notes on the environment of early farming communities in Britain. In Simpson, D. D. A. (ed.) *Economy and Settlement in Neolithic and Early Bronze Age Britain and Europe,* 11–26. Leicester: Leicester UP.

Evans, J. G., 1972. *Land Snails in Archaeology.* London: Seminar Press.

Evans, J. G., 1975. *The Environment of Early Man in the British Isles.* London: Elek.

Evans, J. G. and Valentine, K. W. G., 1974. Ecological changes induced by prehistoric man at Pitstone, Buckinghamshire. *Journ. Archaeol. Science* 1, 343–52.

Evett, D., 1973. Early farming in Europe. *Man,* new series 8, 475–6.

Fahy, E. M., 1960. A hut and cooking places at Dromberg, Co. Cork. *Journ. Cork Hist. Archaeol. Soc.* 62, 65–76.

Fairhurst, H., 1971. The wheelhouse site at Cheardach Bheag, on Drimore machair, South Uist. *Glasgow Archaeol. Journ.* 2, 72–106.

Fairhurst, H. and Taylor D., 1971. A hut-circle settlement at Kilphedir, Sutherland. *Proc. Soc. Antiq. Scotland* 103, 65–99.

Feachem, R., 1960. The palisaded settlements at Harehope, Peeblesshire. Excavations 1960. *Proc. Soc. Antiq. Scotland* 93, 174–91.

Feachem, R., 1973. Ancient agriculture in the highland of Britain, *Proc. Prehist. Soc.* 39, 332–53.

Fenton, A., 1963. Early and traditional cultivating implements in Scotland. *Proc. Soc. Antiq. Scotland* 96, 264–317.

Fenton, A., 1976. Traditional Elements in the Diet of the Northern Isles of Scotland. Reprinted from *The Second International Symposium for Ethnological Food Research,* Helsinki 1973. Lerwick: The Shetland Times.

Field, N. H., Mathews, C. L. and Smith, I. F., 1964. New Neolithic sites in Dorset and Bedfordshire with a note on the distribution of Neolithic storage pits in Britain. *Proc. Prehist. Soc.* 30, 352–81.

Fisher, J. and Lockley, R., 1954. *Sea Birds.* London: Collins.

Flanagan, L., 1962. Flint hollow scrapers and the Irish Neolithic. *Atti del VI Congresso Internazionale delle Scienze Preistoriche e Protostoriche, 2: Comunicazioni sezioni 1–4,* pp. 323–8. Florence: Sansoni Editore.

Fleming, A., 1971a. Bronze Age agriculture on the marginal lands of north-east Yorkshire. *Agric. Hist. Rev.* 19, 1–24.

Fleming, A., 1971b. Territorial patterns in Bronze Age Wessex. *Proc. Prehist. Soc.* 37 (i), 138–66.

Fleming, A., 1972a. The genesis of pastoralism in European prehistory. *World Archaeol.* 4, 179–91.

Fleming, A., 1972b. Vision and design: approaches to ceremonial monument typology. *Man,* new series 7, 57–73.

Fleming, A., 1976. Early settlement and landscape in West Yorkshire. In Sievking, G., Longworth, I. and Wilson, K. (eds) *Problems in Economic and Social Archaeology,* 359–73. London: Duckworth.

Fleming, A., 1977. The Dartmoor reaves. *Current Archaeol.* 55, 250–2.

Forde-Johnston, J., 1976. *Hillforts of the Iron Age in England and Wales.* Liverpool: Liverpool UP.

Foster, J., 1977. *Bronze Boar Figurines in Iron Age and Roman Britain.* Oxford: British Archaeological Reports.

Fowler, P. J., 1967. The archaeology of Fyfield and Overton Downs, Wiltshire: third interim report. *Wilts. Archaeol. Mag.* 62, 16–33.

Fowler, P. J., 1971. Early prehistoric agriculture in western Europe: some archaeological evidence. In Simpson, D. D. A. (ed.) *Economy and Settlement in Neolithic and Early Bronze Age Britain and Europe,* 153–182. Leicester: Leicester UP.

Fowler, P. J., 1975. Paper to CBA Conference, December 1975, *The Effect of Man on the Landscape – the Lowland Zone.*

Fowler, P. J. and Evans, J. G., 1967. Plough marks, lynchets and early fields. *Antiquity* 41, 289–301.

Fox, A., 1954. Celtic fields and farms on Dartmoor. *Proc. Prehist. Soc.* 20, 87–102.

Fox, A., 1961. South western hillforts. In Frere, S. S. (ed.) *Problems of the Iron Age in Southern Britain*, 35–60. London: Council for British Archaeology.

Fox, A., 1964. *South West England*. London: Thames & Hudson.

Fox, A., 1973. *South West England 3500 BC – AD 600*. Newton Abbot: David & Charles.

Fox, C., 1927. An Early Iron Age settlement on Methyr Mawr Warren, Glamorgan. *Archaeol. Cambrensis*, 7th series, 7, 44–66.

Fox, C., 1932. *The Personality of Britain*. Cardiff: National Museum of Wales.

Fox, C., 1939. The socketed bronze sickles of the British Isles. *Proc. Prehist. Soc.* 5, 222–48.

Fox, C., 1959. *Life and Death in the Bronze Age*. London: Routledge & Kegan Paul.

Fox, C. F., 1928. A Bronze Age refuse pit at Swanwick, Hants. *Antiq. Journ.* 8, 331–6.

Fox, C. F., 1930. The Bronze Age pit at Swanwick, Hants: further finds. *Antiq. Journ.* 10, 30–3.

Francis, A. G., 1931. A West Alpine and Hallstatt site at Southchurch, Essex. *Antiq. Journ.* 11, 410–18.

Frenzel, B., 1966. Climatic change at the Atlantic/Sub Boreal transition in the northern hemisphere. *Proc. Roy. Meteorological Soc.* 99.

Froom, F. R., 1972. A Mesolithic site at Wawcott, Kintbury. *Berks. Archaeol. Journ.* 66, 23–44.

Gabel, C., 1976. St Catherine's Hill: a Mesolithic site near Guildford. *Research Volume of the Surrey Archaeological Society* 3, 77–102.

Gailey, A. and Fenton, A. (eds), 1970. *The Spade in Northern and Atlantic Europe*. Belfast: Institute of Irish Studies.

Gardner, K. S., 1972. *Lundy – an Archaeological Field Guide*. Landmark Trust.

Gelling, P. S., 1963. Excavations at the hill fort on South Barrule. *Proc. Isle of Man Nat. Hist. Antiq. Soc.* 6, 313–23.

Gerloff, S., 1975. *The Early Bronze Age Daggers in Great Britain*. Prähistorische Bronzefunde 6, 2. Munich.

Gibson, A., 1972. A Mesolithic site at Stanstead Abbots. *Herts. Archaeol. Rev.* 5, 96–7.

Gilchrist-Shirlaw, D. W., 1966. *An Agricultural Geography of Great Britain*. Oxford: Pergamon.

Gilks, J. A., 1973. The Neolithic and Early Bronze Age pottery from Elbolton Cave, Wharfedale. *Yorks. Archaeol. Journ.* 45, 41–54.

Godwin, H., 1968. Organic deposits at Old Buckenham Mere, Norfolk. *New Phytologist* 67, 95–107.

Godwin, H., 1975. *The History of the British Flora*. 2nd edn. Cambridge: Cambridge UP.

Godwin, H. and Clifford, M., 1938. Studies of the post-glacial history of British vegetation, part 1. *Phil. Trans. Roy. Soc.* B 229, 323.

Graham, A., 1956. Cairnfields in Scotland. *Proc. Soc. Antiq. Scotland* 90, 7–23.

Gray, H. St G. and Bulleid, A., 1953. *The Meare Lake Village* volume 2. Taunton: privately printed.

Gray, M., 1974. The Devil's Quoits, Stanton Harcourt, Oxon. *Oxoniensia* 39, 96–7.

Green, C., 1971. Interim report on excavations at Poundbury, Dorchester, 1971. *Proc. Dorset Natur. Hist. Archaeol. Soc.* 93, 154–6.

Green, H. S., 1974. Early Bronze Age territory and population in Milton Keynes, Buckinghamshire, and the Great Ouse Valley. *Archaeol. Journ.* 131, 75–139.

Green, H. S., 1976. The excavation of a late Neolithic settlement at Stacey Bushes, Milton Keynes, and its significance. In Burgess, C. and Miket, R. (eds) *Settlement and Economy in the Third and Second Millennia BC*, 11–27. Oxford: British Archaeological Reports.

Greenfield, E., 1960. The excavation of Barrow 4 at Swarkestone, Derbyshire. *Derbs. Archaeol. Journ.* 80, 1–48.

Greenwell, W., 1894. Antiquities of the Bronze Age found in the Heathery Burn Cave, County Durham. *Archaeologia* 54, 87–114.

Greig, A. and Rankine, W. F., 1953. A Stone Age settlement system near East Week, Dartmoor: Mesolithic and Post-Mesolithic industries. *Proc. Devon. Archaeol. Exploration Soc.* 5, 8–26.

Gresham, C., 1963. The interpretation of settlement patterns in north west Wales. In Foster, I.Ll. and Alcock, L. (eds) *Culture and Environment*, 263–80. London: Routledge & Kegan Paul.

Griffiths, W. E., 1950. Early settlements in Caernarvonshire. *Archaeol. Cambrensis* 101, 38–71.

Grimes, W. F., 1932. Surface flint industries around Solva, Pembrokeshire. *Archaeol. Cambrensis* 87, 179–92.

Grinsell, L. V., 1964. The Royce Collection at Stow-on-the-Wold. *Trans. Bristol and Gloucs. Archaeol. Soc.* 83, 5–33.

Grinsell, L. V. and Janes, D., 1966. The Royce Collection of Cotswold antiquities: supplement. *Trans. Bristol and Gloucs. Archaeol. Soc.* 85, 209–13.

Groenman-van-Waateringe, W., 1968. The Elm Decline and the first appearance of Plantago maior. *Vegetatio* 15, 292–6.

Groenman-van-Waateringe, W., 1972. Hecken im westeurropäischen Frühneolithikum. *Bericht van de Ryjkdienst Oudkeidkundig Bodemonderzoek* 20/21, 295–9.

Groenman-van-Waateringe, W. and Regteren-Altena, J. F. van, 1961. Een vuurstenen sikkel uit de Voor-Romeinse ijzertijd te den haag. *Helinium* 1, 141–6.

Grundy, J. E., 1970. Notes on the relationship between climate and cattle housing. *Vernacular Architecture*, 1, 2–5.

Guilbert, G., 1975. Planned hill fort interiors. *Proc. Prehist. Soc.* 41, 203–21.

Hachmann, R., 1976. The problem of Belgae seen from the Continent. *Bull. Inst. Archaeol. Univ. London* 13, 117–37.

Hall, D. N., 1972. Modern surveys of medieval field systems. *Beds. Archaeol. Journ.* 7, 53–66.

Hall, D. N. and Hutchings, J. B., 1972. The distribution of archaeological sites between the Nene and the Ouse valleys. *Beds. Archaeol. Journ.* 7, 1–16.

Hallam, J. S., Edwards, B. J. N., Barnes, B. and Stuart, A. J., 1973. A Late Glacial elk with associated barbed points from High Furlong, Lancashire. *Proc. Prehist. Soc.* 39, 100–28.

Hamilton, J. R. C., 1956. *Excavations at Jarlshof, Shetland*. Edinburgh: HMSO.

Harding, A., 1976. Bronze agricultural implements in Bronze Age Europe. In Sievking, G., Longworth, I. and

Wilson, K. (eds) *Problems in Economic and Social Archaeology*, 513–22. London: Duckworth.

Harding, D. W., 1974. *The Iron Age in Lowland Britain*. London: Routledge & Kegan Paul.

Harding, J., 1964. Interim report on the excavation of a Late Bronze Age homestead in Weston Wood, Albury, Surrey. *Surrey Archaeol. Collect.* 61, 10–17.

Harvey, J. C., Morgan, R. and Webley, D. P., 1967. Tooth Cave, Ilston, Gower: an Early Bronze Age occupation. Part I. *Bulletin of the Board of Celtic Studies* 22, 277–85.

Haselgrove, C., 1976. External trade as a stimulus to urbanisation. In Cunliffe, B. W. and Rowley, R. T. (eds) *Oppida in Barbarian Europe*, 25–49. Oxford: British Archaeological Reports.

Hastings, F. A., 1965. Excavation of an Iron Age farmstead at Hawk's Hill, Leatherhead. *Surrey Archaeol. Collect.* 62, 1–43.

Hawkes, C., 1968. New thoughts on the Belgae. *Antiquity*, 42, 6–16.

Hawkes, C. and Dunning, G., 1931. The Belgae of Gaul and Britain. *Archaeol. Journ.* 87, 150–335.

Hedges, J., 1975. Excavation of two Orcadian burnt mounds at Liddle and Beaquoy. *Proc. Soc. Antiq. Scotland* 106, 39–98.

Helbaek, H., 1952. Early crops in southern England. *Proc. Prehist. Soc.* 18, 194–233.

Hemp, W. and Gresham, C., 1953. Hut-circles in north-west Wales. *Antiquity* 27, 29–31.

Hencken, H. O'N., 1938. *Cahercommaum: A Stone Fort in County Clare*. Dublin: Royal Society of Antiquaries of Ireland.

Hencken, H. O'N., 1942. Balinderry crannog no. 2. *Proc. Roy. Irish Acad.* C 47, 1–76.

Henshall, A., 1950. Textiles and weaving appliances in prehistoric Britain. *Proc. Prehist. Soc.* 16, 130–62.

Herity, M., 1974. *Irish Passage Graves*. Dublin: Irish UP.

Herity, M. and Eogan, G., 1976. *Ireland in Prehistory*. London: Routledge & Kegan Paul.

Hewer, T. F., 1925. Second report on excavations in the Wye Valley. *Proc. Univ. Bristol Spelaeological Soc.* 2, 216–28.

Hewson, L. M., 1935. Notes on Irish sandhills. *Journ. Roy. Soc. Antiq. Ireland* 65, 231–44.

Higgs, E. S. and White, J. P., 1963. Autumn killing. *Antiquity* 37, 282–9.

Higham, N. J. and Jones, G. D. B., 1975. Frontier, forts and farmers: Cumbrian aerial survey 1974–5. *Archaeol. Journ.* 132, 16–53.

Hillam, J., 1976. The dating of Cullyhanna hunting lodge. *Irish Archaeol. Research Forum* 3 (i), 17–20.

Hinchcliffe, J., 1975. Excavations at Grims Ditch, Mongewell, 1975. *Oxoniensia* 40, 122–35.

Hodder, I., 1974. Regression analysis of some trade and marketing patterns. *World Archaeol.* 6, 172–89.

Hodder, I., 1977. Some new directions in the spatial analysis of archaeological data at the regional scale. In Clarke, D. L. (ed.) *Spatial Archaeology*, 223–351. London: Academic Press.

Hodder, I. and Orton, C., 1976. *Spatial Analysis in Archaeology*. Cambridge: Cambridge UP.

Hodges, H., 1955. The excavation of a group of cooking places at Ballycroghan, Co. Down. *Ulster Journ. Archaeol.* 18, 17–28.

Hodges, H., 1958. A hunting camp at Cullyhanna Lough. *Ulster Journ. Archaeol.* 21, 7–13.

Hodgson, G. W. I., 1968. A comparative account of the animal remains from Corstopitum and the Iron Age site of Catcote near Hartlepools, County Durham. *Archaeol. Aeliana* 46, 127–62.

Hogg, A. H. A., 1962. Garn Boduan and Tre'r Ceiri, excavations at two Caernarvonshire hill forts, *Archaeol. Journ.* 117, 1–39.

Hogg, A. H. A., 1971. Some applications of surface fieldwork. In Hill, D. and Jesson, M. (eds) *The Iron Age and its Hill Forts*, 105–25. Southampton: Southampton University Archaeological Society.

Hogg, A. H. A., 1972. The size distribution of hill forts in Wales and the Marches. In Burgess, C. and Lynch, F. (eds) *Early Man in Wales and the West*, 293–306. Bath: Adams & Dart.

Hogg, A. H. A., 1975. *Hill Forts of Britain*. London: Hart-Davis MacGibbon.

Hogg, A. H. A. and N., 1956. Doddington and Horton Moors. *Archaeol. Aeliana* 34, 142–9.

Holden, E. W. and Bradley, R. J., 1975. A late Neolithic site at Rackham. *Sussex Archaeol. Collect.* 113, 85–103.

Holleyman, G., 1937. Harrow Hill excavations, 1936. *Sussex Archaeol. Collect.* 78, 230–51.

Houlder, C., 1968. The henge monuments at Llandegai. *Antiquity* 42, 216–21.

Hubbard, R., 1975. Assessing the botanical component of human palaeo-economies. *Bull. Inst. Archaeol. Univ. London* 12, 197–205.

Hubbard, R., 1976. Crops and climate in prehistoric Europe. *World Archaeol.* 8, 159–68.

Hudson, J. C., 1969. A location theory for rural settlement. *Annals of the Association of American Geographers* 59, 365–81.

Isaac, G., 1967. Towards the interpretation of occupation debris: some experiments and observations. *Kroeber Anthropological Society Papers* 37, 31–54.

Iversen, J., 1941. Landnam i Danmarks Stenalder. *Danmarks Geol. Undersgelse.*

Iversen, J., 1956. Forest clearance in the Stone Age. *Scientific American* 194, 36–41.

Jackson, D., 1975. An Iron Age site at Twywell, Northamptonshire. *Northants. Archaeol.* 10, 31–93.

Jackson, D., 1976. The excavation of Neolithic and Bronze Age sites at Aldwincle, Northants, 1967–71. *Northants. Archaeol.* 11, 12–70.

Jacobi, R., 1973. Aspects of the 'Mesolithic Age' in Britain. In Kozlowski, S. K. (ed.) *The Mesolithic in Europe*, 237–65. Warsaw: Warsaw UP.

Jacobi, R., 1976. Britain inside and outside Mesolithic Europe. *Proc. Prehist. Soc.* 42, 67–84.

Jacobi, R., Tallis, J. and Mellars, P., 1976. The Southern Pennine Mesolithic and the archaeological record. *Journ. Archaeol. Science* 3, 307–20.

Jardine, W. and Morrison, A., 1976. The archaeological significance of Holocene coastal deposits in south-western Scotland. In Davidson, D. and Shackley, M. (eds) *Geoarchaeology*, 175–195. London: Duckworth.

Jarman, M., 1972. European deer economies and the advent of the Neolithic. In Higgs, E. S. (ed.) *Papers in Economic Prehistory*, 125–47. Cambridge: Cambridge UP.

Jessen, K. and Helbaek, H., 1944. *Cereals in Great Britain and Ireland in Prehistoric and Early Historic Times.*

Copenhagen: 1 Kommission Hos Ejnar Munksgaard.

Jewell, P., 1963. *Cattle from British Archaeological Sites*. Royal Anthropological Institute of Great Britain occasional paper no. 18, 80–101.

Jobey, G., 1965. Hillforts and settlements in Northumberland. *Archaeol. Aeliana* 43, 21–64.

Jobey, G., 1966. Excavation on palisaded settlements and cairnfields at Alnham, Northumberland. *Archaeol. Aeliana* 44, 5–48.

Jobey, G., 1968. Excavations of cairns at Chatton Sandyford, Northumberland. *Archaeol. Aeliana* 46, 5–50.

Jobey, G., 1970. An Iron Age settlement and homestead at Burradon, Northumberland. *Archaeol. Aeliana* 48, 51–96.

Jobey, G., 1973. A native settlement at Hartburn and the Devil's Causeway, Northumberland, 1971. *Archaeol. Aeliana* 5th series, 1, 11–54.

Jobey, G., 1974. Notes on some population problems in the area between the two Roman walls. *Archaeol. Aeliana*, 5th series 2, 17–26.

Jobey, G., 1976. Traprain Law: a summary. In Harding, D. W. (ed.) *Hillforts – Later Prehistoric Earthworks in Britain and Ireland*, 192–204. London: Academic Press.

Jochim, M., 1975. *Hunter Gatherer Subsistence: A Predictive Model*. New York: Academic Press.

Kelley, T., 1967. A series of late Middle Bronze Age sites, Wilde Street, Mildenhall. *Proc. Suffolk Inst. Archaeol.* 31, 47–56.

Kelly, J. H., 1976. *The Excavations of Wetton Mill Rock Shelter, Manifold Valley, Staffs*. Stoke on Trent: Stoke on Trent City Museum.

Kerney, M. P., Brown, E. H. and Chandler, T. J., 1964. The late-glacial and post-glacial history of the chalk escarpment near Brook, Kent. *Phil. Trans. Roy. Soc.* B 248, 135–204.

Kinnes, I., 1976. The Barnack grave-group. *Durobrivae* 4, 16–17.

Kirk, S. M., 1974. High altitude cereal growing in County Down, Northern Ireland? A note. *Ulster Journ. Archaeol.* 36/37, 99–100.

Lacaille, A. D., 1937. A stone industry, potsherds and a bronze pin from Valtos, Uig, Lewis. *Proc. Soc. Antiq. Scotland* 71, 279–96.

Lacaille, A. D., 1954. *The Stone Age in Scotland*. Oxford: Oxford UP. for the Wellcome Historical Medical Museum.

Lamb, R. G., 1974. Sunburgh multi-period occupation site. *Discovery and Excavation in Scotland* 1974, 87–8.

Langmaid, N., 1971. Norton Fitzwarren. *Current Archaeol.* 28, 116–20.

Leach, E., 1976. A view from the bridge. In Spriggs, M. (ed.) *Archaeology and Anthropology*, 161–76. Oxford: British Archaeological Reports.

Leaf, C. S., 1935. Report on the excavation of two sites in Mildenhall Fen. *Proc. Cambridge Antiq. Soc.* 35, 106–27.

Lee, R. G., 1968. What hunters do for a living, or how to make out on scarce resources. In Lee, R. B. and Devore, I. (eds) *Man the Hunter*. Chicago: Aldine.

Leeds, E. T., 1934. Recent Bronze Age discoveries in Berkshire and Oxfordshire. *Antiq. Journ.* 14, 264–76.

Leeds, E. T., 1938. Beakers of the Upper Thames district. *Oxoniensia* 3, 7–30.

Lethbridge, T. C., 1934. Investigation of the ancient causeway in the fen between Fordy and Little Thetford, Cambridgeshire. *Proc. Cambridge Antiq. Soc.* 35, 86–9.

Limbrey, S., 1975. *Soil Science and Archaeology*. London: Academic Press.

Lindquist, S-O., 1974. The development of the agrarian landscape on Gotland during the Early Iron Age. *Norwegian Archaeological Review* 7, 6–32.

Liversage, G. D., 1958. An island site at Lough Gur. *Journ. Roy. Soc. Antiq. Ireland* 88, 67–81.

Liversage, G. D., 1968. Excavations at Dalkey Island, Co. Dublin, 1956–1959. *Proc. Roy. Irish Academy* C, 66, 53–231.

Lomas, J., 1962. A Bronze Age site at Parwich. *Derbs. Archaeol. Journ.* 82, 90–9.

Longley, D., 1976. Excavation of the site of a Late Bronze Age settlement at Runnymede Bridge, Egham. *London Archaeologist* 3.1, 10–17.

Lynch, F., 1975a. The impact of landscape on prehistoric man. In Evans, J. G., Limbrey, S. and Cleere, H. (eds) *The Effect of Man on the Landscape: The Highland Zone*, 124–7. London: Council for British Archaeology.

Lynch, F., 1975b. Excavations at Cerreg Samson megalithic tomb, Mathry, Pembrokeshire. *Archaeol. Cambrensis* 124, 15–35.

McGrail, S., 1976. Problems in Irish nautical archaeology. *Irish Archaeol. Research Forum* 3 (i), 21–31.

McGrail, S. and Switsur, R., 1975. Early British boats and their chronology. *Int. Journ. Nautical Archaeol.* 4, 191–200.

McGregor, A., 1974. The Broch of Burrian, North Ronaldsay, Orkney. *Proc. Soc. Antiq. Scotland* 105, 63–118.

McGregor, M. and Simpson, D. D. A., 1963. A group of iron objects from Barbury Castle, Wilts. *Wilts. Archaeol. Mag.* 58, 394–402.

McInnes, I., 1964. The Neolithic and Early Bronze Age pottery from Luce Sands, Wigtownshire. *Proc. Soc. Antiq. Scotland* 97, 40–81.

McInnes, I., 1971. Settlements in later Neolithic Britain. In Simpson, D. D. A. (ed.) *Economy and Settlement in Neolithic and Early Bronze Age Britain and Europe*, 113–30. Leicester: Leicester UP.

Mackensen, M., 1974. Die älteste keltische Gold und Silberprägung in England. *Jahrbuch Numismatik und Geldgeschichte* 24, 7–63.

McKie, E. W., 1965. The origin and development of the broch and wheelhouse building cultures of the Scottish Iron Age. *Proc. Prehist. Soc.* 31, 93–146.

McKie, E., 1972a. Continuity in Iron Age fort building traditions in Caithness. In Meldrum, E. (ed.) *The Dark Ages in the Highlands*, 5–23. Inverness: Inverness Field Club.

McKie, E. W., 1972b. Radiocarbon dates for two Mesolithic shell heaps and a Neolithic axe-factory in Scotland. *Proc. Prehist. Soc.* 38, 412–16.

McKie, E. W., 1974. *Dun Mor Vaul – an Iron Age Broch on Tiree*. Glasgow: Glasgow UP.

McKie, E. W., 1977. *Science and Society in Prehistoric Britain*. London: Elek.

Machin, M., 1971. Further excavation at Swine Sty, Big Moor, Baslow. *Trans. Hunter Archaeol. Soc.* 10 (1), 5–13.

Mahr, A., 1937. New aspects and problems in Irish prehistory. *Proc. Prehist. Soc.* 3, 261–436.

Manby, T. G., 1974. *Grooved Ware Sites in the North of*

England. Oxford: British Archaeological Reports.

Mann, L. McL., 1903. Report on the excavation of prehistoric pile-structures in pits in Wigtownshire. *Proc. Soc. Antiq. Scotland* 37, 370–415.

Manning, W. H., 1970. Mattocks, hoes, spades and related tools in Roman Britain. In Gailey, A. and Fenton, A. (eds) *The Spade in Northern and Atlantic Europe*, 18–29. Belfast: Institute of Irish Studies.

Mason, E. J., 1968. Ogof-yr-Esgyrn, Dan-yr-Ogof Caves, Brecknock, excavations 1938–50. *Archaeol. Cambrensis* 117, 18–71.

Mathews, C. L., 1976. *Occupation Sites on a Chiltern Ridge, Part 1*. Oxford: British Archaeological Reports.

Mawer, A. and Stenton, F. M., 1929. *The Place Names of Sussex: Part 1*. Cambridge: Cambridge UP.

May, A. McL., 1953. Neolithic habitation site, stone circles and alignments at Beaghmore, Co. Tyrone. *Journ. Roy. Soc. Antiq. Ireland* 83, 174–97.

May, A. McL. and Batty, J., 1948. The sandhill cultures of the River Bann estuary. *Journ. Roy. Soc. Antiq. Ireland* 78, 130–56.

May, J., 1976. *Prehistoric Lincolnshire*. Lincoln: History of Lincolnshire Committee.

Meek, A., 1916. *The Migrations of Fish*. London: Edward Arnold.

Megaw, J. V. S., 1976. Gwithian, Cornwall: some notes on the evidence for Neolithic and Bronze Age settlement. In Burgess, C. and Miket, R. (eds) *Settlement and Economy in the Third and Second Millennia BC*, 51–66. Oxford: British Archaeological Reports.

Megaw, J. V. S., Thomas, A. C. and Wailes, B., 1961. The Bronze Age settlement at Gwithian, Cornwall: preliminary report on the evidence for early agriculture. *Proc. W. Cornwall Field Club* 2, 200–15.

Mellars, P., 1976a. Fire ecology, animal populations and man: a study of some ecological relationships in prehistory. *Proc. Prehist. Soc.* 42, 15–45.

Mellars, P., 1976b. Settlement patterns and industrial variability in the British Mesolithic. In Sievking, G., Longworth, I. and Wilson, K. (eds) *Problems in Economic and Social Archaeology*, 375–400. London: Duckworth.

Mercer, R., 1975. Carn Brae. *Current Archaeol.* 47, 360–5.

Millar, R., 1967. Land use by summer shielings. *Scottish Studies* 11, 193–221.

Mitchell, G. F., 1956. Post Boreal pollen diagrams from Irish raised bogs. *Proc. Roy. Irish Acad.* 57, 185.

Mitchell, G. F., and O'Riordain, S. P., 1942. Early Bronze Age pottery from Rockbarton Bog, Co. Limerick. *Proc. Roy. Irish Academy* C, 48, 255–72.

Money, J., 1960. Excavations at High Rocks, Tunbridge Wells, 1954–56. *Sussex Archaeol. Collect.* 98, 173–221.

Money, J., 1968. Excavations in the Iron Age hill fort at High Rocks near Tunbridge Wells, 1957–61. *Sussex Archaeol. Collect.* 106, 158–205.

Morgan, F. de M., 1959. The excavation of a long barrow at Nutbane, Hants. *Proc. Prehist. Soc.* 25, 15–51.

Morris, M., 1974. Megalithic exegesis: megalithic monuments as sources of socio-cultural meanings: the Irish case. *Irish Archaeol. Research Forum*, 1.2, 10–28.

Mortimer, J. R., 1911. Dane's Graves. *Trans. E. Riding Archaeol. Soc.* 18, 30–52.

Movius, H., 1936. A Neolithic site on the River Bann. *Proc. Roy. Irish Acad.* C 43, 17–40.

Movius, H., 1940. A Stone Age excavation at Rough Island, Strangford Lough, Co. Down. *Journ. Roy. Soc. Antiq. Ireland* 70, 111–42.

Mueller, J. S. (ed.), 1975. *Sampling in Archaeology*. Tucson: University of Arizona Press.

Munro, R., 1890. *The Lake Dwellings of Europe*. London: Cassell.

Murray, J., 1970. *The First European Agriculture*. Edinburgh: Edinburgh UP.

Musson, C., Smith, A. G. and Girling, M., 1977. Environmental evidence from the Breiddin hillfort. *Antiquity* 51, 147–51.

Newall, F., 1963. Crannog site? Garryeallabus. *Discovery and Excavation in Scotland* 1963, 18–19.

Newall, R. R., 1973. The post-glacial adaptations of the indigenous population of the north west European plain. In Kozlowski, S. K. (ed.) *The Mesolithic in Europe*, 399–440. Warsaw: Warsaw UP.

Newton, R. G. and Renfrew, C., 1970. British faience beads reconsidered. *Antiquity* 44, 199–206.

Oakley, K. P., Rankine, W. F. and Lowther, A. W. G., 1939. *A Survey of the Prehistory of the Farnham District*. Guildford: Surrey Archaeological Society.

O'Kelly, M. J., 1954. Excavations and experiments in ancient Irish cooking-places. *Journ. Roy. Soc. Antiq. Ireland* 84, 105–55.

O'Riordain, S. P., 1954. The Lough Gur excavations: Neolithic and Bronze Age houses on Knockadoon. *Proc. Roy. Irish Acad.* C 56, 297–459.

O'Riordain, S. P. and Lucas, A. T., 1947. Excavation of a small crannog at Rathjordan, Co. Limerick. *N. Munster Antiq. Journ.* 5, 68–77.

Palmer, S., 1968. A Mesolithic site at Portland Bill 1966. *Proc. Dorset Natur. Hist. Archaeol. Soc.* 90, 183–206.

Palmer, S., 1976. The Mesolithic habitation site at Culver Well, Portland, Dorset – interim note. *Proc. Prehist. Soc.* 42, 324–7.

Patrick, J., 1974. Mid-winter sunrise at New Grange. *Nature* 249, 517–19.

Patrick, J., 1975. Megalithic exegesis – a comment. *Irish Archaeol. Research Forum* 2.2, 9–14.

Peacock, D. P. S., 1969. Neolithic pottery production in Cornwall. *Antiquity* 43, 145–9.

Pearsall, W., 1970. *Mountains and Moorland*. London: Collins.

Pennington, W., 1973. Absolute pollen frequencies in the sediments of lakes of different morphometry. In Birks, H. J. B. and West, R. G. (eds) *Quaternary Plant Ecology*, 79–104. Oxford: Blackwell Scientific Publications.

Pennington, W., 1975. The effect of Neolithic man on the environment of north-west England: the use of absolute pollen diagrams. In Evans, J. G., Limbrey, S. and Cleere, H. (eds) *The Effect of Man on the Landscape: The Highland Zone*, 74–85. London: Council for British Archaeology.

Pennington, W., Haworth, E. Y., Bonny, A. P. and Lishman, A. P., 1972. Lake sediments in northern Scotland. *Phil. Trans. Roy. Soc.* 264, 191–294.

Perrin, R., Davies, M. and Fysh, D., 1974. Distribution of late Pleistocene aeolian deposits in eastern and southern England. *Nature* 248, 320–4.

Perry, B., 1969. Iron Age enclosures and settlements on the Hampshire chalklands. *Archaeol. Journ.* 126, 29–43.

Perry, B. T., 1972. Excavations at Bramdean, Hampshire 1965 and 1966 and a discussion of similar sites in southern England. *Proc. Hants. Field Club* 29, 41–77.

Piercy-Fox, N., 1969. Caesar's Camp, Keston. *Archaeol. Cantiana* 84, 185–200.

Piercy-Fox, N., 1970. Excavation of the Iron Age camp at Squerryes, Westerham. *Archaeol. Cantiana* 85, 29–33.

Piggott, C. M., 1938. A Middle Bronze Age barrow and Deverel-Rimbury urnfield at Latch Farm, Christchurch, Hampshire. *Proc. Prehist. Soc.* 4, 169–87.

Piggott, S., 1954. *Neolithic Cultures of the British Isles*. Cambridge: Cambridge UP.

Piggott, S., 1958. Native economies and the Roman occupation of North Britain. In Richmond, I. A. (ed.) *Roman and Native in North Britain*, 1–27. London: Nelson.

Piggott, S., 1962. *The West Kennet Long Barrow*. London: HMSO.

Piggott, S., 1972a. Excavation of the Dalladies long barrow, Fettercairn, Kincardineshire. *Proc. Soc. Antiq. Scotland* 104, 23–47.

Piggott, S., 1972b. A note on climatic deterioration in the first millennium BC in Britain. *Scottish Archaeol. Forum* 4, 109–13.

Piggott, S., 1973. The final phase of bronze technology c.1500–c.500 BC. *Victoria County History of Wiltshire I.i*, 376–407. Oxford: Oxford UP.

Pilcher, J. R., 1969. Archaeology, palaeoecology and C14 dating of the Beaghmore stone circle site. *Ulster Journ. Archaeol.* 32, 73–91.

Pitt-Rivers, A., 1898. *Excavations in Cranborne Chase*, vol. 4. Privately printed.

Pollard, E., 1973. Hedges VII. Woodland relic hedges in Huntingdon and Peterborough. *Journ. Ecol.* 61, 343–52.

Posnansky, M., 1955. The Bronze Age round barrow at Swarkestone. Part 1: the excavation and finds. *Derbs. Archaeol. Journ.* 75, 123–39.

Posnansky, M., 1956. The Bronze Age round barrow at Swarkestone. Part 2. *Derbs. Archaeol. Journ.* 76, 10–26.

Powell, T. G. E., 1969. Introduction to the field study of megalithic tombs. In Powell (ed.) *Megalithic Enquiries*, 1–12. Liverpool: Liverpool UP.

Powell, T. G. E., Oldfield. F. and Corcoran, J., 1971. Excavations in Zone VII peat at Storrs Moss, Lancashire, England. *Proc. Prehist. Soc.*, 37(i), 112–37.

Price, D. G. and Tinsley, H. M., 1976. On the significance of soil profiles at Trowlesworthy Warren and Wigford Down. *Rep. Trans. Devonshire Ass.* 108, 147–57.

Price, T. D., 1973. A proposed model for procurement systems in the Mesolithic of north western Europe. In Kozlowski, S. K. (ed.) *The Mesolithic in Europe*, 455–76. Warsaw: Warsaw UP.

Proudfoot, V. B., 1961. The economy of the Irish rath. *Medieval Archaeol.* 5, 94–122.

Pryor, F., 1974a. *Excavation at Fengate, Peterborough, England: the first report*. Toronto: Royal Ontario Museum.

Pryor, F., 1974b. Fengate 1973: the flint projectile points. *Durobrivae* 2, 10–12.

Pryor, F., 1976a. Fen-edge land management in the Bronze Age: an interim report on excavations at Fengate, Peterborough 1971–5. In Burgess, C. and Miket, R. (eds) *Settlement and Economy in the Third and Second Millennia BC*, 29–49. Oxford: British Archaeological Reports.

Pryor, F., 1976b. A Neolithic multiple burial from Fengate, Peterborough. *Antiquity* 50, 232–3.

RCAHM (Scotland) 1911a. *Sutherland*. Edinburgh: HMSO.

RCAHM (Scotland) 1911b. *Caithness*. Edinburgh: HMSO.

RCAHM (Scotland) 1928. *The Outer Hebrides, Skye and the Small Isles*. Edinburgh: HMSO.

RCAHM (Scotland) 1946. *Orkney and Shetland*. Edinburgh: HMSO.

RCAHM (Scotland) 1967. *Peeblesshire*. Edinburgh: HMSO.

RCAHM (Scotland) 1971. *Argyll* vol. 1. Edinburgh: HMSO.

RCAM (Scotland) 1956. *Roxburghshire*. Edinburgh: HMSO.

RCAM (Scotland) 1957. *Selkirkshire*. Edinburgh: HMSO.

RCAM (Wales) 1964. *Caernarvonshire* vol. 3. London: HMSO.

RCHM (England) 1970. *County of Dorset* vol. 2, part 3. London: HMSO.

RCHM (England) 1972. *County of Dorset* vol. 5. London: HMSO.

Rackham, O., 1976. *Trees and Woodland in the British Landscape*. London: Dent.

Rackham, O., 1977. Neolithic woodland management in the Somerset Levels: Garvin's, Walton Heath and Rowland's tracks. *Somerset Levels Papers* 3, 65–71.

Radley, J. and Cooper, L. B., 1968. A Neolithic site at Elton: an experiment in field recording. *Derbs. Archaeol. Journ.* 88, 37–46.

Raftery, B., 1976. Rathgall and Irish hillfort problems. In Harding, D. W. (ed.) *Hillforts – Later Prehistoric Earthworks in the British Isles*, 339–57. London: Academic Press.

Rahtz, P., 1976. Buildings and rural settlement. In Wilson, D. M. (ed.) *The Archaeology of Anglo-Saxon England*, 49–98. London: Methuen.

Rahtz, P. and ApSimon, A. M., 1962. Excavations at Shearplace Hill, Sydling St Nicholas, Dorset, England. *Proc. Prehist. Soc.* 28, 289–328.

Raistrick, A., 1939. Iron Age settlements in West Yorkshire. *Yorks. Archaeol. Journ.* 34, 115–50.

Ralston, I. and Büchsenschütz, O., 1975. Late pre-Roman Iron Age forts in Berry. *Antiquity* 49, 8–18.

Ramm, H. G., McDowall, R. W. and Mercer, E., 1970. *Shielings and Bastles*. London: HMSO.

Rankine, W. F., 1936. A Mesolithic site at Farnham. *Surrey Archaeol. Collect.* 44, 25–46.

Ratcliffe-Densham, H. and M., 1961. An anomalous earthwork of the Late Bronze Age on Cock Hill. *Sussex Archaeol. Collect.* 99, 78–101.

Ratcliffe-Densham, H. and M., 1966. Amberley Mount: its agricultural story from the late Bronze Age. *Sussex Archaeol. Collect.* 104, 6–25.

Renfrew, C., 1973a. Monuments, mobilisation and social organisation in Neolithic Wessex. In Renfrew, C. (ed.) *The Explanation of Culture Change*, 539–58. London: Duckworth.

Renfrew, C., 1973b. Wessex as a social question. *Antiquity* 47, 221–5.

Renfrew, C., 1974. Beyond a subsistence economy: the evolution of social organisation in prehistoric Europe. In Moore, C. (ed.) *Reconstructing Complex Societies*, 69–85. Massachusetts: School of Oriental Research.

Renfrew, C., 1975. Trade as action at a distance: questions of integration and communication. In Sabloff, J. and Lamberg-Karlowsky, C. (eds) *Ancient Civilisation and Trade*, 3–59. Albuquerque: New Mexico Press.

Renfrew, C., 1976. Megaliths, territories and populations. In De Laet, S. J. (ed.) *Acculturation and Continuity in Atlantic Europe*, 198–220. Bruges: De Tempel.

Reynolds, P. J., 1972. Experimental Archaeology. *Worcestershire Archaeological Newsletter* 9 (whole issue).

Reynolds, P. J., 1974. Experimental Iron Age storage pits: an interim report. *Proc. Prehist. Soc.* 40, 118–31.

Ritchie, A., 1970. Palisaded sites in north Britain: their context and affinities. *Scottish Archaeol. Forum* 2, 48–67.

Ritchie, A., 1971. Settlement archaeology – methods and problems. In Hill, D. and Jesson, M. (eds) *The Iron Age and its Hill Forts*, 91–5. Southampton: Southampton University Archaeological Society.

Ritchie, J., 1940. A keg of butter from Skye and its contents. *Proc. Soc. Antiq. Scotland* 75, 5–22.

Roberts, B., Turner, J. and Ward, P., 1973. Recent forest history and land use in Weardale, Northern England. In Birks, H. and West, R. (eds) *Quaternary Plant Ecology*, 207–21. Oxford: Blackwell Scientific Publications.

Robinson, M. and Hubbard, R., 1977. The transport of pollen in the bracts of hulled cereals. *Journ. Archaeol. Science*, 4, 197–200.

Robinson, R. S. G., 1946. The prehistoric occupation of Cefn Hill, near Craswall. *Trans. Woolhope Club* 32, 32–7.

Robinson, R. S. G., 1950. Notes on Bronze Age settlements on Abbey Farm, Craswall. *Trans. Woolhope Club* 33, 112–17.

Rodwell, W., 1976. Coinage, oppida and the rise of Belgic power in south-eastern Britain. In Cunliffe, B. W. and Rowley, R. T. (eds) *Oppida in Barbarian Europe*, 181–366. Oxford: British Archaeological Reports.

Rosenfeld, A., 1964. Excavations in the Torbryan Caves, Devonshire: Part II. *Trans. Devon Archaeol. Exploration Soc.* 22, 3–26.

Ross, A., 1967. *Pagan Celtic Britain*. London: Routledge & Kegan Paul.

Ross, A., 1968. Shafts, pits, wells – sanctuaries of the Belgic Britons? In Coles, J. M. and Simpson, D. D. A. (eds) *Studies in Ancient Europe*, 255–85. Leicester: Leicester UP.

Roth, H., 1974. Ein Ledermesser der atlantischen Bronzezeit aus Mittelfranken. *Archaeologishce Korrespondenzblatt* 4, 37–47.

Rowlands, M., 1976. *The Organisation of Middle Bronze Age Metalworking*. Oxford: British Archaeological Reports.

Sahlins, M. D., 1968. *Tribesmen*. New Jersey: Prentice Hall.

Savory, H. N., 1960. Excavations at Dinas Emrys, Beddgelert, Caernarvonshire 1954–56. *Archaeol. Cambrensis* 109, 13–77.

Savory, H. N., 1971. A Neolithic stone axe and wooden handle from Port Talbot. *Antiq. Journ.* 51, 296–7.

Savory, H., 1976. Welsh hillforts: a reappraisal of recent research. In Harding, D. W. (ed.) *Hillforts: Later Prehistoric Earthworks in Britain and Ireland*, 237–91. London: Academic Press.

Sayce, R. U., 1945. Canoes, coffins and cooking troughs. *Proc. Soc. Antiq. Scotland* 79, 106–11.

Scott, J., 1969. The Clyde Cairns of Scotland. In Powell, T. G. E. (ed.) *Megalithic Enquiries*, 175–222. Liverpool UP.

Scott, J., 1970. A note on Neolithic settlement in the Clyde region of Scotland. *Proc. Prehist. Soc.* 36, 116–24.

Scott, L., 1934. Excavation of the Ruidh' an Dunain cave, Skye. *Proc. Soc. Antiq. Scotland* 68, 200–23.

Scott, L., 1948. Gallo-British colonies: the aisled round-house culture in the north. *Proc. Prehist. Soc.* 14, 46–125.

Scott-Elliott, J., 1967. The small cairnfields of Dumfriesshire. *Trans. Dumfriesshire and Galloway Antiq. Soc.* 44, 99–116.

Scott-Elliott, J. and Rae, I., 1965. Whitestanes Moor Sites 1 and 80 – an enclosed cremation cemetery. *Trans. Dumfriesshire and Galloway Antiq. Soc.* 42, 51–60.

Selkirk, A., 1976. Mesolithic or Neothermal? *Current Archaeol.* 54, 206.

Shaw, T., 1969. Tree felling by fire. *Antiquity* 43, 52.

Shepherd, I., 1976. Preliminary results from the Beaker settlement at Rosinish, Benbecula. In Burgess, C. and Miket, R. (eds) *Settlement and Economy in the Third and Second Millennia BC*, 209–20. Oxford: British Archaeological Reports.

Sherratt, A. G., 1976. Resources, technology and trade: an essay in early European metallurgy. In Sievking, G., Longworth, I. and Wilson, K. (eds) *Problems in Economic and Social Archaeology*, 557–81. London: Duckworth.

Simmons, I., 1969. Environment and early man on Dartmoor, Devon, England. *Proc. Prehist. Soc.* 35, 203–19.

Simpson, D. D. A., 1969. Excavations at Kaimes hillfort, Midlothian 1964–1968. *Glasgow Archaeol. Journ.* 1, 7–28.

Simpson, D. D. A., 1971. Beaker houses and settlements in Britain. In *id* (ed.) *Economy and Settlement in Neolithic and Early Bronze Age Britain and Europe*, 131–52. Leicester: Leicester UP.

Simpson, D. D. A., 1976. The later Neolithic and Beaker settlement at Northton, Isle of Harris. In Burgess, C. and Miket, R. (eds) *Settlement and Economy in the Third and Second Millennia BC*, 221–31. Oxford: British Archaeological Reports.

Sims, R., 1973. The anthropogenic factor in East Anglian vegetational history: an approach using A.P.F. techniques. In Birks, H. J. B. and West, R. G. (eds) *Quaternary Plant Ecology*, 223–36. Oxford: Blackwell Scientific Publications.

Skenlář, K., 1975. Palaeolithic and Mesolithic dwellings: problems of interpretation. *Památky Archeologické* 66, 266–304.

Skenlář, K., 1976. Palaeolithic and Mesolithic dwellings: an essay in classification. *Památky Archeologické* 67, 249–340.

Smith, A. G., 1970. The influence of Mesolithic and Neolithic man on British vegetation: a discussion. In Walker, D. and West, R. G. (eds) *The Vegetational History of the British Isles*, 81–96. Cambridge UP.

Smith, A. G., 1975. Neolithic and Bronze Age landscape changes in Northern Ireland. In Evans, J. G., Limbrey, S. and Cleere, H. (eds) *The Effect of Man on the Landscape: The Highland Zone*, 64–73. London: Council for British Archaeology.

Smith, A. G. and Pilcher, J. R., 1973. Radiocarbon dates and vegetational history of the British Isles. *New Phytologist* 72, 903–13.

Smith, C., 1974. A morphological analysis of late prehistoric and Romano-British settlements in north-west Wales. *Proc. Prehist. Soc.* 40, 157–69.

Smith, I. F., 1965. *Windmill Hill and Avebury*. Oxford: Oxford UP.

Smith, I. F., 1974. The Neolithic. In Renfrew, C. (ed.) *British Prehistory – A New Outline*, 100–36. London: Duckworth.

Smith, I. F. and Simpson, D. D. A., 1966. Excavations of a round barrow on Overton Hill, North Wiltshire, England. *Proc. Prehist. Soc.* 32, 122–55.

Smith, R. A., 1911. Lake dwellings in Holderness, Yorks. discovered by Thos. Boynton Esq., F.S.A., 1880–1. *Archaeologia* 62, 593–610.

Smith, R. A., 1924. Pottery finds at Wisley. *Antiq. Journ.* 4, 40–5.

Snow, D. W. (ed.), 1971. *The Status of Birds in Britain and Ireland*. Oxford: Blackwell.

Sonnenfeld, J., 1963. Interpreting the function of primitive stone implements. *Amer. Antiq.* 28, 56–65.

Spratt, D. A. and Simmons, I. G., 1976. Prehistory activity and environment on the North York Moors. *Journ. Archaeol. Science* 3, 193–210.

Stanford, S., 1972. The function and populations of hill forts in the Central Marches. In Burgess, C. and Lynch, F. (eds) *Early Man in Wales and the West*, 307–20. Bath: Adams & Dart.

Stanford, S., 1974. *Croft Ambrey*. Hereford: privately published.

Startin, W., 1976. *Mathematics and Manpower in Archaeological Explanation*. B. Litt. thesis, University of Oxford.

Stead, I. M., 1968. An Iron Age hill fort at Grimthorpe, Yorkshire, England. *Proc. Prehist. Soc.* 34, 148–90.

Stead, I., 1976. The earliest burials of the Aylesford Culture. In Sievking, G., Longworth, I. and Wilson, K. (eds) *Problems in Economic and Social Archaeology*, 401–16. London: Duckworth.

Stevenson, R. B. K., 1945. A shell-heap at Polmonthill, Falkirk. *Proc. Soc. Antiq. Scotland* 80, 135–9.

Stone, J. F. S., 1936. An enclosure on Boscombe Down East. *Wilts. Archaeol. Mag.* 47, 466–89.

Stone, J. F. S., 1941. The Deverel-Rimbury settlement on Thorny Down, Winterbourne Gunner, S. Wilts. *Proc. Prehist. Soc.* 7, 114–33.

Stone, J. F. S. and Gray-Hill, N., 1938. A Middle Bronze Age site at Stockbridge, Hampshire. *Proc. Prehist. Soc.* 4, 249–57.

Storrs-Fox, W., 1911. Derbyshire cave-men of the Roman period. *Derbs. Archaeol. Journ.* 33, 115–26.

Tangye, M., 1973. 'Hulls' in Cornwall: a survey and discussion. *Cornish Archaeol.* 12, 31–52.

Taylor, C. C., 1972. The study of settlement patterns in pre-Saxon Britain. In Ucko, P., Tringham, R. and Dimbleby, G. (eds) *Man, Settlement and Urbanism*, 109–13. London: Duckworth.

Taylor, H., 1925. Fifth report on Rowbarrow Cavern. *Proc. Univ. Bristol Spelaeological Soc.* 2, 190–210.

Taylor, W. W., 1948. *A Study of Archaeology*. Memoirs of the American Anthropological Association No. 69.

Tebbutt, C. F., 1974. The prehistoric occupation of the Ashdown Forest area of the Weald. *Sussex Archaeol. Collect.* 112, 34–43.

Thom, A., 1967. *Megalithic Sites in Britain*. Oxford: Oxford UP.

Thomas, A. S., 1960. Chalk, heather and man. *Agric. Hist. Rev.* 8, 57–65.

Thomas, C., 1966. The character and origins of Roman Dumnonia. In Thomas (ed.) *Rural Settlement in Roman Britain*, 74–98. London: Council for British Archaeology.

Thomas, C., 1970. Bronze Age spade marks at Gwithian, Cornwall. In Gailey, A. and Fenton, A. (eds) *The Spade in Northern and Atlantic Europe*, 1–9. Belfast: Institute of Irish Studies.

Thomas, C., 1972. Souterrains in the Irish Sea Province: a note. In Thomas (ed.) *The Iron Age in the Irish Sea Province*, 75–8. London: Council for British Archaeology.

Thompson, M. W. and Ashbee, P., 1957. Excavation of a barrow near the Hardy Monument, Black Down, Portesham, Dorset. *Proc. Prehist. Soc.* 23, 124–36.

Toms, H., 1925. Bronze Age or earlier lynchets. *Proc. Dorset Natur. Hist. Archaeol. Soc.* 46, 89–100.

Tratman, E. K., 1931. Read's Cavern – final report: excavation of the exterior. *Proc. Univ. Bristol Spelaeological Soc.* 4, 8–10.

Tratman, E. K., 1967. The Priddy Circles, Mendip, Somerset: henge monuments. *Proc. Univ. Bristol Spelaeological Soc.* 11, 97–125.

Tratman, E. K., 1970. The Glastonbury Lake Village: a reconsideration. *Proc. Univ. Bristol Spelaeological Soc.* 12, 143–67.

Tratman, E. K. and Henderson, G. T. D., 1926. First report on the excavations at Sun Hole, Cheddar. *Proc. Univ. Bristol Spelaeological Soc.* 3, 84–97.

Troels Smith, J., 1960. Ivy, mistletoe and elm: climatic indicators – fodder plants. *Danmarks Geol. Undersgelse* 4R, 4, no 4, 1–32.

Turk, F. A., 1967. Report on the animal remains from Nornour. *Journ. Roy. Inst. Cornwall* 5, 250–66.

Turner, D. J. (ed.), 1975. *Archaeology and the M25, 1971–1975*. Guildford: Surrey Archaeological Society.

Turner, J., 1962. The *Tilia* decline: an anthropogenic interpretation. *New Phytologist* 61, 328–41.

Turner, J., 1965. A contribution to the history of forest clearing. *Proc. Roy. Soc.* B, 161, 343–53.

Tyler, A., 1976. *Neolithic Flint Axes from the Cotswold Hills*. Oxford: British Archaeological Reports.

Tyson, N., 1972. *A Bronze Age Cairn at Wind Hill, Heywood, Lancs.* Bury: Bury Archaeological Group.

Uerpmann, H. P., 1976. Comments on Jarman, M., Early animal husbandry. *Phil. Trans. Roy. Soc.* 275, 96.

Usher, G., 1974. *A Dictionary of Plants Used by Man.* London: Constable.

Van der Velde, P., 1973. Rituals, Skins and Homer: the Danubian tan-pits. *Analecta Praehistorica Leidensia* 6, 50–68.

Varley, W. J., 1968. Barmston and the Holderness crannogs. *East Riding Archaeologist* 1.1, 11–26.

Varley, W. J., 1976. A summary of the excavations at Castle Hill, Almondbury, 1939–1972. In Harding, D. W. (ed.) *Hillforts – Later Prehistoric Earthworks in Britain and Ireland*, 119–131. London: Academic Press.

Wace, A. J. B. and Jehu, no initial given, 1915. Cave excavations in east Fife. *Proc. Soc. Antiq. Scotland* 49, 233–55.

Wainwright, G. J., 1962. The excavation of an earthwork at Castell Bryn-Gwyn, Llanidan parish, Anglesey. *Archaeol. Cambrensis* 111, 25–58.

Wainwright, G. J., 1968. The excavation of a Durotrigian farmstead near Tollard Royal in Cranbourne Chase, Southern England. *Proc. Prehist. Soc.* 34, 102–47.

Wainwright, G. J., 1970. Mount Pleasant. *Current Archaeol.* 23, 320–4.

Wainwright, G. J., 1972. The excavation of a Neolithic settlement on Broome Heath, Ditchingham, Norfolk. *Proc. Prehist. Soc.* 38, 1–97.

Wainwright, G. J., 1973. The excavation of prehistoric and Romano-British settlements at Eaton Heath, Norwich. *Archaeol. Journ.* 130, 1–43.

Wainwright, G. J., 1975. Religion and settlement in Wessex c. 3000–1700 bc. In Fowler, P. J. (ed.) *Recent Work in Rural Archaeology*, 57–71. Bradford-on-Avon: Moonraker Press.

Wainwright, G. J. and Longworth, I. H., 1971. *Durrington Walls: Excavations 1966–1968.* London: Society of Antiquaries.

Wainwright, G. J. and Switsur, V. R., 1976. Gussage All Saints – a chronology. *Antiquity* 50, 32–9.

Walker, D., 1966. The Late Quaternary history of the Cumberland lowland. *Phil. Trans. Roy. Soc.* B, 251, 1–210.

Ward, J. E., 1974. Wooden objects uncovered at Branthwaite, Workington, in 1956 and 1971. *Trans. Cumberland and Westmorland Archaeol. Soc.* 74, 18–27.

Warren, S. H., 1932. Prehistoric timber structures associated with a briquetage site in Lincolnshire. *Antiq. Journ.* 12, 254–6.

Waterbolk, H., 1972. Pfein and Niederwell. Lecture to Prehistoric Society, spring 1972.

Waterbolk, H., 1975. Evidence of cattle stalling in excavated pre- and protohistoric houses. In Clason, A. T. (ed.) *Archaeozoological Studies*, 383–94. Amsterdam: North Holland Publishing Company.

Webster, R. A., 1971. A morphological study of Roman-British settlements in Westmorland. *Trans. Cumberland and Westmorland Antiq. Archaeol. Soc.* 71, 64–74.

Welinder, S., 1975. *Prehistoric Agriculture in Eastern Middle Sweden.* Lund: Gleerup.

Wells, C., 1974. Osteochondritis dissecans in ancient British skeletal material. *Medical History* 18, 365–9.

Whelan, C. B., 1952. *A Bone Industry from the Lower Bann.* Belfast: HMSO.

Whittington, G., 1973. Field systems of Scotland. In Baker, A. and Butlin, R. (eds) *Studies of Field Systems in the British Isles*, 530–79. Cambridge: Cambridge UP.

Whittle, A., 1977. *The Earlier Neolithic of Southern England and its Continental Background.* Oxford: British Archaeological Reports.

Wijngaarden-Bakker, L. H. van, 1974. The animal bones from the Beaker settlement at New Grange, Co. Meath: first report. *Proc. Roy. Irish Acad.* C, 74, 313–83.

Williams, A., 1941. The excavation of High Penard promontory fort, Glamorgan. *Archaeol. Cambrensis* 96, 23–30.

Williams, J., 1966. A sample of bog butter from Lochar Moss, Dumfriesshire. *Trans. Dumfriesshire and Galloway Antiq. Soc.* 43, 153–4.

Wilmer, H. and Reader, F. W., 1907. Report of the Red Hills Excavation Committee 1906–7. *Proc. Soc. Antiq. London* 22, 164–214.

Wilson, A. E., 1940. Report on the excavations at Highdown Hill, Sussex, August 1939. *Sussex Archaeol. Collect.* 81, 173–204.

Wilson, A. E., 1950. Excavations on Highdown Hill, 1947. *Sussex Archaeol. Collect.* 89, 163–78.

Woodman, P. C., 1974a. Settlement patterns of the Irish Mesolithic. *Ulster Journ. Archaeol.* 36/37, 1–16.

Woodman, P. C., 1974b. The chronological position of the latest phases of the Larnian. *Proc. Roy. Irish Acad.* C. 74, 237–58.

Woodman, P. C., 1976. The Irish Mesolithic/Neolithic transition. In De Laet, S. J. (ed.) *Acculturation and Continuity in Atlantic Europe*, 296–307. Bruges: De Tempel.

Woolridge, S. and Linton, D., 1933. The loam terrains of south east England and their relation to its early history. *Antiquity* 7, 297–310.

Worth, R. H., 1945. The Dartmoor hut circles. *Rep. Trans. Devon Ass.* 77, 225–56.

Wymer, J. J., 1962. Excavations at the Maglemosian sites at Thatcham, Berkshire, England. *Proc. Prehist. Soc.* 28, 329–61.

Bibliographical Index

General Index